The Challenge of Employment in India

An Informal Economy Perspective

Volume II - Annexures

NATIONAL COMMISSION FOR ENTERPRISES
IN THE UNORGANISED SECTOR,
GOVERNMENT OF INDIA

Chairman

Arjun K. Sengupta

ACADEMIC FOUNDATION
NEW DELHI

www.academicfoundation.com

First Published in 2009
by

ACADEMIC FOUNDATION
4772-73 / 23 Bharat Ram Road, (23 Ansari Road),
Darya Ganj, New Delhi - 110 002 (India).
Phones : 23245001 / 02 / 03 / 04.
Fax : +91-11-23245005.
E-mail : books@academicfoundation.com
www.academicfoundation.com

The Challenge of Employment in India: An Informal Economy Perspective
ISBN 13: 9788171887774 (set of 2 volumes)
ISBN 10: 8171887775

Printed and bound in India.

Contents

List of Tables

List of Figures

List of Boxes

List of Appendix

Volume II - Annexures

Annex 1.1: Past and Present Composition of the Commission

The composition of the Commission is as follows:

Professor Arjun Sengupta Chairman, Centre for Development and Human Rights, New Delhi	**Chairman,** [From 20.09.2004 to 01.07.2005 and from 17.11.2005 till date]
Professor K. P. Kannan Fellow, Centre for Development Studies, Ulloor, Thiruvananthapuram 695011, Kerala	**Full-time Member** [From 01.11.2004 till date]
Professor Ravi S. Srivastava Professor, Centre for Studies in Regional Development, Jawaharlal Nehru University, New Delhi 110067	**Full-time Member** [From 01.05.2006 till date]
Shri V.K. Malhotra, IAS (Retd.)	**Member Secretary** [From 01. 03.2006 till date]
Shri B.N. Yugandhar Member, Planning Commission, New Delhi 110001	**Part-time Member** [From 05.11.2004 till date]
Professor T.S. Papola Director, Institute for Studies in Industrial Development, Vasant Kunj Institutional Area, New Delhi.110070	**Part-time Member** [From 06.04.2005 till date]
Professor K. Jayashankar Former Vice Chancellor, Kakatiya University, Warangal, Andhra Pradesh	**Full-time Member** [From 01.12.2004 to 9.03.2006]
Shri Bibek Debroy, Director, Rajiv Gandhi Institute for Contemporary Studies, New Delhi 110001.	**Part-time Member** [From 27.10.2004 to 20.12.2005]
Shri K.K. Jaswal, IAS (Retd.)	**Member Secretary** [From 01.11.2004 to 18.02.2006]

Annex 1.2: Composition of the Advisory Board

1. **Professor Bhalchandra Mungekar,**
Member, Planning Commission,
Yojana Bhavan, New Delhi.

2. **Swami Agnivesh,**
President, Bonded Labour Liberation Front,
13, South Avenue, New Delhi.

3. **Professor Sheila Bhalla,**
(Formerly Professsor of Economics,
Jawaharlal Nehru University, New Delhi)
Institute of Human Development,
Old IAMI Building (3rd Floor).
I.P.Estate, Mahatma Gandhi Marg,
New Delhi-110002.

4. **Professor Mahendra Dev,**
Director, Centre for Economic and Social Studies,
Begumpet, Hyderabad.

5. **Ms. Madhu Kishwar,**
Editor, Manushi
C-1/3 Sangam Estate, 1, Underhill Road, Civil Lines,
Delhi-110054.

6. **Ms. Mirai Chatterjee,**
Self-Employed Women's Association (SEWA)
Opposite Victoria Garden, Bhadra, Ahmedabad-380001.

7. **Shri Joginder Kumar**
President,
Federation of Tiny & Small Scale Industries of India (FTSSI),
General Metal Industries, B-189, Industrial Estate,
Ludhiana, Punjab.

8. **Professor Jean Dreze,**
Delhi School of Economics, Department of Economics,
Delhi University, Delhi-110007.

9. **Professor Amit Bhaduri,**
Council for Social Development,
53, Lodhi Estate, New Delhi - 110003.

10. **Secretary,** Special Invitee
Ministry of Micro, Small and Medium Enterprises
Udyog Bhawan, New Delhi

11. **Secretary,** Special Invitee
Ministry of Labour & Employment
Shram Shakti Bhwan, New Delhi

Annex 1.3: Task Forces and Technical Expert Groups Constituted

File No.A-25022/11/2005-NCEUS
NCEUS

19th Floor, Jawahar Vyapar Bhavan
1 Tolstoy Marg, New Delhi-110 001
Dated the 16th May, 2005

ORDER

Subject:- Constitution of Task Force on Social Security for Workers in the Unorganised Sector

1.	**Professor K.P. Kannan,** Member, National Commission for Enterprises In the Unorganised Sector, 19th Floor, Jawahar Vyapar Bhavan, New Delhi-110001	**Chairman**
2.	**Ms. Mirai Chatterjee,** Self Employed Women's Association (SEWA), Opposite Victoria Garden, Bhadra, Ahmedabad-380001	**Member**
3.	**Professor S. Mahendra Dev,** Director, Centre for Economic and Social Studies, Begumpet, Hyderabad	**Member**
4.	**Professor Ravi Srivastava** Professor of Economics, Centre for Studies in Regional Development, School of Social Sciences, Jawaharlal Nehru University, New Delhi-110067	**Member**
5.	**Professor Alakh N, Sharma,** Director, Institute for Human Development, NIDM Building, 3rd Floor, IIPA Campus, IP Estate, New Delhi-2	**Member**
6.	**Dr. N. Vijayamohanan Pillai,** Associate Fellow, Centre for Development Studies, Prasanth Nagar, Ulloor, Thiruvananthapuram-695011, Kerala	**Member**
7.	**Professor Jeemol Unni,** Professor, Gujarat Institute of Development Research, Gota, Ahmedabad-380 060 (India)	**Member**

8. **Swami Agnivesh,** **Member**
Member, Advisory Board, NCEUS,
13, South Avenue, New Delhi-110001

9. **Director General (Labour Welfare),** **Member**
Ministry of Labour and Employment,
Government of India,
Shramshakti Bhavan,
New Delhi-110001

10. **Professor Achin Chakraborty,** **Member**
Professor of Economics,
Institute of Development Studies,
1, Reformatory Street, Kolkata University
Alipur Campus, 5th Floor, Kolkata

11. **Shri Mahesh Kumar,** **Convenor**
Director, NCEUS

Annex 1.3 Contd

File No.A-25022/11/2005-NCEUS
NCEUS

19th Floor, Jawahar Vyapar Bhavan
1 Tolstoy Marg, New Delhi-110 001
Dated the 16th May, 2005

ORDER

Subject:- Constitution of Task Force on Definitional and Statistical Issues relating to the Unorganised Sector.

It has been decided that a Task Force on Definitional and Statistical Issues relating to the Unorganised Sector be set up.

2. The composition of the Task Force shall be as follows:

1. **Professor Arjun K. Sengupta, Chairman** — **Chairman**
National Commission for Enterprises in the UnorganisedSector,(NCEUS)
19th Floor, 1, Tolstoy Marg, Jawahar Vyapar Bhavan,
New Delhi-110001

2. **Professor K.P. Kannan,** — **Member**
Member, NCEUS,
19th Floor, 1, Tolstoy Marg,
Jawahar Vyapar Bhavan, New Delhi-110001.

3. **Professor T.S. Papola,** — **Member**
Part Time Member, NCEUS,
Director, Labour Expert,
Institute for Studies for Industrial Development,
Narendra Niketan, I.P. Estate, New Delhi-110002

4. **Dr. N.S. Sastry,** — **Member**
Parsila Bhavan, N.C.A.E.R. 11,
I.P. Estate, M.G. Road, New Delhi-110002

5. **Professor Sheila Bhalla,** — **Member**
Member, Advisory Board, NCEUS,
Institute for Human Development,
NIDM, Building, (3rd Floor), I.P. Estate,
Mahatma Gandhi Marg, New Delhi-2

6. **Ms. Renana Jhabwala,** — **Member**
President, SEWA BHARAT,
7/5, First Floor, South Patel Nagar, New Delhi – 08.

7. **Dr. G. Raveendran,** **Member**
Additional Director General, Central Statatistical
OrganisationSardar Patel Bhavan,
Parliament Street, New Delhi-110001

8. **Shri S.V. Ramana Murthy** **Convenor**
Deputy Secretary, NCEUS
19th Floor, 1 Tolstoy Marg,
Jawahar Vyapar Bhavan, New Delhi-110001.

Annex 1.3 Contd

A-25024/9/2005-NCEUS
Government of India
National Commission for Enterprises in the Unorganized Sector

16th /19th Floor, Jawahar Vyapar Bhawan,
1, Tolstoy Marg, New Delhi 110001
Dated the 9th June, 2005

ORDER

Subject: Constitution of Task Force on Skill Formation in the Unorganised Sector.

It has been decided to set up a Task force on Skill Formation in the Unorganised Sector.

The composition of the Task Force shall be as follows:

1.	**Shri K.K.Jaswal,** Member Secretary, NCEUS	Chairman
2.	**Shri B.N.Yugandhar,** Part Time Member, NCEUS Member, Planning Commission, Yojana Bhawan, Sansad Marg, New Delhi	Member
3.	**Dr.Madhav Chavan,** Director, PRATHAM B3/3, Safdarjung Enclave, 1st Floor, New Delhi	Member
4.	**Lt.General (Retd.) S.S.Mehta,** Principal Adviser,CII India Development Foundation 249F, Sector 18, Udyog Vihar, Phase IV, Gurgaon	Member
5.	**Ms.Nalini Gangadharan,** Executive Director Dr. Reddy's Foundation 6-3-668/10/77&78, Durganagar Colony Punjagutta, Hyderabad-	Member
6.	**Shri K. K.Mittal,** DGE&T, M/o Labour & Employment Shram Shakti Bhawan, Rafi Marg, New Delhi	Member
7.	**Dr.S.D.Awale,** Joint Education Advisor (Technical), D/o Secondary & Higher Education, Ministry of Human Resource Development, Shastri Bhawan, New Delhi	Member

8.	**Shri Sharda Prasad,** Labour Commissioner, Government of Uttar Pradesh, G.T.Road, Kanpur	Member
9.	**Smt.Neelam Nath,** Joint Secretary, NCEUS	Member Secretary
10	**Shri J .D. Hajela,** Director NCEUS	Convenor

Annex 1.3 Contd

A-25022/ 26/2005-NCEUS
Government of India
National Commission for Enterprises in the Unorganised Sector

16th /19th Floor, Jawahar Vyapar Bhawan,
1, Tolstoy Marg, New Delhi 110001
Dated the 20th April, 2006

ORDER

Subject:- **Constitution of Task Force on Access to Finance, Raw Materials and Marketing relating to the Unorganised Sector.**

It has been decided that a Task Force on Access to Finance, Raw Materials, and Marketing relating to the Unorganised Sector be set up.

1. **Professor V.S. Vyas,** — Chairman
Institute of Development Studies,
8-B, Jhalna Institutional Area, Jaipur.

2. **Professor K P Kannan,** — Member
Member, NCEUS.

3. **Shri V.K. Malhotra** — Member
Member, NCEUS.

4. **Dr. Y.S. P. Thorat,** — Member
Managing Director,
National Bank for Agriculture and Rural Development, (NABARD),
Plot C-24, Bandra-Kurla Complex P.B. No. 8121,
Bandra (E) Mumbai

5. **Shri. N. Balasubramanian,** — Member
Chairman & Managing Director,
Small Industries Development Bank of India (SIDBI),
SIDBI Tower, 15, Ashok Marg, Lucknow-

6. **Shri. A.V. Sardesai,** — Member
C-16, Kumar Elixir, Banner Road, PUNE.

7. **Dr. S.L. Shetty,** — Member
Director,
Economic and Political Weekly Research Foundation, (EPW),
C-212, Akurli Industrial Estate,
Kandivali (East), Mumbai.

8. **Shri Nachiket Mor,** Member
Advisory Board Member, (NCEUS).
Exe. Director, ICICI Bank Ltd.,
ICICI Tower, Bandra Kurla Complex, Mumba

9. **Shri Kamal Taori,** Member
Director General,
National Productivity Council,
5&6, Institutional area, Lodhi Road,
New Delhi

10. **Shri Joginder Kumar,** Member
President,
Federation of Tiny & Small Industries of India, Mg. Partner,
General Metal Industries, B-189,
Industrial estate, LUDHIANA

11. **Shri. C. Chandran, IAS,** Member
Chief Executive Officer and Commissioner,
Khadi & Village Industries Commission,
Irla Road, Vile Parle (W), Mumbai

12. **Ms. Achala,** Member
SADAN,
12&13, 2nd Floor, MPTCD Building,
Special Institutional Area,
Shaheed Jeet Sing Marg,
New Delh

13. **Ms. Jayashree Vyas,**
Member
MD,
Self Employed Women's Association (SEWA) Bank,
Ellis Bridge, Ahmedabad

14. **Secretary,** Member
Ministry of Textiles, Udyog Bhawan , New Delhi

15. **Shri Vipin Sharma,** Member
Director,
CARE India, 27, Hauz Khas Village, New Delhi

16. **Shri Mahesh Kumar,** Convenor
Director, (NCEUS).

Annex 1.3 Contd

No. A-25022/29/2005-NCEUS
Government of India
National Commission for Enterprises in the Unorganized Sector

16th /19th Floor, Jawahar Vyapar Bhawan,
1, Tolstoy Marg, New Delhi 110001
Dated the 20th April, 2006

ORDER

Subject :Constitution of Task Force on Review of Indian Labour Laws.

It has been decided to set up a Task Force on Review of Indian Labour Laws.

The composition of the Task Force shall be as follows:

1.	**Professor T.S. Papola,** Delhi Government Chair in Human Development Institute for Human Development NIDM Building, IIPA Campus, IP Estatem M G Marg, New Delhi	Chairman
2.	**Professor K.P. Kannan,** Member, NCEUS	Member
3.	**Professor Ravi Shankar Srivastava,** Member, NCEUS	Member
4.	**Professor Navin Chandra,** Senior Fellow, Flat No. 119, A, Sipra Sun City Indrapuram, Ghaziabad	Member
5.	**Dr. Kamala Sankaran,** Research Professor Indian Law Institute, Bhagwandas Road, New Delhi	Member
6.	**Dr. Praveen Jha,** Associate Professor, School of Social Sciences, Jawaharlal Nehru University, New Mehrauli Road, New Delhi	Member

7.	**Dr. C.S. Venkata Ratnam,** Director, International Management Institute, B-10, Qutab Institutional Area, Tara Crescent, New Delhi	Member
8.	**Shri Joginder Kumar,** President, Federation of Tiny & Small Scale Industries of India (FTSSI), General Metal Industries, B-189, Industrial Estate, Ludhiana	Member
9.	**Shri Swami Agnivesh,** President, Bonded Labour Liberation Front, 7, Jantar Mantar Road, New Delhi	Member
10.	**Shri B. P Pant,** Joint Director, All India Organization of Employers (AIOE), Federation House, Tansen Marg, New Delhi	Member
11.	**Shri Anil Bhardwaj,** Secretary General, Federation of Indian Micro and Small & Medium Enterprises (FISME), B-4/161, Safdarjung Enclave, New Delhi-	Member
12	**Shri J .D. Hajela ,** Director NCEUS	Convenor

Annex 1.3 Contd

F. No. A-25024/4/2005-NCEUS
Government of India
National Commission for Enterprises in the Unorganized Sector
****

16th /19th Floor, Jawahar Vyapar Bhawan,
1 Tolstoy Marg, New Delhi 110001
Dated : 10th November ,2006

ORDER

Subject: Constitution of Technical Experts Group on Growth Pole.

It has been decided to set up a Technical Experts Group to take their inputs on Growth Pole proposals and other relevant issues.

2. The composition of the Group shall be as follows:

1. **Professor Dinesh N. Awasthi, Director,** - Member
Entrepreneurship Development Institute of India,
Near Village Bhat, via Ahmedabad Airport & Indira Bridge,
P.O. Bhat-382428, District- Gandhinagar, Gujarat.

2. **Dr. Sarita Nagpal,** - Member
Confederation of Indian Industry (CII),
The Mantosh Sondhi Centre,
23, Institutional Area, Lodi Road, New Delhi

3. **Shri Mukesh Gulati,** - Member
Focal Point Manager, CDP,
U.N. Industrial Development Organization House,
6 Special Institutional Areas, New Delhi

4. **Development Commissioner (SSI),** - Member
Office of the Development Commissioner,
Small Scale Industries,
7th Floor, A-Wing, Nirman Bhavan, New Delhi

5. **Secretary,** Ministry of Commerce & Industry, - Member
Department Of Industrial Policy & Promotion,
Udyog Bhawan, New Delhi

6. **CMD,** - Member
Housing & Urban Development Corporation Ltd. (HUDCO]
HUDCO Bhawan, India Habitat Centre,
Lodhi Road, New Delhi

Annex 1.3 Contd

F. No. A-25024/4/2005-NCEUS
Government of India
National Commission for Enterprises in the Unorganized Sector
****

16th /19th Floor, Jawahar Vyapar Bhawan,
1, Tolstoy Marg, New Delhi 110001
Dated the 4th February, 2008

REVISED ORDER

Subject: Constitution of Task Force on Enterprise Development in the Unorganized Sector.

In supersession of Order of even no. dated 1st October, 2007, the following changes have been made.

It has been decided to change the name as "Task Force on Enterprise Development in the Unorganized Sector" to examine the issues related to the Development of Enterprise in the Unorganized Sector and other relevant issues.

The composition of the Task Force shall be as follows:

1.	**Professor K. P. Kannan** Member, NCEUS	-	Chairman
2.	**Professor Ravi Shankar Srivastava,** Member, NCEUS	-	Member
3.	**Shri V. K. Malhotra** Member Secretary, NCEUS	-	Member
4.	**Professor T.S. Papola,** Part Time Member, NCEUS, Director, Labour Expert, Institute for Studies for Industrial Development, Narendra Niketan, I.P. Estate, New Delhi-110002	-	Member
5.	**Professor Dinesh N. Awasthi,** Director, Entrepreneurship Development Institute of India, Gandhi Nagar, Ahemdabad.	-	Member
6.	**Professor Rakesh Basant** Indian Institute of Management, Ahemadabad.	-	Member
7.	**Shri Mukesh Gulati,** Focal Point Manager, UNIDO, New Delhi.	-	Member

8.	**Professor Padmini Swaminathan,** Director, MIDS	-	Member
9.	**Professor Pankaj Chandra,** IIM, Vastrapur, Ahmedabad	-	Member
10.	**Shri DE. Ramakrishnan,** President, IFRASTE, Paramount Gardens, no. 11, Arunachalam Road, Saligramam, Chennai	-	Member
11.	**DC, MSME and / or his representative** Nirman Bhawan, New Delhi	-	Member
12.	**Secretary** Ministry of Commerce & Industry, Department Of Industrial Policy & Promotion, Udyog Bhawan, New Delhi	-	Member
13.	**Shri Ashutosh Mishra** Director, NCEUS	-	Convener

Annex 1.3 Contd

F. No. A-25024/3/2008-NCEUS
Government of India
National Commission for Enterprises in the Unorganized Sector
****

16th Floor, Jawahar Vyapar Bhawan,
1 Tolstoy Marg,
New Delhi - 110 001.
Dated: 30th July, 2008

ORDER

Subject : Constitution of Technical Experts Group on Marginal and Small Farmers

It has been decided to set up a Technical Experts Group on Marginal and Small Farmers to take their inputs on Special Programme for Marginal and Small farmers and other related issues.

The composition of the Group shall be as follows:

1.	**Professor Arjun Sengupta,** Chairman, NCEUS	-	Chairperson
2.	**Professor Ravi Srivastava,** Member, NCEUS	-	Member Convener
3.	**Professor K.P. Kannan,** Member, NCEUS	-	Member
4.	**Shri V.K. Malhotra,** Member Secretary, NCEUS	-	Member
5.	**Professor V.S. Vyas,** Chairman Institute of Development Studies, 8-B, Jhalna Institutional Area, Jaipur	-	Member
6.	**Professor Surjit Singh,** Director, IDS, Jaipur Institute of Development Studies, 8B, Jhalana Institutional Area, Jaipur	-	Member
7.	**Professor Alakh Narain Sharma,** Director, Institute of Human Development, NIDM Building, IIPA Campus, IP Estate, M.G. Marg, New Delhi	-	Member
8.	**Professor D.N. Reddy,** Former Dean and Professor, Central University, 3-33-33, Venkat Reddy Colony, Lingam Palli, Hyderabad.	-	Member

9.	**Professor G. Vallabh,** Circuit House Area (East), Jamshedpur	-	Member
10.	**Professor Kanchan Chopra,** Director Institute of Economic Growth, University of Delhi Enclave, North Campus, Delhi	-	Member
11.	**Dr. Mahendra Dev,** Chairman, CACP, Krishi Bhawan, Delhi	-	Member
12.	**Dr. P.K. Joshi,** NCAP, P. B. No. 11305, Library Avenue, Pusa, New Delhi	-	Member
13.	**Secretary,** Ministry of Agriculture or his Representative. (Dr. S.M. Jharwal, Principal Advisor) Krishi Bhawan, Delhi	-	Member
14.	**Secretary,** Department of Agriculture, Govt.of Madhya Pradesh, or his Representative	-	Member
15.	**Secretary,** Department of Agriculture, Govt. of West Bengal, or his Representative	-	Member
16.	**Secretary,** Department of Agriculture Govt. of Andhra Pradesh, or his Representative	-	Member
17.	**Shri S.V. Ramana Murthy,** Director, NCEUS	-	Co-ordinator

Annex 3.1: Measures of Labour Force Participation and Utilisation

J. Krishnamurthy and G. Raveendran
Senior Consultants, NCEUS

1. Introduction

There is a continuing debate in India among economists, planners and policy-makers on the best measure of labour force participation and utilization. This is despite the fact that the Committee of Experts on Unemployment Estimates, constituted by the Planning Commission in 1968 under the chairmanship of Prof. M.L. Dantwala, has clearly indicated[1] that it would not be justified to aggregate labour force, employment and unemployment into single dimensional magnitudes in view of inherent socio-economic conditions prevailing in the country.

In this paper a new set of measures of labour force, employment and unemployment has been suggested which we believe would be better suited for many purposes than those currently in use. We also propose new measures of labour time utilization and underemployment.

2. The Existing Measures of Labour Force

The Labour Force Participation Rate (LFPR), obtained by dividing the number of persons in the labour force by total population, is an important parameter in employment projections and formulation of employment strategies. The crucial issue, however, is the basis, or the decision rule, on which a person is classified as belonging to the labour force. There are four different concepts used in India in this regard. These are:

Usual Principal Status (UPS)
Usual Principal and Subsidiary Status (UPSS)
Current Weekly Status (CWS), and
Current Daily Status (CDS).

2.1 *Usual Principal Status*

For several purposes, we need to relate social and economic variables to the enduring characteristics of the population and labour force. The labour force, in this context, is typically measured through the usual principal activity status (UPS) which reflects the status of an individual over a reference period of one year. Thus a person is classified as belonging to labour force, if s/he had been either working or looking for work during longer part of the 365 days preceding the survey. In case the total period of being within the labour force is equal to the total period out of it, priority is given to labour force participation. Again, for a person already identified as belonging to the labour force, s/he would be labeled as employed or unemployed depending on which category accounted for more days. In the event of a tie, employed would get priority over unemployed. However, if a person has a very complex pattern of labour force and work participation, the UPS measure cannot fully reflect it.

The UPS measure excludes from the labour force all those who are employed and/or unemployed for a total of less than six months. Thus persons who work intermittently, either because of the pattern of work in the household farm or enterprise or due to economic compulsions and other reasons, would not be included in the labour force unless their days at work and unemployment totalled over half the reference year.

2.2 *Usual Principal and Subsidiary Status*

The Usual Principal and Subsidiary Status (UPSS) concept was introduced to widen the UPS concept to include even those who were outside the labour force on the basis of the majority time criterion but had been employed during some part of the year on a usual basis. In the NSS 61st Round Survey, all those who were either un-employed or out of labour force but had worked for at least 30 days over the reference year were treated as subsidiary status workers. UPSS is thus a hybrid concept incorporating both the major time criterion and priority to work status.

The UPSS measure was used on the ground that it was stable and inclusive: it related to a picture emerging from

[1] The Report of the Committee of Experts on Unemployment Estimates submitted to the Planning Commission in 1970 states that "In our complex economy, the character of the labour force, employment and unemployment, is too heterogeneous to justify aggregation into single-dimensional magnitudes".

a long reference period, and even persons working for 30 days or more, but not working for the major part of the year, were included. However, those outside the UPS labour force, seeking or available for work for more than 30 days during the preceding 365 days, were not included in the UPSS labour force.[2]

By including as workers those outside the UPS labour force but had worked for 30 days or more, the UPSS estimates of work participation (which included some of the UPS unemployed and outside the labour force) exceeded the corresponding UPS estimates. However, the number of unemployed got reduced and their share in the expanded UPSS labour force became much lower.

It is important to stress the difference between the UPS and UPSS measures as the latter has been used for employment projections in all the recent Plan exercises except the Tenth Plan document. The basic differences between UPS and UPSS measurements are the following:

- The enduring characteristic sought to be captured in UPS is how the person spends the major part of the year. The UPSS, on the other hand, seeks to place as many persons as possible under the category of employed by assigning priority to work
- While the notion of long term attachment to particular activity status may be a valid generalization, there may be a considerable number of persons for whom no single long-term activity status is applicable as they move between statuses over a long period of one year depending on a variety of factors, including cyclical patterns and random events. This possibility is eliminated from our purview when a statistical straight-jacket like UPS or UPSS is applied and a person has to select one and only one status (employed, unemployed, out of the labour force) as her/his enduring status.
- Usual status requires a recall over a whole year of what the person did. For those in regular employment this is easy to do, but for those who take whatever work opportunities they can find over the year or have prolonged spells out of the labour force, a very complex pattern has to be recalled in order to decide what their usual status is. In this respect, a short reference period of a week has advantages.

2.3 *Current Weekly Status*

The concept of Current Weekly Status (CWS) has been in use in the labour force surveys in India even before 1970, when the recommendations of the Dantwala Committee became available. It was primarily because the agencies like International Labour Organization (ILO) use estimates of employment and unemployment rates based on weekly reference period for international comparisons. Under CWS, a person is classified to be in labour force, if s/he has either worked or is seeking and/or available for work at least one hour during the reference period of one week preceding the date of survey.

The CWS participation rates also relate to persons and hence may be roughly compared with those obtained by using UPS and UPSS measurements. However, the reference periods are different and UPS, unlike UPSS and CWS, is based on majority time and does not accord priority to work and unemployment. The classification under CWS is based on the status of each person during the last seven days and priority is assigned to "working" over "not working but seeking or available for work" and to both "working" and "not working but seeking or available for work" over "neither working nor available for work". The advantage of CWS is that it uses a shorter reference period of seven days and as such recall lapses are expected to be comparatively lower. Further, it facilitates easy classification and analysis by sub-rounds to identify seasonal patterns. The major disadvantage of CWS is that it classifies persons with very nominal work of even one hour during the reference week into work force and labour force. Similarly, a person is treated as unemployed only if s/he has been unemployed on all the days on which s/he has been in the labour force.

2 The 30 day rule was introduced in the 61st Round. In earlier Rounds, no such minimum cut off point was prescribed. For strict consistency, all those who were outside the labour force on the basis of principal status, but who were in the labour force on the basis of their subsidiary status, should have been included in the UPSS labour force. If the 30 day cut-off rule was applied it should have related to labour force participation, not only to work participation.

2.4 *Current Daily Status*

The Dantwala Committee proposed the use of Current Daily Status (CDS) rates for studying intensity of work. These are computed on the basis of the information on employment and unemployment recorded for the 14 half days of the reference week. The employment statuses during the seven days are recorded in terms of half or full intensities. An hour or more but less than four hours is taken as half intensity and four hours or more is taken as full intensity.

> An advantage of this approach was that it was based on more complete information; it embodied the time utilisation, and did not accord priority to labour force over outside the labour force or work over unemployment, except in marginal cases. A disadvantage was that it related to person-days, not persons. Hence it had to be used with some caution.

3. Labour Force Measures Used in Recent Plan Exercises

The Task Force on Employment Opportunities set up by the Planning Commission and chaired by Dr Montek Singh Ahluwalia, which reported in July 2001, examined estimates of employment and unemployment generated by the National Sample Survey, based on different concepts developed by the Dantwala Committee. All four measures, UPS, UPSS, CWS and CDS were reviewed and estimates based on all four measures featured in the analysis. It was stated that:

> the CDS measure of unemployment is widely agreed to be the one that most fully captures open unemployment in the country.[3]

The projections of the labour force were, however, based on the UPSS concept, perhaps because it related to persons rather than person-day units.

The Planning Commission's Special Group on Targeting Ten Million Employment Opportunities Per Year over the Tenth Plan Period, chaired by Dr S P Gupta, which reported in May 2002, took a different view. It argued that:

> the method of estimation of employment and unemployment on the basis of the usual and subsidiary status (UPSS) used during the Ninth Plan formulation would not be of help to get any realistic estimate of the quantum of generating gainful employment in order to fulfill the Tenth Plan targets, especially given the promise for gainful nature of employment, as per the Group's terms of reference. This is because on the basis of UPSS calculation, the volume of unemployment shown is always under-estimated since it excludes a large number who are significantly under-employed or unemployed over a major part of the referred period.[4]

It was therefore decided to switch over to the CDS. The rationale was as follows:

> Hence, we switched over to what is called the Current Daily Status (CDS), which is conveniently one of the other options provided by the National Sample Survey Organisation for measurement of employment and unemployment. If the gainfully employed are defined as those who are near fulltime employed, then the CDS definition on employment given by the NSSO will give more realistic estimate at least directionally. Most countries across the globe use the concept close to weekly status, which again is closer to that of CDS used in this report. Within India almost all other reports from alternate sources agree that the CDS concept of unemployment is the most realistic.[5]

This approach was later adopted in the Tenth Plan (2002-2007) document for projecting labour force and employment generation. It was justified on the ground that (a) CDS was a better measure than the UPSS to capture unemployment and under-employment and (b) it took into account seasonal variations as the samples

---

3 See Government of India, Planning Commission: Report of the Task Force on Employment Opportunities, New Delhi, July 2001, pp. 14-15.

4 See Government of India, Planning Commission: Report of the Special Group on Targeting Ten Million Employment Opportunities Per Year over the Tenth Plan Period, New Delhi, July 2002, p. 12.

5 Ibid, p.21.

were surveyed uniformly over the year. A review of these developments brings out the following points.

First, the Special Group is right in stressing that the gainfully employed should be those who have a strong involvement in employment, i.e. that they should be "near fulltime employed." It does not follow, however, as the Special Group claims, that the CDS definition on employment will give a more realistic estimate at least directionally, for it cannot yield an estimate of *persons* gainfully employed. Under CDS, the basic classificatory unit is a person-day and the status of the same person on all the seven days is recorded. It thus relates to a composite unit of person-day and not to persons or individuals. Aggregates of person-days cannot be readily related to characteristics of individuals who contribute to it.

Secondly, the UPSS-based projections may be questioned for using a concept that overstates employment and understates unemployment. Many persons included as workers under UPSS are not really gainfully employed for much of the time.

Thirdly, the argument of the Task Force that "the difference between the unemployment rates on the Current Weekly and that on the Usual Status would provide one measure of seasonal unemployment" is difficult to sustain. The two unemployment rates are based on different labour force denominators, and many reported as working on UPSS may be outside the labour force on CWS. Seasonality in labour force characteristics is better captured by variations in CDS rates over the four sub-rounds.

4. Requirements of a Good Measure

From the preceding discussion we may attempt to highlight some of the requirements of a good measure.

- A good employment/unemployment measure should be able to depict the baseline situation in a realistic and consistent manner, identifying those individuals who have a substantial attachment to the labour force and who spend a good part of their time at work or in unemployment.
- In our predominantly rural, agrarian economy, it should enable us to identify patterns of seasonal change over the different parts of the year.
- It should provide a basis for projecting the growth of labour force, employment and unemployment over time and facilitate comparisons with expected employment generation in the economy.

5. Modified Current Weekly Status (MCWS)

In both UPSS and CWS, the priority criterion results in overestimation of the labour force and work force. It is essentially because persons who normally remain outside the labour force (work force) most of the time would get included in the labour force (work force) if they spent just above 30 days in a year (UPSS) or one hour in a week (CWS) in an economic activity like gathering of uncultivated crops, collection of firewood, cleaning of household enterprise premises, etc. The UPSS and CWS as currently used, therefore, have only limited value in estimating trends in employment and unemployment and projecting labour force. This paper proposes a modified CWS (hereafter MCWS) based on major time criterion. This approach had been used many years ago by Prof. Pravin Visaria in an exercise involving re-tabulation of NSS data for some States.

Unlike CWS, the MCWS takes better account of the time disposition of each individual over the 14 half days. It follows a two step procedure. *First*, it assigns individuals to the labour force if the majority of their half-days were in the labour force. *Second*, within the labour force, it uses the majority time principle to classify individuals among the two activity statuses, employed and unemployed. Only in a few cases, where the majority time rule does not give a unique solution, is the criterion of priority for labour force and employment invoked.

Under MCWS, each surveyed individual is uniquely classified as within or outside the labour force, and again as employed or unemployed by consistently applying the majority time principle to the time disposition information relating to all the 14 half-days of the week. The labour force estimates based on MCWS includes only those who were in the labour force during major part of the week. A member of the MCWS labour force would have been working or unemployed or a combination of both *for at least 3.5 days in the reference week.*

In contrast to the CWS, under MCWS a person will not be classified as worker, if that person has worked only for half-a-day during the reference week. Any person classified as a member of the MCWS labour force can be further classified as a worker only if s/he has worked for at least two days in the reference week. This may be established in the following way. Consider individual, A, who has spent the minimum qualifying period of 3.5 days in the labour force.

- If A spent 2 or more days at work, this would be the majority of her/his labour force days and s/he would be classified as a worker.
- If A spent less than 2 days at work i.e. 1.5 days or less, A must have been unemployed for 2 days or more out of her/his 3.5 days in the labour force. A would then be classified as unemployed.

To generalize, if the number of days of any person in the labour force is 3.5 or more, the majority rule would ensure that if the person was classified as a worker s/he would have worked for 2 or more days and if the person was classified as unemployed, s/he would have been unemployed for 2 or more days.

In the above classification, we follow the analogy of the usual principal status and *first* classify according to whether or not in the labour force on the basis of majority time, and *then* apply the same majority time criterion to decide whether the person is employed or unemployed. This MCWS procedure has a definite advantage over the CWS as any person classified as employed (or unemployed) would have recorded a significant involvement (at least 2 days) in that activity and at least 3.5 days in the labour force. The concept thus enables us to focus on persons with a significant involvement in the labour force and in work or unemployment.

6. Comparison of Rates from the Different Measures

In this Section we examine labour force and unemployment rates derived from unit level data sets by different measures in use and compare them with rates obtained using the MCWS. Before making the comparison, it is important to note that the rates are obtained on very different bases. The UPS and UPSS relate to usual status with a reference period of one year, while the other rates relate to current status, relating to the reference week. The UPS, and MCWS embody the majority time criterion, while the UPSS and CWS embody the priority criterion, assigning priority to work over unemployment and unemployment over being outside the labour force. Unlike UPS, UPSS, CWS and MCWS which relate to persons, the CDS relates to person-days. The CWS and the MCWS apply two different principles, priority and majority time respectively, to the same set of labour-time disposition particulars.

Since different reports have used one or other of the earlier measures, it is useful to look at these results in relation to MCWS. One must not forget that the bases for the different measures differ greatly and the reasons for these differences are complex. The labour force participation rates estimated by using the different measures listed above on the data sets relating to NSS 50th, 55th and 61st Round Surveys on Employment – Unemployment are given in Table 1 and the corresponding worker participation and unemployment rates are given in Tables 2 and 3 respectively.

6.1 *Labour force participation rates*

Considering the labour force participation rates reported in Table 1, all have a common denominator, viz. the population, although the CDS uses a variant, viz. total person days. The following generalizations may be made:

<u>Usual status</u>

UPSS>UPS (i)

This is obvious since UPSS adds to the labour force those outside the UPS labour force with subsidiary work.

<u>Current status</u>

CWS>MCWS (ii)

CWS results in a higher labour participation rate than MCWS. This is due to the inclusion in CWS of some persons who were not in the labour force for the majority of the week.

CWS> CDS (iii)

The CWS labour force participation rates are higher than the CDS as the half-days outside the labour force of persons in the CWS labour force are ignored under CWS but included in CDS.

The relation between MCWS and CDS labour force participation rates cannot be predicted. The MCWS rate could exceed the CDS since it ignores half-days of outside the labour force reported by persons in the MCWS labour force; on the other hand, CDS could exceed MCWS as it includes half-days in the labour force of persons outside the MCWS labour force. Hence, the relation between MCWS and CDS depends on the relative magnitudes of these two factors.

Looking at Table 1, we find that for all India for 1993-94, 1999-2000 and 2004-05, for all segments (i.e. rural males, rural females, urban males and urban females) labour force participation rates under UPSS are consistently higher than under UPS. Again, CWS rates are higher than MCWS rates which, in turn are higher than CDS rates.

6.2 *Work participation rates*

The work participation rates estimated by using different concepts are given in Table 2.

<u>Usual status</u>

UPSS>UPS (iv)

As one would expect, WPRs are higher under UPSS as compared to UPS as the former includes subsidiary work.

<u>Current status</u>

CWS>MCWS (v)

As in the case of labour force participation rates, the CWS work participation rates, based on priority for employment, are consistently higher than MCWS rates, based on majority time.

CWS>CDS (vi)

The CWS rates are higher than those under CDS, as persons with minimal days of employed would be classified as employed under CWS and no account would be taken of their unemployed days.

The relation between MCWS and CDS WPRs is, in theory, unclear. The MCWS, in its estimation, ignores the non-work time of MCWS workers. Against this, the work time of MCWS non-workers is also ignored by MCWS. In practice, it would appear that the former factor outweighs the latter, and MCWS WPRs generally exceed CDS WPRs.

As Table 2 shows, for all persons in 2004-05, the UPSS based WPR is the highest at 420 per thousand of population and the CDS based WPR is the lowest at 350. The UPS and CWS based WPRs are 380 and 389 respectively, while that based on MCWS is 368.

6.3 *Unemployment rates*

Turning to comparisons of unemployment rates (which are proportions to the labour force) it is important to note that, unlike the labour force participation rates which are proportions of the population, differences in unemployment rates could be due to the numerator and/ or the denominator.

<u>Usual status</u>

UPS> UPSS (vii)

Under UPSS, the priority for work over unemployment results in unemployment being smaller than in UPS. Further, the UPSS labour force is larger than the UPS labour force as some persons outside the UPS labour force are included in the UPSS labour force. Hence, the UPS unemployment rate, with a larger numerator and a smaller denominator, will be higher than the corresponding UPSS rate.

<u>Current status</u>

MCWS>CWS (viii)

MCWS unemployed would be greater than the corresponding number for CWS as persons in the MCWS labour force who were unemployed for the major part of the week, but had also done some work, would be classified as unemployed; but such persons would have been included among the employed under CWS. The labour force, as we have seen in (ii) above, would be larger under CWS. Hence, with a larger numerator and a smaller denominator the MCWS unemployment rate would be higher compared to the CWS rate.

CWS<CDS (ix)

As CWS, unlike CDS, assigns priority to employment over unemployment a smaller number of unemployed would be obtained under CWS than under CDS. We already know that CWS would result in a larger labour force than CDS. Hence the unemployment rate under CDS (with more unemployed and less in the labour force) would be more than under CWS.

MCWS unemployment would be larger than CWS unemployment, since the former is based on majority time and does not assign priority to work over unemployment. But, as we have already shown, labour force participation rates under MCWS may be higher, equal or less than the corresponding CDS rates. Hence no conclusion may be drawn on comparing MCWS and CDS unemployment rates.

Looking at Table 2, we find that CDS rates are the highest, followed in descending order by MCWS, CWS, UPS, and UPSS. In the case of urban females, UPS and CWS rates are rather close and in 2004-05, it appears that the UPS rates slightly exceeded the CWS rate. However, in the preceding discussion we made no predictions regarding the relationship between usual and current status rates as their bases are very different.

7. Advantages of the MCWS Approach to Labour Force Measurement

The MCWS participation and unemployment rates, which relate to persons by majority time, are better aggregates of current daily status information. They are based on the actual status of the person during the last seven days and not based on a long recall memory of the informant as in the case of UPS and UPSS. They do not classify a person into one of the categories of employed, unemployed and out of labour force on an a priori basis but do so only after ascertaining the daily status on each of the last seven days. Thus the classification errors are significantly reduced. The unemployment rates estimated by using MCWS are a better reflection of the situation than those based on CWS as the former is on the basis of major time disposition within the labour force.

Since MCWS estimates relate to persons, they can be used to project the size and composition of the labour force. They can also be used to examine labour force characteristics, using cross classifications based on individual and household characteristics.

While the different approaches and the resulting estimates are useful in illuminating different characteristics of labour force participation and utilization, we believe that the analysis should be built around the MCWS estimates, drawing in, as required, results based on the other approaches and estimates. This would provide the best use of the available detailed information for policy analysis including planning exercises.

In a sense the time disposition module of the NSSO makes it possible to apply a host of alternative definitions of labour force, employment and unemployment resulting in a family of estimates. The task of the analyst is to select those among these estimates that are best suited to specific purposes. We illustrate this point in the next section by considering, in more detail, different ways of identifying and measuring underemployment and unemployment.

8. Impact of Use of Different Concepts in the Classification of Persons

In this section we examine how the use of different concepts impact on the classification of persons into labour force and work force. Since the first basic classification is that of labour force, the analysis mainly focuses on the same, though it can be repeated for work force classification. The two basic parameters which differ between different concepts and contribute to variation in the classification are: (i) the reference period and (ii) the classification rule. The specific parameters in use in each of the concepts are summarised in the Statement 1.

As stated earlier, the UPS concept is based on a notion of stable attachment to labour force which is one of the desirable characteristics of a good measure. A long reference period of 365 days and major time criterion are therefore, used for determining the status of a person under the UPS concept. It, however, needs to be investigated whether the use of a long reference period is capable of discriminating long term stable labour force attachment from casual and | or intermittent attachments. It is done by comparing the profiles of persons identified to be in labour force as per UPS but not as per CWS as

Statement 1: Parameters for Labour Force Classification

Sl. No	Concept	Reference Period	Classification Rule
1.	UPS	Last 365 days	Major time criterion
2.	UPSS	Last 365 days	Major time criterion and priority criterion with a minimum threshold of 30 days in work
3.	CWS	Last 7 days	Priority criterion with a minimum threshold of one hour in labour force
4.	MCWS	Last 7 days	Major time criterion
5.	CDS	Each day of the last week	Persons are not classified but mandays are classified

well as those identified to be in labour force as per CWS but not as per UPS. The discriminatory power of MCWS in identifying stable labour force attachments is thus analysed by comparing the profiles of those included in CWS labour force but not in MCWS labour force.

8.1 Comparison Between UPS and CWS

The estimated UPS labour force as per Seventh Quinquennial Employment-Unemployment Survey conducted during 2004-05 was 428.29 million. In comparison, the estimated labour force as per CWS concept was 444.76 million. The cross classification of population by UPS and CWS concepts is given in Statement 2.

The above statement indicates that the classification is essentially the same both by UPS and CWS in 96.3 per cent of the cases. Of the remaining 3.7 per cent, 11.86 million persons (1.1%) are in labour force as per UPS concept though not as per CWS concept. On the other hand 28.33 million persons (2.6%) are in labour force as per CWS concept but not as per UPS concept.

By including the subsidiary status workers also in the labour force, the variations in classification get reduced to 2.6 per cent of the cases. However, percentage of persons who are in labour force as per UPSS but not as per CWS increases to 2.4 per cent while the percentage of persons in labour force as per CWS concept but not as per UPSS get reduced to just 0.2 per cent. It implies that about 2.4 per cent of persons in the CWS labour force get classified into UPSS labour force due to subsidiary status work. The details are given in Statement 3.

We may now examine the profile of the 28.33 million persons who get classified into labour force as per CWS but not as per UPS. The percentage distribution of these persons by CWS and UPS activity statuses is given in Table 4. It indicates that about 57.0 per cent of the

Statement 2: Distribution of Persons by UPS and CWS Concepts (in million)

CWS	UPS		
	In Labour Force	Out of Labour Force	Total
In Labour Force	416.43 (38.2)	28.33 (2.6)	444.76 (40.8)
Out of Labour Force	11.86 (1.1)	632.99 (58.1)	644.85 (59.2)
Total	**428.29** **(60.7)**	**661.32** **(100.0)**	**1089.61**

Figures in brackets indicate percentage shares.
Source: NSSO 61st Round Survey on Employment-Unemployment. Computed.

Statement 3: Distribution of Persons by UPSS and CWS Concepts (in million)

CWS	UPSS		
	In Labour Force	Out of Labour Force	Total
In Labour Force	442.84 (40.6)	1.92 (0.2)	444.76 (40.8)
Out of Labour Force	25.79 (2.4)	619.06 (56.8)	644.85 (59.2)
Total	**468.63** **(43.0)**	**620.98** **(57.0)**	**1089.61** **(100.0)**

Figures in brackets indicate percentage shares.
Source: ibid

persons classified are unpaid family workers, 26.2 per cent are self-employed own account workers and 10.4 per cent are casual workers as per CWS. These three categories taken together account for 93.6 per cent. Of the remaining, 3.3 per cent are unemployed, 1.9 per cent are regular salaried and the rest are either those who did not work during the week due to illness or other reason or self-employed employers. By usual status, about 59.7 per cent of them were classified as those attending domestic duties and also engaged in free collection of goods, 27.2 per cent as those attending domestic duties only and 10.5 per cent as those attending educational institutions. These three categories taken together account for about 97.4 per cent of the persons classified. It is thus clear that most of those classified as unpaid family workers, self-employed own account workers and casual workers as per CWS were classified as those attending domestic duties with or without free collection of goods and attending educational institutions as per UPS. It will be difficult to assume that all these persons are without any stable attachment to labour force. The problem is primarily because of a priori classification of persons under UPS based on the perceptions of time utilisation of individual members of households over a period of last 365 days. In the case of persons with multiple roles, there is always a tendency to report only the status which is traditionally recognised as more important in the household hierarchy. It is also not feasible for the field investigators to physically record all the activities of each person in the surveyed households over a period of 365 days and then decide the exact classification. The point becomes more clear, if we look at the rural-urban and male-female break-up of the group. The distribution of these persons by area, gender and weekly status is given in Table 5.

Table 5 is quite revealing. About 90 per cent of those classified into labour force by CWS but not by UPS are females and among them 78 per cent are in rural areas. Of the remaining ten per cent of males also about 8 per cent are in rural areas. Thus the use of UPS concept in the measurement of labour force excludes a significant share of persons in rural areas, particularly women.

Among the 90 per cent strong female labour force, about 72.6 per cent are engaged in agriculture with a break-up of 69.2 per cent in rural areas and 3.4 per cent in urban areas. The remaining 17.4 per cent of the women in labour force are distributed among manufacture of textiles (3.5), manufacture of wearing apparel (2.5 %), retail trade (2.2 %), manufacture of tobacco products (2.1 %), education (1.1 %) and others (6.0 %). Among the ten per cent men also 5.9 per cent are in agriculture, 0.9 per cent in retail trade, 0.5 per cent in education and the remaining 2.7 per cent in all other industries.

About 41 per cent of the women among female labour force are farmers engaged in livestock, poultry, fruit cultivation, etc. Another 23 per cent of them are cultivators of crops and vegetables and 7.4 per cent are agricultural labourers. The other major occupations in which the women in CWS work force but not in UPS work force are engaged are (i) tailoring and dress making (4.9 %), (ii) tobacco preparation and making (2.2 %), (iii) sales workers (1.5 %), (iv) teaching (1.2%) and (v) the rest others (16.2 %).

The above analysis brings out clearly that the persons not included in the labour force as per UPS concept, but captured by the CWS concept are not those having weak attachment to labour force. The concept of subsidiary status bring almost all of them into labour force along with others who do not have such stable attachments with labour force.

We may also examine the profiles of 11.85 million persons in the labour force as per UPS concept but not as per CWS concept. The percentage distribution of these persons by UPS and CWS statuses are given in Table 6. As per UPS, about 43.9 per cent of them were casual workers, 33.7 per cent unpaid family workers, 13.1 per cent self-employed own account workers and 6.1 per cent unemployed. About 16.4 per cent of those classified as casual workers by UPS were classified under CWS as those attending domestic duties, 9.9 per cent as those attending domestic duties along with free collection of goods, 11 per cent as those who did not work due to temporary sickness and 5.8 per cent as 'others' consisting of too young, too old and those not engaged in any specific activity. In other words, these persons neither did work nor did seek work during the entire seven days of reference week. The person who is really a casual worker as per UPS cannot afford to remain idle for seven days even without looking for a job. Similarly, those classified as unpaid family worker and self-employed own account worker as per UPS also cannot remain outside labour force for a full week. Among all those included in the labour force under UPS, 15.4 per cent were classified under 'others' and about three-fourth of them were males. It indicates that the classification these persons in work and labour force as per UPS is largely due to 'stylish' responses of the informants to summarise their activity status over the last one year rather than based on a realistic assessment of the duration in different activities. It also indicates that the persons involved did not have a stable labour force attachment.

Again, 91 per cent of the persons classified to be in labour force as per UPS but not as per CWS are in rural areas and 67 per cent of them were females. Out of the remaining 9 per cent in urban areas, 5 per cent were females. In total, 72 per cent were females and 28 per cent were males. About 83.8 per cent of them were engaged in agriculture, 5.3 per cent in construction and 1.9 per cent in retail trade as per UPS. In terms of occupation 43.8 per cent were cultivators of crop, 37.6 per cent were farmers engaged in livestock, poultry, etc and 3 per cent were in construction work. In case these persons had long term attachment to labour force, they should not have been classified as those engaged in domestic duties, attending educational institution, etc., on the basis of their activity. It re-confirms the point that persons with intermittent/non-regular attachment can also get classified into labour force by UPS due to 'stylish' responses.

The above analysis based on 61st Round Employment Un-employment survey data makes it clear that UPS concept can fail in identifying those having stable attachment to labour force, particularly in the case of rural women. It can also wrongly classify, though to a lesser extent, those not having stable attachment to labour force. In the case of CWS on the other hand, the classification is done after recording the actual activity status of each person over a period of seven days and as such the responded biases are eliminated. The weakness of CWS, however, is the priority criteria under which even persons with one hour of 'seeking work' in the reference week will be classified into 'labour force'. The MCWS measure is to remove this weakness by introducing the major time criterion.

8.2 Comparison Between CWS and MCWS

As mentioned earlier, the application of major time criterion instead of priority criterion in the activity status records of each person over a period of seven days provides MCWS based classification of labour force. In other words, MCWS labour force is invariably a sub-set of CWS labour force. The estimated MCWS labour force in 2004-05 was 431.6 million as compared to the estimated CWS labour force of 444.76 million. Thus about 3 per cent of the CWS labour force got excluded from the MCWS labour force. By analysing the profiles of the persons who gets excluded on the application of major time criterion, it can be seen that the group generally consists of those having marginal or weak attachment to labour force. The distribution of persons in the CWS labour force by days of attachment is given in Table 7. It may be seen that about 98 per cent of those in the labour force for less than half the week were working on all the days. It implies that they were generally not in the labour force on the days on which they were not working. Thus their labour force attachment is intermittent and | or unstable.

The group of persons with labour force days upto 3 days in a week according to CWS concept consists of about 13.15 million. The percentage distribution of these persons by sector and gender is given in Table 9. About 87.5 per cent are in rural areas and the rest 12.5 per cent in urban areas. Both in rural and urban areas females dominated. In the aggregate 27.6 per cent of them were males and the remaining 72.4 per cent were females consisting of 43.8 per cent illiterates, 6.7 per cent literates but below primary and another 8.9 per cent with primary level education. By weekly activity status, 41.6 per cent of them were unpaid family workers, 35.4 per cent casual workers and 20.2 per cent self-employed own account workers. Females dominated in each group with 34.8 per cent females in unpaid family workers, 23.4 per cent in casual workers and 12.3 per cent in self-employed own account workers.

It is thus evident that, in general, women in rural areas who do not have a stable attachment get rightly excluded from the CWS labour force if major time criterion is applied.

9. Measures of Non-utilization of Labour Time

Examination of the time disposition of persons over the reference week indicates that for many individuals time is divided between employment, unemployment and being outside the labour force. There are several useful ways in which this information could be summarized.

9.1 Severe Unemployment

We could identify as "severely unemployed" (SUE) persons reporting unemployment for 3.5 days or more, i.e. half or more days of the week. Whatever they may have done for the rest of the week, these are people who have been in the labour market and have clearly not done well. Their characteristics warrant further analysis. The SUE group is not identical to the MCWS unemployed, but a slightly different sub-set of the MCWS labour force. This is because persons who worked 3.5 days and were unemployed on 3.5 days would be classified as MCWS workers, but, for our present purpose, they would be classified as SUE, i.e. unemployed on 3.5 days. Further MCWS unemployed would also include those unemployed for major part of their labour force days though less than 3.5 days. To obtain incidence rates, the number of persons unemployed for 3.5 or more days could be divided by either the number in the CWS or in the MCWS labour force, as SUE persons would be members of the labour force under both concepts.

In Table 9 we present the estimated number of persons with severe unemployment, i.e. those who report 3.5 or more days of unemployment in the week. We also look at rates of severe unemployment in relation to the MCWS labour force. Severe unemployment rates appear to have been rising over the period from 1993-94 to 2004-05. For all persons, the rate rises from 5.14% to 6.66%, the absolute number increasing from 18.4 to 28.6 million over the period. Roughly two-thirds are male and about 70% are in rural areas.

9.2 Part-time Workers

A completely different approach would be to identify persons who worked for 0.5 to 3 days in the week. These are part-time workers (PTWs): they may be interested in additional work or they may not; some may report availability on non-working days while others may not. Also some may not report availability as they have been discouraged by their past labour market experiences. The incidence of part-time work is best measured in relation to the CWS work force, for not all part-time workers would be categorized as workers under the MCWS approach, but all of them would be included in the CWS work force, given its priority for work.

As Table 10 shows, persons working 0.5 to 3 days during the week account for a significant part of the CWS work force. In 2004-05, PTWs accounted for 5.34% of the total CWS work force. The percentages are higher for rural areas and among females. Among rural females, for instance, around 10.4% of the CWS work force comprised of PTWs. Between the 50th Round (1993-94) and the 61st Round (2004-05), PTWs to have increased both in absolute and in relative terms.

It might be argued that only those PTWs who express an interest in undertaking additional work should be considered when formulating employment policies. In practice, some may report non-availability for additional work on account of discouragement resulting from past efforts to find work or due to the weak link with the labour market, especially among non-wage earners. Hence, estimates of the size and characteristics of PTWs should be analyzed irrespective of their declared intentions regarding availability for additional work.

9.3 Underemployment

In the past, persons employed but interested in additional work were described as underemployed. Before 1972-73, the NSS results provided current status data on hours worked and hours available. It was possible to identify those who worked for a relatively short time (typically 28 hours or less per week) and were seeking and/or available for work. The latter were described as underemployed and this practice continues in several other Asian countries. This approach is, however, no longer feasible in India as time use is now done on a person-day basis, in terms of half days rather than clock time.

To estimate underemployment, we therefore propose a new measure. We take the ratio to the workforce of those who have worked for 3 days or less but more than 0.5 days in the week and who were unemployed for 0.5 days or more as per CWS. This will have the effect of excluding those who did not report any availability for additional work. The measure of underemployment used here is similar to the earlier measure based on the number of persons working 28 hours or less and available for additional work.

As Table 11 shows, the rate of underemployment for all persons rises from 1.65% of the CWS work force in 1993-94 to 2.26% in 2004-05. With the exception of urban females, the rates appear to be increasing over time for the other segments of the work force. While these results may reflect increasing underemployment, it may also capture the process of growing labour market orientation over time, whereby more and more PTWs report time outside the work force as being unemployment rather than outside the labour force.

9.4 Under-employment by Level of Earning

The frame work given by the 'Committee of Experts on Unemployment Estimates' under the Chairmanship of Prof. M.L. Dantwala for the measurement of labour force, work force and unemployment is purely based on time utilisation although the participation of any person in the labour force / work force is guided by the level of earning. In other words, the labour force participation rate without specifying the level of wages/earnings is only of limited value. This is one of the major short comings of the above frame work and labour statistics in the country.

The Employment-unemployment surveys being conducted by the National Sample Survey Organisation (NSSO) do collect wage and salary earnings received or receivable for the work done during the reference week for those employed on regular or casual basis These are collected separately for each of the activities pursued by each of the person in the sample households. Bonus received or to be received and perquisites evaluated at retail prices duly apportioned for the reference week are included in the salary / wages but overtime allowance received or receivable is excluded. The average earning per day for each worker can be estimated from these data sets in the case of employees.

The underemployment by level of earning can be therefore computed in the case of employee by comparing their daily wages with a minimum wage or standard which is expected or required for sustenance. An exercise in this regard has been undertaken by using the data sets of the latest Quinquennial Employment-Unemployment Survey. The percentage of workers receiving an average daily salary / wage of less than the national minimum wage of Rs. 66 per day has been computed both for casual workers and regular / salaried by using the data. The results are given in Table 12. It reveals that about 80 per cent of the casual workers and 31 per cent of the regular salaried / wage workers are under-employed in the sense that they do not receive the minimum daily wage of Rs. 66. The differentials between rural and urban areas and between the males and females are significantly large. In the case of casual workers, those not receiving the minimum daily wage of Rs. 66 in rural areas was 84.4 per cent as against 57.2 per cent in the case of urban areas in 2004-05. Similarly, the percentage of females receiving less than the minimum was 95.0 per cent as against 74.0 per cent in the case of males. The trend is similar even in the case of regular salaried / wage employed. While the under-employment ratio for rural and urban areas were 41.8 per cent and 25.4 per cent, the same in respect of males and females were 26.2 per cent and 53.7 per cent respectively.

In the case of self-employed including unpaid family workers, data on earnings / income are not being collected in the employment - unemployment surveys. This is a serious data gap on labour and employment which are important macro-economic variables and the national statistical system needs to be revamped to bridge this gap in line with the international conventions on labour statistics. In fact, the consumer expenditure block in the employment - unemployment survey schedule can be slightly expanded to collect income from self - employment and other sources.

In the 61st Round Survey on Employment - Unemployment, specific questions were asked about perceptions of remunerative income to all the self-employed persons including unpaid family workers as per usual principal or subsidiary statuses. The questions asked were the following:

(i) Do you regard the current earning from self-employment as remunerative, and

(ii) What amount per month would you regard as remunerative?

For the purpose of classification, the earning from self-employment was considered as remunerative, if the total earnings from self-employment were able to meet the desired level of income of the individual under the existing situation in respect of type of activity, scale of operation of the business, market condition, location of the business, etc. If the actual earnings from self-employment fell short of the desired level, the employment was regarded as non-remunerative. In the case of partnerships if the owners of the enterprises were from the same household, earning was judged by considering equal distribution of income among all the owners including the helpers irrespective of the shares held by the individual members. If the owners were from different households, earning from the partnership business was distributed first according to the agreement among the partner households. Then, the share of each household was to be distributed among its owners including the helpers equally. The perception about remunerative income is assessed on the basis of individual share of such income.

A monthly income upto Rs. 1000 was reported to be remunerative by 16.3 per cent of the self-employed, while 17.9 per cent reported as income between Rs. 1001 and 1500 as remunerative and another 15.3 per cent between Rs. 1501 and 2000. The minimum daily wage of Rs. 66 is equivalent to a monthly income of about Rs. 2000. Thus, even the perceptions of remunerative income were lower than the national minimum daily wage of Rs. 66 in the case of 49.4 per cent of the self-employed. The percentage of self-employed persons under-employed based on their perception of remunerative income itself thus constituted about 49.4 per cent.

10. Conclusion

The principal aim of this paper is to suggest new ways of analyzing labour force data. An important principle adopted is to retain the identity of the individual in the analysis as other characteristics of the individual can then be related to her/his labour force behaviour. The use of the majority time current weekly status measure is recommended as it fulfils this requirement, and implies a more substantial degree of involvement in the labour force and, within the labour force, in employment or unemployment. This measure should be used also for labour force projections, instead of the UPSS and CDS measures presently in use.

Three types of underutilization of labour time are identified for use in analysis and policy. All relate to persons. These are the ***severely unemployed***, persons who are unemployed for 3.5 days or more in the week; the ***part-time workers***, persons who work 0.5 to 3 days in the week, and the ***underemployed***, persons who are part-time workers reporting 0.5 or more days of unemployment. While the employment needs of these three groups of persons are likely to be different, we need to look at their other characteristics before formulating policy responses. This lies outside the scope of the present paper.

Table.1: Labour Force Participation Rates under Different Concepts

Category	Year	Per Thousand Participation Rates				
		UPS	UPSS	CWS	MCWS	CDS
Rural Males	1993-94	549	561	547	539	534
	1999-00	533	540	531	522	515
	2004-05	546	555	545	537	531
Rural Females	1993-94	237	330	276	254	232
	1999-00	235	302	263	240	220
	2004-05	249	333	287	265	237
Rural Persons	1993-94	398	449	415	401	387
	1999-00	387	423	400	384	370
	2004-05	401	446	418	403	387
Urban Males	1993-94	538	543	538	535	532
	1999-00	539	542	539	535	528
	2004-05	566	570	566	564	561
Urban Females	1993-94	132	165	152	143	132
	1999-00	126	147	138	129	123
	2004-05	148	178	168	159	150
Urban Persons	1993-94	345	363	355	349	343
	1999-00	342	354	347	341	334
	2004-05	366	382	375	370	364
All Males	1993-94	546	556	555	538	533
	1999-00	535	540	533	525	518
	2004-05	551	559	550	544	539
All Females	1993-94	211	290	245	227	208
	1999-00	208	263	231	212	196
	2004-05	224	294	257	233	215
All Persons	1993-94	384	423	400	388	376
	1999-00	376	406	386	373	361
	2004-05	392	430	407	395	381

Source: NSSO 50th, 55th and 61st Round Survey on Employment-Unemployment. Computed.

Table.2: Work Participation Rates Using Different Concepts

Category	Year	Per Thousand Participation Rates				
		UPS	UPSS	CWS	MCWS	CDS
Rural Males	1993-94	538	553	531	513	504
	1999-00	522	531	510	491	478
	2004-05	535	546	524	503	488
Rural Females	1993-94	234	328	267	242	219
	1999-00	231	299	253	227	204
	2004-05	242	327	275	247	216
Rural Persons	1993-94	390	444	403	381	366
	1999-00	380	417	384	362	344
	2004-05	391	439	402	377	355
Urban Males	1993-94	513	521	511	502	496
	1999-00	513	518	509	500	490
	2004-05	541	549	537	527	519
Urban Females	1993-94	121	155	139	129	120
	1999-00	117	139	128	118	111
	2004-05	135	166	152	142	133
Urban Persons	1993-94	327	347	334	325	317
	1999-00	324	337	327	318	309
	2004-05	346	365	353	343	334
All Males	1993-94	532	545	526	511	502
	1999-00	520	527	510	493	481
	2004-05	536	547	527	509	496
All Females	1993-94	206	286	236	214	195
	1999-00	203	259	222	200	181
	2004-05	215	287	244	216	195
All Persons	1993-94	375	420	386	367	354
	1999-00	365	397	370	350	335
	2004-05	380	420	389	368	350

Source: NSSO 50th, 55th and 61st Round Survey on Employment-Unemployment. Computed.

Table.3: Unemployment Rates Using Different Concepts

Category	Year	Percentage Unemployment Rates				
		UPS	UPSS	CWS	MCWS	CDS
Rural Males	1993-94	2	1.4	3	4.8	5.6
	1999-00	2.1	1.7	3.9	5.9	7.2
	2004-05	2.2	1.6	3.8	6.4	8
Rural Females	1993-94	1.4	0.8	3	4.9	5.6
	1999-00	1.5	1	3.7	5.6	7
	2004-05	3.1	1.8	4.2	6.8	8.7
Rural Persons	1993-94	1.8	1.2	3	4.8	5.6
	1999-00	1.9	1.5	3.8	5.8	7.1
	2004-05	2.5	1.7	3.9	6.5	8.2
Urban Males	1993-94	4.5	4.1	5.2	6.1	6.7
	1999-00	4.8	4.5	5.6	6.5	7.3
	2004-05	4.4	3.8	5.2	6.6	7.5
Urban Females	1993-94	8.2	6.2	8.4	10	10.5
	1999-00	7.1	5.7	7.3	8.6	9.4
	2004-05	9.1	6.9	9	10.5	11.6
Urban Persons	1993-94	5.2	4.5	5.8	6.8	7.4
	1999-00	5.2	4.8	5.9	6.9	7.7
	2004-05	5.3	4.5	6	7.4	8.3
All Males	1993-94	2.6	2.1	3.5	5.1	5.9
	1999-00	2.8	2.4	4.4	6.1	7.2
	2004-05	2.7	2.2	4.2	6.4	7.8
All Females	1993-94	2.4	1.5	3.8	5.7	6.3
	1999-00	2.3	1.7	4.2	6	7.4
	2004-05	4.1	2.6	5	7.4	9.2
All Persons	1993-94	2.6	1.9	3.6	5.3	6
	1999-00	2.7	2.2	4.3	6.1	7.3
	2004-05	3.1	2.3	4.4	6.7	8.2

Source: ibid

Table 4: Percentage Distribution of Persons in CWS Labour Force but not in UPS Labour Force by Activity Status

CWS	UPS						
	91	92	93	94	95	97	Total
11	1.4	7.2	16.8	0.4	0.1	0.4	26.2
12	0.0	0.2	0.1	0.1	0.0	0.0	0.4
21	6.0	15.3	34.9	0.2	0.0	0.6	57.0
31	0.8	0.6	0.4	0.0	0.0	0.0	1.9
41	0.0	0.0	0.2	0.0	0.0	0.0	0.2
51	1.0	2.9	5.9	0.1	0.0	0.3	10.2
61	0.0	0.1	0.1	0.0	0.0	0.0	0.3
62	0.1	0.1	0.2	0.0	0.0	0.0	0.5
71	0.0	0.0	0.0	0.0	0.1	0.0	0.1
72	0.0	0.0	0.0	0.0	0.0	0.0	0.0
81	1.0	0.5	0.6	0.0	0.1	0.1	2.3
82	0.2	0.4	0.4	0.0	0.0	0.1	1.0
Total	**10.5**	**27.2**	**59.7**	**0.9**	**0.3**	**1.6**	**100.0**

Source: ibid

Table 5: Percentage Distribution of Persons in CWS Labour Force but not in UPS Labour Force by Area, Gender and Weekly Status

Area & Gender	Weekly Status				
	11	21	41 & 51	Others	Total
Rural male	1.2	4.6	0.8	1.2	7.8
Rural Female	19.2	47.3	8.3	2.7	77.5
Rural Persons	20.4	51.9	9.1	3.9	85.3
Urban Male	0.5	0.7	0.2	1.0	2.4
Urban Female	5.3	4.4	1.1	1.6	12.4
Urban Persons	5.8	5.1	1.3	2.5	14.74
Total Male	1.6	5.3	1.0	2.3	10.2
Total Female	24.5	51.7	9.4	4.2	89.8
Total Persons	**26.2**	**57.0**	**10.4**	**6.4**	**100.0**

Source: ibid

Table 6: Percentage Distribution of Persons in UPS Labour Fore but not in CWS by Activity Status

UPS	CWS							
	91	92	93	94	95	97	98	Total
11	0.5	4.5	2.9	0.2	0.3	4.4	0.4	13.1
12	0.0	0.5	0.1	0.1	0.1	0.4	0.0	1.2
21	0.4	16.4	12.7	0.0	0.1	3.9	0.1	33.7
31	0.1	0.9	0.0	0.5	0.1	0.4	0.0	2.0
41	0.0	0.0	0.0	0.0	0.0	0.0	0.0	0.1
51	0.2	16.4	9.9	0.1	0.4	5.8	11.0	43.8
81	1.4	3.5	0.5	0.0	0.0	0.4	0.2	6.1
Total	2.6	42.3	26.1	0.9	1.1	15.4	11.7	100.0

Source: ibid

Table 7: Distribution of CWS Labour Force by Days in Labour Force

Days in Labour Force	No: of Persons		Percentage to total	Percentage in work force on all days
	In labour force	in work force on all days		
0.5	77693	77693	0.02	100
1	1296344	1270635	0.29	98.0
1.5	1110660	1092289	0.25	98.3
2	4271906	4234209	0.96	99.1
2.5	1407828	1377478	0.32	97.8
3	4983691	4904584	1.12	98.4
3.5	22636751	22248770	5.09	98.3
4	8150728	8002236	1.83	98.2
4.5	1048676	1013408	0.24	96.6
5	9374025	8964461	2.11	95.6
5.5	924587	889008	0.21	96.2
6	7452229	6967084	1.68	93.5
6.5	291502	270084	0.07	92.7
7	381735693	327073674	85.83	85.7
Total	444762313	388385613	100.00	87.3

Source: ibid

Table 8: Percentage Distribution of Persons with 0.5-3 days in Labour Force by Literacy Status

Literacy	Rural			Urban			Rural + Urban		
Status	Male	Female	Persons	Male	Female	Persons	Male	Female	Persons
Illiterates	8.51	40.72	49.23	0.62	3.12	3.74	9.13	43.84	52.97
Below Primary Literate	3.39	5.81	9.20	0.36	0.93	1.29	3.75	6.74	10.49
Primary	4.23	7.29	11.52	0.40	1.60	2.00	4.63	8.89	13.52
Middle	4.10	6.38	10.48	0.69	1.65	2.33	4.78	8.03	12.81
Secondary	2.40	2.02	4.42	0.40	0.69	1.10	2.80	2.71	5.51
Higher Secondary	1.18	0.73	1.92	0.54	0.72	1.26	1.73	1.45	3.18
Graduate & above	0.47	0.24	0.71	0.27	0.49	0.75	0.73	0.73	1.46
Non Reporting	0.05	0.01	0.06	0.00	0.00	0.00	0.05	0.01	0.06
Total	**24.32**	**63.20**	**87.52**	**3.28**	**9.20**	**12.48**	**27.60**	**72.40**	**100.00**

Source: ibid

Table 9: Persons (in millions) reporting at least 3.5 days of unemployment in a week.

Segment/ Year	Absolute Number			Percentage to MCWS Labourforce		
	1983	1993-94	2004-05	83 to 93-94	93-94 to 04-05	83 to 04-05
Rural Males	8.82	11.47	13.52	4.75	5.83	6.30
Rural Females	3.95	4.66	6.64	4.48	5.10	6.69
Rural Persons	12.76	16.13	20.16	4.66	5.60	6.42
Urban Males	4.02	5.17	6.10	6.02	6.44	6.57
Urban Females	1.59	1.52	2.39	9.43	8.12	10.37
Urban Persons	5.61	6.69	8.49	6.71	6.76	7.32
All Males	12.84	16.64	19.63	5.08	6.01	6.38
All Females	5.54	6.18	9.03	5.28	5.61	7.38
All Persons	18.38	22.82	28.65	5.14	5.89	6.66

Source: NSSO 50th, 55th and 61st Round Survey on Employment-Unemployment. Computed.

Table 10: Estimates of Part Time Workers (in million) and Rates of Part Time Workers (%)

Segment / Year	1993-94	1999-2000	2004-05
Rural Males	5.97 (3.31)	7.19 (3.80)	8.70 (4.15)
Rural Females	8.37 (9.80)	9.26 (10.51)	10.76 (10.42)
Rural Persons	14.33 (5.40)	16.44 (5.93)	19.46 (6.22)
Urban Males	1.09 (1.72)	1.33 (1.76)	1.69 (1.91)
Urban Females	1.16 (7.53)	1.30 (7.45)	1.48 (6.69)
Urban Persons	2.26 (2.86)	2.63 (2.82)	3.17 (2.87)
All Males	7.06 (2.90)	8.52 (3.22)	10.39 (3.49)
All Females	9.53 (9.45)	10.55 (10.01)	12.23 (9.77)
All Persons	**16.59 (4.82)**	**19.07 (5.15)**	22.63 (5.34)

Note: Figures in brackets are percentages of CWS workers who worked for 0.5 to 3.0 days in the reference week.
Source: ibid

Table 11: Estimates of Underemployed (in million) and Underemployment Rates (%)

Segment/ Year	1993-94	1999-2000	2004-05
Rural Males	3.40 (1.89)	3.91 (2.07)	5.56 (2.65)
Rural Females	1.48 (1.73)	1.55 (1.76)	2.46 (2.39)
Rural Persons	4.88 (1.84)	5.47 (1.97)	8.02 (2.56)
Urban Males	0.60 (0.95)	0.71 (0.94)	1.28 (1.45)
Urban Females	0.21 (1.36)	0.21 (1.19)	0.27 (1.24)
Urban Persons	0.81 (1.03)	0.92 (0.99)	1.55 (1.41)
All Males	4.00 (1.64)	4.62 (1.75)	6.84 (2.29)
All Females	1.69 (1.67)	1.76 (1.67)	2.74 (2.18)
All Persons	5.69 (1.65)	6.38 (1.72)	9.57 (2.26)

[Figures in brackets are percentages of CWS Workers who worked for 0.5 to 3.0 days in a week and reported 0.5 or more days of unemployment to CWS Workers.]
Source: NSSO 50th, 55th and 61st Round Survey on Employment-Unemployment. Computed.

References

1. GOI, 1970. "Report *of the Expert Group on Unemployment Estimate (Dantwala Committee)*", Planning Commission, Government of India.
2. GOI, 2001. "*Report of the Task Force on Employment Opportunities (Ahluwalia Committee)*", Planning Commission, Government of India.
3. GOI, 2002. "*Report of the Special Group on Targeting Ten Million Employment Opportunities per Year over the Tenth Plan Period (S.P. Gupta Committee)*", Planning Commission, Government of India.
4. NSSO 1996. "*Key results on Employment-Unemployment*", Report No: 406, Ministry of Statistics and Program Implementation. Government of India. New Delhi.
5. NSSO 1997. "*Employment-Unemployment Situation in India 1999-2000*", Report No. 409, Ministry of Statistics and Program Implementation. Government of India. New Delhi.
6. NSSO 2001a. "*Employment and Unemployment in India 1999-2000*", Round 55th, Report No. 455, Ministry of Statistics and Program Implementation. Government of India. New Delhi.
7. NSSO 2001b. "*Employment-Unemployment Situation in India 1999-2000*", Round 55th, Report No. 458 – I and II (55/10/2), Ministry of Statistics and Program Implementation. Government of India. New Delhi.
8. NSSO 2001c. "*Non-agricultural workers in Informal Sector Based on Employment and Unemployment Survey in India 1999-2000*", Report No. 460, Ministry of Statistics and Program Implementation. Government of India. New Delhi.
9. NSSO 2001d. "*Informal Sector in India 1999-2000*", Report No. 459, Ministry of Statistics and Program Implementation. Government of India. New Delhi.
10. NSSO 2006. "*Employment-Unemployment Situation in India 2004 – 2005*", Round 61st, Report No. 515 – I and II (61/10/1&2), Ministry of Statistics and Program Implementation. Government of India. New Delhi.

Annex 5.1: State-wise UPSS Labour Force by Sector and Sex as on 1st April of 2007, 2012 and 2017.

Table 1: State-wise Labour Force Projections for 2007 (in million)

State/Union	Rural			Urban			Total		
Territory	Male	Female	Persons	Male	Female	Persons	Male	Female	Persons
Andhra Pradesh	18.41	14.30	32.70	6.90	2.46	9.36	25.30	16.76	42.07
Assam	7.16	2.58	9.74	1.33	0.22	1.55	8.48	2.80	11.28
Bihar	22.06	6.39	28.45	2.60	0.40	2.99	24.66	6.79	31.44
Gujarat	10.49	6.94	17.43	7.06	1.65	8.70	17.55	8.59	26.13
Haryana	4.57	2.52	7.09	2.67	0.47	3.14	7.24	2.99	10.23
Himachal Pradesh	1.75	1.50	3.25	0.25	0.08	0.34	2.00	1.58	3.58
Jammu & Kashmir	2.42	1.30	3.72	0.96	0.17	1.13	3.39	1.47	4.86
Karnataka	11.39	8.13	19.53	6.31	2.05	8.36	17.70	10.19	27.89
Kerala	7.38	4.08	11.47	2.60	1.31	3.90	9.98	5.39	15.37
Madhya Pradesh	13.73	8.81	22.55	5.53	1.39	6.92	19.26	10.21	29.47
Maharashtra	17.38	13.39	30.76	15.28	4.20	19.48	32.66	17.59	50.24
Orissa	10.11	5.80	15.90	1.97	0.57	2.54	12.07	6.37	18.44
Punjab	5.19	2.64	7.83	3.25	0.71	3.96	8.45	3.35	11.79
Rajasthan	13.06	9.42	22.48	4.42	1.34	5.76	17.48	10.76	28.24
Tamil Nadu	9.91	7.51	17.43	10.44	4.15	14.59	20.36	11.66	32.02
Uttar Pradesh	39.89	16.67	56.56	11.85	2.17	14.03	51.74	18.84	70.58
West Bengal	18.86	5.49	24.36	8.16	1.91	10.07	27.02	7.40	34.42
Jharkhand	6.30	3.40	9.69	1.93	0.42	2.36	8.23	3.82	12.05
Chhattisgarh	5.01	4.07	9.08	1.52	0.42	1.95	6.54	4.49	11.03
Uttarakhand	1.88	1.50	3.38	0.79	0.17	0.96	2.67	1.67	4.33
Other NE States	2.99	1.71	4.70	0.83	0.35	1.18	3.82	2.06	5.88
Other states	0.89	0.29	1.18	5.67	0.92	6.59	6.56	1.21	7.77
Total	**230.84**	**128.44**	**359.27**	**102.31**	**27.55**	**129.86**	**333.15**	**155.98**	**489.13**

Source: Computed & Projected by NCEUS.

Table 2: State-wise Labour Force Projections for 2012(in million)

State/Union	Rural			Urban			Total		
Territory	Male	Female	Persons	Male	Female	Persons	Male	Female	Persons
Andhra Pradesh	19.70	15.20	34.91	7.38	2.77	10.15	27.09	17.97	45.06
Assam	7.98	3.07	11.05	1.56	0.28	1.84	9.54	3.35	12.89
Bihar	24.89	6.46	31.35	2.92	0.45	3.37	27.81	6.91	34.72
Gujarat	11.42	7.54	18.96	8.07	1.83	9.90	19.49	9.37	28.86
Haryana	5.03	2.95	7.98	3.15	0.57	3.72	8.18	3.52	11.70
Himachal Pradesh	1.88	1.63	3.52	0.30	0.10	0.40	2.18	1.73	3.91
Jammu & Kashmir	2.61	1.36	3.96	1.11	0.19	1.30	3.72	1.54	5.26
Karnataka	12.15	8.71	20.85	7.09	2.23	9.32	19.23	10.94	30.17
Kerala	7.79	4.11	11.90	2.69	1.34	4.03	10.48	5.45	15.93
Madhya Pradesh	15.22	9.42	24.64	6.41	1.62	8.03	21.63	11.04	32.67
Maharashtra	18.53	14.03	32.57	17.42	4.96	22.38	35.95	19.00	54.94
Orissa	10.80	6.39	17.18	2.21	0.73	2.93	13.00	7.11	20.12
Punjab	5.46	2.80	8.26	3.78	0.83	4.61	9.24	3.63	12.87
Rajasthan	14.72	10.33	25.04	5.06	1.53	6.59	19.77	11.86	31.63
Tamil Nadu	9.30	7.13	16.42	11.93	4.83	16.77	21.23	11.96	33.19
Uttar Pradesh	44.57	19.02	63.59	13.57	2.51	16.08	58.14	21.53	79.67
West Bengal	20.81	5.77	26.58	8.67	2.07	10.74	29.48	7.84	37.32
Jharkhand	7.17	3.73	10.91	2.15	0.48	2.63	9.33	4.21	13.54
Chhattisgarh	5.45	4.32	9.77	1.80	0.50	2.30	7.25	4.82	12.07
Uttarakhand	2.07	1.65	3.73	0.91	0.20	1.11	2.99	1.85	4.84
Other NE States	3.44	2.06	5.50	0.94	0.41	1.36	4.39	2.47	6.86
Other states	0.99	0.33	1.32	6.95	1.07	8.01	7.94	1.40	9.34
Total	251.99	138.01	390.00	116.08	31.51	147.58	368.06	169.52	537.58

Source: ibid

Table 3: State-wise Labour Force Projections for 2017 (in million)

State/Union Territory	Rural			Urban			Total		
	Male	Female	Persons	Male	Female	Persons	Male	Female	Persons
Andhra Pradesh	20.86	15.98	36.84	7.78	2.94	10.72	28.64	18.92	47.57
Assam	8.76	3.56	12.33	1.77	0.32	2.09	10.53	3.88	14.42
Bihar	27.88	6.52	34.39	3.19	0.51	3.70	31.07	7.03	38.10
Gujarat	12.30	8.17	20.48	8.99	2.01	10.99	21.29	10.18	31.47
Haryana	5.46	3.42	8.87	3.65	0.66	4.30	9.11	4.07	13.18
Himachal Pradesh	2.01	1.73	3.74	0.33	0.11	0.44	2.34	1.84	4.18
Jammu & Kashmir	2.85	1.46	4.30	1.24	0.20	1.43	4.08	1.65	5.74
Karnataka	12.68	9.28	21.96	7.79	2.47	10.26	20.47	11.76	32.22
Kerala	8.14	4.25	12.39	2.77	1.35	4.12	10.92	5.59	16.51
Madhya Pradesh	16.85	10.15	27.00	7.21	1.81	9.02	24.06	11.96	36.02
Maharashtra	19.65	14.78	34.44	19.40	5.51	24.92	39.06	20.30	59.36
Orissa	11.42	6.90	18.31	2.40	0.83	3.23	13.82	7.73	21.55
Punjab	5.68	2.91	8.59	4.26	0.93	5.19	9.94	3.84	13.78
Rajasthan	16.61	11.45	28.06	5.61	1.71	7.32	22.22	13.16	35.38
Tamil Nadu	8.50	6.57	15.07	13.36	5.39	18.75	21.85	11.97	33.82
Uttar Pradesh	49.32	21.28	70.60	15.12	2.76	17.89	64.45	24.04	88.49
West Bengal	22.59	5.97	28.56	9.01	2.12	11.13	31.60	8.09	39.69
Jharkhand	8.08	4.20	12.28	2.37	0.54	2.91	10.45	4.74	15.19
Chhattisgarh	5.90	4.58	10.47	2.08	0.58	2.66	7.98	5.16	13.14
Uttarakhand	2.26	1.79	4.05	1.03	0.22	1.25	3.29	2.01	5.30
Other NE States	3.85	2.40	6.25	1.06	0.49	1.54	4.90	2.89	7.79
Other states	1.08	0.33	1.41	7.98	1.18	9.16	9.06	1.51	10.57
Total	**272.72**	**147.68**	**420.40**	**128.41**	**34.64**	**163.04**	**401.12**	**182.32**	**583.44**

Source: ibid

Table 4: Growth Rate in Labour Force Between 2007 and 2012

State/Union	Rural			Urban			Total		
Territory	Male	Female	Persons	Male	Female	Persons	Male	Female	Persons
Andhra Pradesh	1.36	1.23	1.32	1.35	2.40	1.63	1.38	1.40	1.38
Assam	2.19	3.54	2.56	3.24	4.94	3.49	2.38	3.65	2.70
Bihar	2.44	0.22	1.96	2.35	2.38	2.42	2.43	0.35	2.00
Gujarat	1.71	1.67	1.70	2.71	2.09	2.62	2.12	1.75	2.01
Haryana	1.94	3.20	2.39	3.36	3.93	3.45	2.47	3.32	2.72
Himachal Pradesh	1.44	1.68	1.61	3.71	4.56	3.30	1.74	1.83	1.78
Jammu & Kashmir	1.52	0.91	1.26	2.95	2.25	2.84	1.88	0.93	1.59
Karnataka	1.30	1.39	1.32	2.36	1.70	2.20	1.67	1.43	1.58
Kerala	1.09	0.15	0.74	0.68	0.45	0.66	0.98	0.22	0.72
Madhya Pradesh	2.08	1.35	1.79	3.00	3.11	3.02	2.35	1.58	2.08
Maharashtra	1.29	0.94	1.15	2.66	3.38	2.81	1.94	1.55	1.80
Orissa	1.33	1.96	1.56	2.33	5.07	2.90	1.50	2.22	1.76
Punjab	1.02	1.18	1.07	3.07	3.17	3.09	1.80	1.62	1.77
Rajasthan	2.42	1.86	2.18	2.74	2.69	2.73	2.49	1.97	2.29
Tamil Nadu	-1.26	-1.03	-1.19	2.70	3.08	2.82	0.84	0.51	0.72
Uttar Pradesh	2.24	2.67	2.37	2.75	2.95	2.77	2.36	2.71	2.45
West Bengal	1.99	1.00	1.76	1.22	1.62	1.30	1.76	1.16	1.63
Jharkhand	2.62	1.87	2.40	2.18	2.71	2.19	2.54	1.96	2.36
Chhattisgarh	1.70	1.20	1.48	3.44	3.55	3.36	2.08	1.43	1.82
Uttarakhand	1.94	1.92	1.99	2.87	3.30	2.95	2.29	2.07	2.25
Other NE States	2.84	3.79	3.19	2.52	3.22	2.88	2.82	3.70	3.13
Other states	2.15	2.62	2.27	4.16	3.07	3.98	3.89	2.96	3.75
Total	**1.77**	**1.45**	**1.65**	**2.56**	**2.72**	**2.59**	**2.01**	**1.68**	**1.91**

Source: ibid

Table 5: Growth Rate in Labour Force Between 2012 and 2017

State/Union	Rural			Urban			Total		
Territory	Male	Female	Persons	Male	Female	Persons	Male	Female	Persons
Andhra Pradesh	1.15	1.01	1.08	1.06	1.20	1.10	1.12	1.04	1.09
Assam	1.88	3.01	2.22	2.56	2.71	2.58	1.99	2.98	2.27
Bihar	2.29	0.19	1.87	1.78	2.53	1.89	2.24	0.34	1.88
Gujarat	1.50	1.62	1.55	2.18	1.89	2.11	1.78	1.67	1.75
Haryana	1.65	3.00	2.14	2.99	2.98	2.94	2.18	2.95	2.41
Himachal Pradesh	1.35	1.20	1.22	1.92	1.92	1.92	1.43	1.24	1.34
Jammu & Kashmir	1.77	1.43	1.66	2.24	1.03	1.92	1.86	1.39	1.76
Karnataka	0.86	1.28	1.04	1.90	2.07	1.94	1.26	1.46	1.32
Kerala	0.88	0.67	0.81	0.59	0.15	0.44	0.83	0.51	0.72
Madhya Pradesh	2.06	1.50	1.85	2.38	2.24	2.35	2.15	1.61	1.97
Maharashtra	1.18	1.05	1.12	2.18	2.13	2.17	1.67	1.33	1.56
Orissa	1.12	1.55	1.28	1.66	2.60	1.97	1.23	1.69	1.38
Punjab	0.79	0.77	0.79	2.42	2.30	2.40	1.47	1.13	1.38
Rajasthan	2.45	2.08	2.30	2.09	2.25	2.12	2.36	2.10	2.27
Tamil Nadu	-1.78	-1.62	-1.70	2.29	2.22	2.26	0.58	0.02	0.38
Uttar Pradesh	2.05	2.27	2.11	2.19	1.92	2.16	2.08	2.23	2.12
West Bengal	1.66	0.68	1.45	0.77	0.48	0.72	1.40	0.63	1.24
Jharkhand	2.42	2.40	2.39	1.97	2.38	2.04	2.29	2.40	2.33
Chhattisgarh	1.60	1.18	1.39	2.93	3.01	2.95	1.94	1.37	1.71
Uttarakhand	1.77	1.64	1.66	2.51	1.92	2.40	1.93	1.67	1.83
Other NE States	2.28	3.10	2.59	2.43	3.63	2.52	2.22	3.19	2.58
Other states	1.76	0.00	1.33	2.80	1.98	2.72	2.67	1.52	2.51
Total	**1.59**	**1.36**	**1.51**	**2.04**	**1.91**	**2.01**	**1.74**	**1.47**	**1.65**

Source: ibid

Annex 5.2: State and Age Group-wise UPSS Labour Force by Sector and Sex as on 1st April of 2007, 2012 and 2017.

Projected Age-Sex UPSS Labour Force of Andhra Pradesh in 2007 (in million)

Age Group	Rural			Urban			Rural + Urban		
	Male	Female	Person	Male	Female	Person	Male	Female	Person
0-4	0.00	0.00	0.00	0.00	0.00	0.00	0.00	0.00	0.00
5-9	0.01	0.01	0.02	0.00	0.00	0.00	0.01	0.01	0.02
10-14	0.30	0.45	0.75	0.06	0.05	0.11	0.36	0.51	0.86
15-19	1.98	1.52	3.50	0.50	0.21	0.71	2.48	1.72	4.21
20-24	2.66	1.79	4.44	0.94	0.30	1.24	3.59	2.09	5.68
25-29	2.42	1.90	4.32	1.05	0.31	1.36	3.46	2.21	5.68
30-34	2.19	1.92	4.11	0.96	0.38	1.34	3.16	2.30	5.45
35-39	2.03	1.76	3.79	0.85	0.32	1.17	2.88	2.08	4.96
40-44	1.84	1.48	3.32	0.77	0.28	1.05	2.60	1.77	4.37
45-49	1.58	1.23	2.81	0.67	0.22	0.89	2.25	1.44	3.70
50-54	1.27	0.91	2.19	0.53	0.17	0.71	1.80	1.09	2.89
55-59	0.93	0.66	1.59	0.34	0.10	0.44	1.27	0.76	2.03
60+	1.21	0.67	1.88	0.23	0.11	0.34	1.44	0.78	2.22
Total	**18.41**	**14.30**	**32.70**	**6.90**	**2.46**	**9.36**	**25.30**	**16.76**	**42.07**

Source: ibid

Projected Age-Sex UPSS Labour Force of Andhra Pradesh in 2012 (in million)

Age Group	Rural			Urban			Rural + Urban		
	Male	Female	Person	Male	Female	Person	Male	Female	Person
0-4	0.00	0.00	0.00	0.00	0.00	0.00	0.00	0.00	0.00
5-9	0.00	0.00	0.00	0.00	0.00	0.00	0.00	0.00	0.00
10-14	0.05	0.26	0.31	0.02	0.04	0.06	0.07	0.29	0.37
15-19	1.84	1.43	3.27	0.43	0.18	0.61	2.27	1.61	3.88
20-24	2.99	1.92	4.91	0.90	0.32	1.22	3.89	2.23	6.12
25-29	2.73	1.96	4.69	1.10	0.35	1.45	3.83	2.31	6.14
30-34	2.37	1.99	4.36	1.07	0.45	1.52	3.44	2.44	5.88
35-39	2.14	1.93	4.07	0.94	0.40	1.35	3.09	2.33	5.41
40-44	1.93	1.66	3.59	0.83	0.33	1.17	2.76	2.00	4.76
45-49	1.75	1.43	3.18	0.76	0.24	1.00	2.51	1.67	4.19
50-54	1.46	1.07	2.53	0.63	0.21	0.84	2.09	1.28	3.37
55-59	1.11	0.77	1.87	0.43	0.12	0.55	1.54	0.89	2.43
60+	1.33	0.79	2.12	0.26	0.13	0.40	1.60	0.92	2.52
Total	**19.70**	**15.20**	**34.91**	**7.38**	**2.77**	**10.15**	**27.09**	**17.97**	**45.06**

Source: ibid

Projected Age-Sex UPSS Labour Force of Andhra Pradesh in 2017 (in million)

Age Group	Rural			Urban			Rural + Urban		
	Male	Female	Person	Male	Female	Person	Male	Female	Person
0-4	0.00	0.00	0.00	0.00	0.00	0.00	0.00	0.00	0.00
5-9	0.00	0.00	0.00	0.00	0.00	0.00	0.00	0.00	0.00
10-14	0.00	0.09	0.09	0.00	0.03	0.03	0.00	0.12	0.12
15-19	1.52	1.20	2.72	0.36	0.16	0.52	1.89	1.35	3.24
20-24	2.96	1.94	4.90	0.82	0.29	1.11	3.78	2.23	6.01
25-29	3.10	2.22	5.32	1.11	0.35	1.45	4.20	2.57	6.78
30-34	2.68	2.07	4.74	1.14	0.46	1.61	3.82	2.53	6.35
35-39	2.31	1.97	4.28	1.05	0.43	1.49	3.36	2.40	5.76
40-44	2.04	1.80	3.84	0.94	0.38	1.31	2.97	2.18	5.15
45-49	1.85	1.60	3.45	0.83	0.28	1.12	2.69	1.88	4.57
50-54	1.62	1.27	2.88	0.71	0.25	0.96	2.33	1.52	3.85
55-59	1.28	0.90	2.18	0.51	0.15	0.67	1.80	1.05	2.85
60+	1.51	0.92	2.43	0.30	0.16	0.46	1.80	1.09	2.89
Total	**20.86**	**15.98**	**36.84**	**7.78**	**2.94**	**10.72**	**28.64**	**18.92**	**47.57**

Source: ibid

Projected Age-Sex UPSS Labour Force of Assam in 2007 (in million)

Age Group	Rural			Urban			Rural + Urban		
	Male	Female	Person	Male	Female	Person	Male	Female	Person
0-4	0.00	0.00	0.00	0.00	0.00	0.00	0.00	0.00	0.00
5-9	0.00	0.00	0.00	0.00	0.00	0.00	0.00	0.00	0.01
10-14	0.08	0.03	0.10	0.00	0.00	0.00	0.08	0.03	0.11
15-19	0.71	0.30	1.00	0.07	0.01	0.08	0.77	0.31	1.08
20-24	1.01	0.35	1.36	0.14	0.05	0.19	1.15	0.40	1.55
25-29	0.96	0.33	1.29	0.20	0.04	0.24	1.16	0.37	1.53
30-34	0.88	0.38	1.26	0.20	0.03	0.23	1.08	0.41	1.49
35-39	0.83	0.40	1.23	0.19	0.03	0.22	1.02	0.43	1.45
40-44	0.76	0.30	1.06	0.17	0.02	0.19	0.93	0.32	1.24
45-49	0.62	0.19	0.81	0.14	0.02	0.16	0.76	0.21	0.97
50-54	0.47	0.14	0.62	0.11	0.01	0.12	0.58	0.16	0.74
55-59	0.35	0.06	0.41	0.07	0.01	0.07	0.42	0.07	0.49
60+	0.49	0.09	0.58	0.04	0.00	0.04	0.53	0.09	0.62
Total	**7.16**	**2.58**	**9.74**	**1.33**	**0.22**	**1.55**	**8.48**	**2.80**	**11.28**

Source: ibid

Projected Age-Sex UPSS Labour Force of Assam in 2012 (in million)

Age Group	Rural			Urban			Rural + Urban		
	Male	Female	Person	Male	Female	Person	Male	Female	Person
0-4	0.00	0.00	0.00	0.00	0.00	0.00	0.00	0.00	0.00
5-9	0.00	0.00	0.00	0.00	0.00	0.00	0.00	0.00	0.00
10-14	0.06	0.02	0.07	0.00	0.00	0.00	0.06	0.02	0.07
15-19	0.72	0.31	1.03	0.06	0.01	0.08	0.78	0.32	1.10
20-24	1.21	0.44	1.65	0.17	0.06	0.23	1.37	0.50	1.88
25-29	1.10	0.37	1.47	0.23	0.05	0.28	1.33	0.42	1.75
30-34	0.92	0.41	1.34	0.23	0.04	0.28	1.16	0.46	1.61
35-39	0.84	0.47	1.31	0.22	0.04	0.26	1.06	0.51	1.58
40-44	0.80	0.38	1.17	0.19	0.02	0.21	0.99	0.40	1.39
45-49	0.72	0.25	0.97	0.17	0.03	0.20	0.89	0.29	1.17
50-54	0.58	0.21	0.79	0.14	0.01	0.15	0.72	0.22	0.94
55-59	0.45	0.08	0.53	0.09	0.01	0.10	0.54	0.09	0.63
60+	0.60	0.12	0.72	0.04	0.00	0.05	0.64	0.13	0.77
Total	**7.98**	**3.07**	**11.05**	**1.56**	**0.28**	**1.84**	**9.54**	**3.35**	**12.89**

Source: ibid

Projected Age-Sex UPSS Labour Force of Assam in 2017 (in million)

Age Group	Rural			Urban			Rural + Urban		
	Male	Female	Person	Male	Female	Person	Male	Female	Person
0-4	0.00	0.00	0.00	0.00	0.00	0.00	0.00	0.00	0.00
5-9	0.00	0.00	0.00	0.00	0.00	0.00	0.00	0.00	0.00
10-14	0.03	0.01	0.04	0.00	0.00	0.00	0.03	0.01	0.04
15-19	0.67	0.29	0.97	0.06	0.01	0.08	0.74	0.31	1.04
20-24	1.25	0.49	1.74	0.18	0.07	0.25	1.43	0.55	1.98
25-29	1.30	0.45	1.75	0.27	0.06	0.33	1.56	0.51	2.07
30-34	1.06	0.47	1.53	0.27	0.05	0.32	1.33	0.52	1.85
35-39	0.88	0.52	1.40	0.26	0.04	0.30	1.14	0.56	1.70
40-44	0.82	0.44	1.26	0.22	0.02	0.24	1.03	0.46	1.50
45-49	0.76	0.32	1.07	0.19	0.04	0.23	0.95	0.35	1.30
50-54	0.68	0.29	0.97	0.16	0.01	0.18	0.85	0.30	1.15
55-59	0.56	0.12	0.68	0.12	0.01	0.13	0.68	0.13	0.80
60+	0.75	0.17	0.92	0.05	0.01	0.05	0.80	0.17	0.97
Total	**8.76**	**3.56**	**12.33**	**1.77**	**0.32**	**2.09**	**10.53**	**3.88**	**14.42**

Source: ibid

Projected Age-Sex UPSS Labour Force of Bihar in 2007 (in million)

Age Group	Rural			Urban			Rural + Urban		
	Male	Female	Person	Male	Female	Person	Male	Female	Person
0-4	0.00	0.00	0.00	0.00	0.00	0.00	0.00	0.00	0.00
5-9	0.00	0.00	0.00	0.00	0.00	0.00	0.00	0.00	0.00
10-14	0.19	0.04	0.23	0.02	0.01	0.03	0.22	0.04	0.26
15-19	2.52	0.42	2.94	0.15	0.01	0.17	2.67	0.43	3.11
20-24	3.16	0.58	3.74	0.34	0.05	0.38	3.49	0.63	4.12
25-29	2.71	0.82	3.53	0.39	0.05	0.44	3.10	0.87	3.98
30-34	2.46	0.91	3.37	0.35	0.05	0.40	2.81	0.96	3.77
35-39	2.34	1.01	3.35	0.31	0.05	0.37	2.65	1.06	3.71
40-44	2.18	0.85	3.03	0.29	0.05	0.34	2.47	0.90	3.37
45-49	1.87	0.58	2.45	0.25	0.03	0.28	2.12	0.61	2.73
50-54	1.52	0.47	1.99	0.21	0.03	0.24	1.73	0.50	2.23
55-59	1.18	0.33	1.51	0.15	0.03	0.17	1.32	0.36	1.68
60+	1.93	0.39	2.32	0.14	0.03	0.17	2.06	0.42	2.48
Total	**22.06**	**6.39**	**28.45**	**2.60**	**0.40**	**2.99**	**24.66**	**6.79**	**31.44**

Source: ibid

Projected Age-Sex UPSS Labour Force of Bihar in 2012 (in million)

Age Group	Rural			Urban			Rural + Urban		
	Male	Female	Person	Male	Female	Person	Male	Female	Person
0-4	0.00	0.00	0.00	0.00	0.00	0.00	0.00	0.00	0.00
5-9	0.00	0.00	0.00	0.00	0.00	0.00	0.00	0.00	0.00
10-14	0.03	0.00	0.03	0.01	0.00	0.01	0.04	0.00	0.04
15-19	2.58	0.28	2.86	0.12	0.00	0.12	2.70	0.28	2.98
20-24	4.19	0.64	4.83	0.36	0.06	0.42	4.56	0.70	5.25
25-29	3.39	0.84	4.23	0.47	0.07	0.53	3.86	0.91	4.76
30-34	2.62	0.83	3.45	0.43	0.06	0.48	3.05	0.89	3.94
35-39	2.36	1.01	3.37	0.36	0.06	0.42	2.73	1.06	3.79
40-44	2.25	0.91	3.16	0.32	0.06	0.38	2.57	0.97	3.53
45-49	2.09	0.62	2.71	0.28	0.03	0.31	2.37	0.66	3.02
50-54	1.77	0.50	2.27	0.24	0.04	0.28	2.00	0.55	2.55
55-59	1.40	0.37	1.78	0.18	0.04	0.22	1.59	0.41	2.00
60+	2.21	0.45	2.66	0.15	0.04	0.19	2.36	0.49	2.85
Total	**24.89**	**6.46**	**31.35**	**2.92**	**0.45**	**3.37**	**27.81**	**6.91**	**34.72**

Source: ibid

Projected Age-Sex UPSS Labour Force of Bihar in 2017 (in million)

Age Group	Rural			Urban			Rural + Urban		
	Male	Female	Person	Male	Female	Person	Male	Female	Person
0-4	0.00	0.00	0.00	0.00	0.00	0.00	0.00	0.00	0.00
5-9	0.00	0.00	0.00	0.00	0.00	0.00	0.00	0.00	0.00
10-14	0.00	0.00	0.00	0.00	0.00	0.00	0.00	0.00	0.00
15-19	2.39	0.08	2.47	0.09	0.00	0.09	2.48	0.08	2.56
20-24	4.61	0.59	5.20	0.34	0.06	0.40	4.95	0.65	5.60
25-29	4.49	1.05	5.54	0.51	0.08	0.59	5.00	1.12	6.12
30-34	3.29	0.84	4.13	0.51	0.07	0.58	3.80	0.91	4.71
35-39	2.53	0.96	3.48	0.44	0.07	0.51	2.97	1.02	3.99
40-44	2.27	0.90	3.17	0.37	0.06	0.43	2.64	0.96	3.60
45-49	2.17	0.63	2.79	0.30	0.04	0.34	2.47	0.66	3.13
50-54	1.98	0.53	2.51	0.26	0.05	0.31	2.24	0.58	2.81
55-59	1.64	0.41	2.05	0.21	0.05	0.26	1.85	0.46	2.31
60+	2.52	0.53	3.05	0.17	0.05	0.21	2.68	0.58	3.26
Total	**27.88**	**6.52**	**34.39**	**3.19**	**0.51**	**3.70**	**31.07**	**7.03**	**38.10**

Source: ibid

Projected Age-Sex UPSS Labour Force of Chhattisgarh in 2007 (in million)

Age Group	Rural			Urban			Rural + Urban		
	Male	Female	Person	Male	Female	Person	Male	Female	Person
0-4	0.00	0.00	0.00	0.00	0.00	0.00	0.00	0.00	0.00
5-9	0.00	0.00	0.00	0.00	0.00	0.00	0.00	0.00	0.00
10-14	0.05	0.10	0.14	0.01	0.01	0.01	0.05	0.10	0.16
15-19	0.54	0.47	1.01	0.10	0.04	0.13	0.64	0.50	1.14
20-24	0.72	0.51	1.23	0.21	0.05	0.26	0.93	0.56	1.48
25-29	0.61	0.46	1.07	0.24	0.06	0.30	0.85	0.52	1.37
30-34	0.57	0.53	1.10	0.22	0.05	0.27	0.79	0.58	1.37
35-39	0.56	0.49	1.05	0.19	0.06	0.25	0.75	0.55	1.30
40-44	0.51	0.48	0.99	0.17	0.05	0.22	0.68	0.53	1.21
45-49	0.43	0.37	0.80	0.14	0.05	0.19	0.57	0.42	0.98
50-54	0.34	0.27	0.60	0.10	0.03	0.13	0.44	0.29	0.73
55-59	0.27	0.19	0.46	0.07	0.02	0.09	0.34	0.21	0.55
60+	0.42	0.21	0.63	0.07	0.02	0.09	0.49	0.23	0.72
Total	**5.01**	**4.07**	**9.08**	**1.52**	**0.42**	**1.95**	**6.54**	**4.49**	**11.03**

Source: ibid

Projected Age-Sex UPSS Labour Force of Chhattisgarh in 2012 (in million)

Age Group	Rural			Urban			Rural + Urban		
	Male	Female	Person	Male	Female	Person	Male	Female	Person
0-4	0.00	0.00	0.00	0.00	0.00	0.00	0.00	0.00	0.00
5-9	0.00	0.00	0.00	0.00	0.00	0.00	0.00	0.00	0.00
10-14	0.01	0.04	0.05	0.01	0.00	0.01	0.02	0.04	0.06
15-19	0.54	0.45	0.98	0.10	0.04	0.14	0.64	0.49	1.13
20-24	0.85	0.59	1.44	0.23	0.07	0.29	1.08	0.65	1.74
25-29	0.71	0.49	1.21	0.29	0.07	0.36	1.01	0.56	1.57
30-34	0.57	0.52	1.09	0.27	0.06	0.33	0.84	0.58	1.42
35-39	0.55	0.50	1.04	0.23	0.07	0.30	0.78	0.56	1.34
40-44	0.54	0.53	1.07	0.19	0.06	0.25	0.73	0.59	1.32
45-49	0.49	0.44	0.93	0.17	0.05	0.22	0.66	0.49	1.15
50-54	0.40	0.31	0.71	0.13	0.03	0.16	0.53	0.34	0.87
55-59	0.31	0.22	0.53	0.09	0.02	0.11	0.40	0.24	0.65
60+	0.48	0.24	0.72	0.09	0.03	0.12	0.56	0.27	0.83
Total	**5.45**	**4.32**	**9.77**	**1.80**	**0.50**	**2.30**	**7.25**	**4.82**	**12.07**

Source: ibid

Projected Age-Sex UPSS Labour Force of Chhattisgarh in 2017 (in million)

Age Group	Rural			Urban			Rural + Urban		
	Male	Female	Person	Male	Female	Person	Male	Female	Person
0-4	0.00	0.00	0.00	0.00	0.00	0.00	0.00	0.00	0.00
5-9	0.00	0.00	0.00	0.00	0.00	0.00	0.00	0.00	0.00
10-14	0.00	0.00	0.00	0.00	0.00	0.01	0.00	0.00	0.01
15-19	0.51	0.40	0.91	0.10	0.04	0.15	0.62	0.44	1.06
20-24	0.87	0.60	1.47	0.25	0.07	0.32	1.12	0.67	1.79
25-29	0.85	0.58	1.43	0.34	0.09	0.43	1.19	0.66	1.86
30-34	0.67	0.57	1.24	0.32	0.08	0.40	1.00	0.64	1.64
35-39	0.55	0.49	1.04	0.27	0.07	0.35	0.82	0.57	1.39
40-44	0.53	0.54	1.07	0.22	0.06	0.29	0.75	0.61	1.36
45-49	0.52	0.49	1.01	0.19	0.06	0.25	0.71	0.55	1.26
50-54	0.46	0.37	0.83	0.15	0.04	0.20	0.61	0.41	1.02
55-59	0.37	0.26	0.63	0.12	0.03	0.14	0.49	0.29	0.77
60+	0.56	0.28	0.84	0.11	0.03	0.14	0.67	0.32	0.98
Total	**5.90**	**4.58**	**10.47**	**2.08**	**0.58**	**2.66**	**7.98**	**5.16**	**13.14**

Source: ibid

Projected Age-Sex UPSS Labour Force of Gujarat in 2007 (in million)

Age Group	Rural			Urban			Rural + Urban		
	Male	Female	Person	Male	Female	Person	Male	Female	Person
0-4	0.00	0.00	0.00	0.00	0.00	0.00	0.00	0.00	0.00
5-9	0.00	0.00	0.00	0.01	0.00	0.01	0.01	0.00	0.01
10-14	0.07	0.07	0.14	0.03	0.02	0.05	0.10	0.09	0.19
15-19	1.23	0.77	2.00	0.51	0.14	0.65	1.74	0.92	2.66
20-24	1.52	0.94	2.45	1.01	0.19	1.20	2.53	1.13	3.66
25-29	1.37	0.85	2.22	1.13	0.18	1.31	2.51	1.02	3.53
30-34	1.24	0.88	2.12	1.01	0.24	1.25	2.25	1.12	3.37
35-39	1.17	0.87	2.03	0.88	0.24	1.12	2.04	1.11	3.15
40-44	1.06	0.78	1.84	0.77	0.22	0.98	1.83	1.00	2.82
45-49	0.88	0.70	1.58	0.66	0.16	0.82	1.54	0.86	2.40
50-54	0.71	0.49	1.20	0.49	0.10	0.59	1.20	0.59	1.79
55-59	0.51	0.32	0.83	0.31	0.08	0.39	0.82	0.40	1.22
60+	0.74	0.27	1.01	0.24	0.08	0.32	0.99	0.35	1.34
Total	**10.49**	**6.94**	**17.43**	**7.06**	**1.65**	**8.70**	**17.55**	**8.59**	**26.13**

Source: ibid

Projected Age-Sex UPSS Labour Force of Gujarat in 2012 (in million)

Age Group	Rural			Urban			Rural + Urban		
	Male	Female	Person	Male	Female	Person	Male	Female	Person
0-4	0.00	0.00	0.00	0.00	0.00	0.00	0.00	0.00	0.00
5-9	0.00	0.00	0.00	0.01	0.00	0.01	0.01	0.00	0.01
10-14	0.00	0.00	0.00	0.01	0.02	0.02	0.01	0.02	0.03
15-19	1.22	0.74	1.95	0.50	0.13	0.63	1.71	0.87	2.58
20-24	1.61	0.96	2.57	1.10	0.22	1.32	2.71	1.18	3.89
25-29	1.51	0.88	2.40	1.28	0.22	1.50	2.79	1.10	3.89
30-34	1.34	0.94	2.28	1.19	0.27	1.47	2.53	1.21	3.75
35-39	1.22	0.93	2.15	1.02	0.28	1.30	2.24	1.21	3.45
40-44	1.14	0.88	2.02	0.87	0.22	1.09	2.01	1.10	3.11
45-49	1.01	0.86	1.87	0.77	0.19	0.96	1.78	1.05	2.83
50-54	0.85	0.63	1.47	0.60	0.11	0.72	1.45	0.74	2.19
55-59	0.63	0.40	1.04	0.42	0.10	0.52	1.05	0.51	1.56
60+	0.90	0.31	1.21	0.30	0.07	0.37	1.20	0.38	1.58
Total	**11.42**	**7.54**	**18.96**	**8.07**	**1.83**	**9.90**	**19.49**	**9.37**	**28.86**

Source: ibid

Projected Age-Sex UPSS Labour Force of Gujarat in 2017 (in million)

Age Group	Rural			Urban			Rural + Urban		
	Male	Female	Person	Male	Female	Person	Male	Female	Person
0-4	0.00	0.00	0.00	0.00	0.00	0.00	0.00	0.00	0.00
5-9	0.00	0.00	0.00	0.01	0.00	0.01	0.01	0.00	0.01
10-14	0.00	0.00	0.00	0.00	0.02	0.02	0.00	0.02	0.02
15-19	1.13	0.66	1.78	0.50	0.12	0.62	1.63	0.78	2.41
20-24	1.56	0.94	2.50	1.16	0.23	1.39	2.72	1.17	3.89
25-29	1.62	0.93	2.54	1.38	0.23	1.62	3.00	1.16	4.16
30-34	1.50	1.03	2.54	1.32	0.30	1.62	2.83	1.33	4.16
35-39	1.34	1.01	2.36	1.18	0.30	1.48	2.53	1.31	3.84
40-44	1.21	0.96	2.16	0.99	0.25	1.24	2.20	1.20	3.40
45-49	1.10	1.00	2.09	0.86	0.21	1.07	1.95	1.21	3.16
50-54	0.98	0.78	1.76	0.69	0.14	0.83	1.67	0.92	2.59
55-59	0.76	0.51	1.26	0.52	0.13	0.64	1.28	0.63	1.91
60+	1.10	0.36	1.46	0.38	0.10	0.47	1.48	0.46	1.94
Total	**12.30**	**8.17**	**20.48**	**8.99**	**2.01**	**10.99**	**21.29**	**10.18**	**31.47**

Source: ibid

Projected Age-Sex UPSS Labour Force of Haryana in 2007 (in million)

Age Group	Rural			Urban			Rural + Urban		
	Male	Female	Person	Male	Female	Person	Male	Female	Person
0-4	0.00	0.00	0.00	0.00	0.00	0.00	0.00	0.00	0.00
5-9	0.00	0.00	0.00	0.00	0.00	0.00	0.00	0.00	0.00
10-14	0.02	0.03	0.05	0.13	0.00	0.13	0.14	0.03	0.18
15-19	0.36	0.24	0.60	0.33	0.05	0.38	0.68	0.29	0.98
20-24	0.79	0.34	1.14	0.43	0.06	0.49	1.22	0.40	1.63
25-29	0.70	0.32	1.02	0.40	0.06	0.46	1.10	0.38	1.48
30-34	0.60	0.36	0.96	0.34	0.07	0.41	0.94	0.43	1.36
35-39	0.51	0.34	0.85	0.29	0.07	0.36	0.80	0.41	1.21
40-44	0.45	0.31	0.76	0.25	0.07	0.33	0.71	0.39	1.09
45-49	0.37	0.24	0.61	0.20	0.04	0.24	0.58	0.27	0.85
50-54	0.27	0.13	0.40	0.14	0.03	0.16	0.41	0.16	0.57
55-59	0.19	0.09	0.28	0.04	0.01	0.05	0.23	0.10	0.33
60+	0.30	0.12	0.42	0.12	0.01	0.13	0.42	0.13	0.55
Total	**4.57**	**2.52**	**7.09**	**2.67**	**0.47**	**3.14**	**7.24**	**2.99**	**10.23**

Source: ibid

Projected Age-Sex UPSS Labour Force of Haryana in 2012 (in million)

Age Group	Rural			Urban			Rural + Urban		
	Male	Female	Person	Male	Female	Person	Male	Female	Person
0-4	0.00	0.00	0.00	0.00	0.00	0.00	0.00	0.00	0.00
5-9	0.00	0.00	0.00	0.00	0.00	0.00	0.00	0.00	0.00
10-14	0.00	0.01	0.01	0.11	0.00	0.11	0.11	0.01	0.11
15-19	0.29	0.23	0.52	0.34	0.05	0.39	0.63	0.28	0.91
20-24	0.84	0.40	1.24	0.51	0.07	0.58	1.35	0.47	1.82
25-29	0.81	0.37	1.19	0.49	0.08	0.57	1.31	0.45	1.76
30-34	0.68	0.42	1.10	0.43	0.09	0.52	1.12	0.50	1.62
35-39	0.57	0.37	0.94	0.36	0.09	0.45	0.93	0.46	1.39
40-44	0.50	0.39	0.88	0.30	0.09	0.38	0.79	0.47	1.27
45-49	0.43	0.32	0.75	0.24	0.05	0.29	0.67	0.37	1.04
50-54	0.34	0.17	0.52	0.17	0.04	0.20	0.51	0.21	0.72
55-59	0.25	0.12	0.37	0.04	0.02	0.06	0.29	0.14	0.43
60+	0.31	0.16	0.47	0.16	0.01	0.16	0.47	0.16	0.63
Total	**5.03**	**2.95**	**7.98**	**3.15**	**0.57**	**3.72**	**8.18**	**3.52**	**11.70**

Source: ibid

Projected Age-Sex UPSS Labour Force of Haryana in 2017 (in million)

Age Group	Rural			Urban			Rural + Urban		
	Male	Female	Person	Male	Female	Person	Male	Female	Person
0-4	0.00	0.00	0.00	0.00	0.00	0.00	0.00	0.00	0.00
5-9	0.00	0.00	0.00	0.00	0.00	0.00	0.00	0.00	0.00
10-14	0.00	0.00	0.00	0.09	0.00	0.09	0.09	0.00	0.09
15-19	0.22	0.20	0.42	0.35	0.05	0.41	0.57	0.25	0.82
20-24	0.80	0.38	1.18	0.57	0.08	0.65	1.38	0.46	1.83
25-29	0.88	0.43	1.31	0.58	0.10	0.68	1.47	0.52	1.99
30-34	0.80	0.55	1.35	0.53	0.11	0.63	1.33	0.66	1.98
35-39	0.66	0.41	1.07	0.45	0.10	0.55	1.11	0.51	1.62
40-44	0.56	0.46	1.02	0.36	0.10	0.46	0.92	0.55	1.47
45-49	0.48	0.40	0.88	0.28	0.05	0.33	0.76	0.45	1.21
50-54	0.40	0.23	0.63	0.19	0.04	0.23	0.59	0.27	0.86
55-59	0.30	0.17	0.48	0.04	0.02	0.06	0.35	0.19	0.54
60+	0.34	0.20	0.55	0.20	0.01	0.21	0.54	0.21	0.76
Total	**5.46**	**3.42**	**8.87**	**3.65**	**0.66**	**4.30**	**9.11**	**4.07**	**13.18**

Source: ibid

Projected Age-Sex UPSS Labour Force of Himachal Pradesh in 2007 (in million)

Age Group	Rural			Urban			Rural + Urban		
	Male	Female	Person	Male	Female	Person	Male	Female	Person
0-4	0.00	0.00	0.00	0.00	0.00	0.00	0.00	0.00	0.00
5-9	0.00	0.00	0.00	0.00	0.00	0.00	0.00	0.00	0.00
10-14	0.01	0.01	0.02	0.00	0.00	0.00	0.01	0.01	0.02
15-19	0.11	0.10	0.21	0.02	0.00	0.02	0.12	0.10	0.23
20-24	0.24	0.21	0.45	0.03	0.01	0.04	0.27	0.22	0.48
25-29	0.24	0.20	0.45	0.04	0.02	0.06	0.29	0.22	0.51
30-34	0.22	0.19	0.41	0.04	0.01	0.05	0.26	0.20	0.46
35-39	0.19	0.17	0.36	0.03	0.01	0.04	0.22	0.19	0.41
40-44	0.17	0.16	0.32	0.03	0.01	0.04	0.20	0.17	0.36
45-49	0.15	0.13	0.27	0.02	0.01	0.03	0.17	0.13	0.30
50-54	0.13	0.10	0.23	0.02	0.01	0.03	0.15	0.11	0.25
55-59	0.10	0.08	0.18	0.01	0.00	0.02	0.11	0.08	0.20
60+	0.20	0.14	0.34	0.01	0.01	0.02	0.21	0.15	0.36
Total	**1.75**	**1.50**	**3.25**	**0.25**	**0.08**	**0.34**	**2.00**	**1.58**	**3.58**

Source: ibid

Projected Age-Sex UPSS Labour Force of Himachal Pradesh in 2012 (in million)

Age Group	Rural			Urban			Rural + Urban		
	Male	Female	Person	Male	Female	Person	Male	Female	Person
0-4	0.00	0.00	0.00	0.00	0.00	0.00	0.00	0.00	0.00
5-9	0.00	0.00	0.00	0.00	0.00	0.00	0.00	0.00	0.00
10-14	0.00	0.00	0.00	0.00	0.00	0.00	0.00	0.00	0.00
15-19	0.09	0.08	0.16	0.02	0.00	0.02	0.10	0.08	0.19
20-24	0.24	0.22	0.46	0.03	0.01	0.04	0.27	0.23	0.50
25-29	0.27	0.22	0.49	0.04	0.02	0.06	0.31	0.24	0.55
30-34	0.25	0.21	0.46	0.04	0.01	0.06	0.29	0.22	0.52
35-39	0.22	0.20	0.41	0.04	0.01	0.05	0.26	0.21	0.47
40-44	0.19	0.18	0.36	0.03	0.01	0.05	0.22	0.19	0.41
45-49	0.16	0.15	0.31	0.03	0.01	0.04	0.19	0.15	0.35
50-54	0.14	0.12	0.26	0.02	0.01	0.03	0.17	0.13	0.29
55-59	0.11	0.09	0.21	0.02	0.01	0.02	0.13	0.10	0.23
60+	0.22	0.17	0.39	0.02	0.01	0.02	0.23	0.18	0.41
Total	**1.88**	**1.63**	**3.52**	**0.30**	**0.10**	**0.40**	**2.18**	**1.73**	**3.91**

Source: ibid

Projected Age-Sex UPSS Labour Force of Himachal Pradesh in 2017 (in million)

Age Group	Rural			Urban			Rural + Urban		
	Male	Female	Person	Male	Female	Person	Male	Female	Person
0-4	0.00	0.00	0.00	0.00	0.00	0.00	0.00	0.00	0.00
5-9	0.00	0.00	0.00	0.00	0.00	0.00	0.00	0.00	0.00
10-14	0.00	0.00	0.00	0.00	0.00	0.00	0.00	0.00	0.00
15-19	0.07	0.06	0.12	0.02	0.00	0.02	0.09	0.06	0.15
20-24	0.21	0.20	0.41	0.04	0.01	0.04	0.25	0.21	0.46
25-29	0.28	0.23	0.51	0.05	0.02	0.06	0.33	0.25	0.57
30-34	0.28	0.22	0.50	0.05	0.01	0.06	0.33	0.24	0.56
35-39	0.25	0.21	0.46	0.04	0.02	0.06	0.29	0.23	0.52
40-44	0.21	0.20	0.41	0.04	0.01	0.05	0.25	0.21	0.46
45-49	0.18	0.16	0.34	0.03	0.01	0.04	0.21	0.17	0.39
50-54	0.16	0.13	0.29	0.03	0.01	0.04	0.19	0.14	0.33
55-59	0.13	0.11	0.24	0.02	0.01	0.03	0.15	0.11	0.27
60+	0.25	0.21	0.46	0.02	0.01	0.03	0.27	0.22	0.48
Total	**2.01**	**1.73**	**3.74**	**0.33**	**0.11**	**0.44**	**2.34**	**1.84**	**4.18**

Source: ibid

Projected Age-Sex UPSS Labour Force of Jammu & Kashmir in 2007 (in million)

Age Group	Rural			Urban			Rural + Urban		
	Male	Female	Person	Male	Female	Person	Male	Female	Person
0-4	0.00	0.00	0.00	0.00	0.00	0.00	0.00	0.00	0.00
5-9	0.00	0.00	0.00	0.00	0.00	0.00	0.00	0.00	0.00
10-14	0.01	0.01	0.02	0.00	0.02	0.02	0.01	0.03	0.04
15-19	0.26	0.18	0.44	0.02	0.02	0.04	0.28	0.20	0.48
20-24	0.37	0.20	0.57	0.12	0.03	0.15	0.49	0.23	0.72
25-29	0.33	0.18	0.51	0.15	0.03	0.18	0.48	0.20	0.68
30-34	0.28	0.15	0.43	0.14	0.02	0.16	0.42	0.17	0.59
35-39	0.25	0.16	0.40	0.13	0.02	0.15	0.38	0.17	0.56
40-44	0.22	0.14	0.36	0.12	0.01	0.13	0.35	0.15	0.49
45-49	0.20	0.11	0.30	0.10	0.01	0.11	0.29	0.12	0.41
50-54	0.16	0.08	0.24	0.08	0.01	0.09	0.23	0.09	0.32
55-59	0.11	0.06	0.17	0.05	0.00	0.05	0.17	0.06	0.23
60+	0.24	0.04	0.28	0.05	0.00	0.06	0.29	0.04	0.34
Total	**2.42**	**1.30**	**3.72**	**0.96**	**0.17**	**1.13**	**3.39**	**1.47**	**4.86**

Source: ibid

Projected Age-Sex UPSS Labour Force of Jammu & Kashmir in 2012 (in million)

Age Group	Rural			Urban			Rural + Urban		
	Male	Female	Person	Male	Female	Person	Male	Female	Person
0-4	0.00	0.00	0.00	0.00	0.00	0.00	0.00	0.00	0.00
5-9	0.00	0.00	0.00	0.00	0.00	0.00	0.00	0.00	0.00
10-14	0.00	0.00	0.00	0.00	0.01	0.01	0.00	0.01	0.01
15-19	0.20	0.15	0.36	0.01	0.02	0.02	0.21	0.17	0.38
20-24	0.39	0.23	0.63	0.13	0.03	0.16	0.52	0.26	0.79
25-29	0.40	0.20	0.59	0.17	0.04	0.21	0.56	0.24	0.80
30-34	0.32	0.17	0.48	0.16	0.02	0.18	0.48	0.19	0.67
35-39	0.26	0.15	0.41	0.15	0.02	0.17	0.41	0.17	0.59
40-44	0.23	0.13	0.37	0.14	0.01	0.15	0.37	0.15	0.52
45-49	0.21	0.11	0.32	0.12	0.02	0.14	0.33	0.13	0.46
50-54	0.18	0.09	0.27	0.10	0.01	0.11	0.28	0.10	0.38
55-59	0.14	0.07	0.21	0.07	0.00	0.07	0.20	0.07	0.28
60+	0.28	0.04	0.32	0.07	0.00	0.07	0.35	0.05	0.40
Total	**2.61**	**1.36**	**3.96**	**1.11**	**0.19**	**1.30**	**3.72**	**1.54**	**5.26**

Source: ibid

Projected Age-Sex UPSS Labour Force of Jammu & Kashmir in 2017 (in million

Age Group	Rural			Urban			Rural + Urban		
	Male	Female	Person	Male	Female	Person	Male	Female	Person
0-4	0.00	0.00	0.00	0.00	0.00	0.00	0.00	0.00	0.00
5-9	0.00	0.00	0.00	0.00	0.00	0.00	0.00	0.00	0.00
10-14	0.00	0.00	0.00	0.00	0.01	0.01	0.00	0.01	0.01
15-19	0.19	0.14	0.32	0.00	0.01	0.01	0.19	0.15	0.34
20-24	0.37	0.22	0.59	0.13	0.03	0.16	0.50	0.25	0.75
25-29	0.45	0.22	0.68	0.18	0.04	0.22	0.63	0.27	0.90
30-34	0.39	0.20	0.59	0.18	0.03	0.21	0.57	0.23	0.80
35-39	0.30	0.18	0.47	0.17	0.02	0.20	0.47	0.20	0.67
40-44	0.25	0.14	0.39	0.15	0.01	0.17	0.40	0.16	0.56
45-49	0.22	0.12	0.34	0.13	0.02	0.15	0.35	0.14	0.49
50-54	0.20	0.11	0.30	0.12	0.01	0.13	0.31	0.12	0.43
55-59	0.16	0.08	0.24	0.08	0.00	0.09	0.24	0.09	0.33
60+	0.33	0.05	0.38	0.09	0.00	0.09	0.42	0.05	0.47
Total	**2.85**	**1.46**	**4.30**	**1.24**	**0.20**	**1.43**	**4.08**	**1.65**	**5.74**

Source: ibid

Projected Age-Sex UPSS Labour Force of Jharkhand in 2007 (in million)

Age Group	Rural			Urban			Rural + Urban		
	Male	Female	Person	Male	Female	Person	Male	Female	Person
0-4	0.00	0.00	0.00	0.00	0.00	0.00	0.00	0.00	0.00
5-9	0.00	0.00	0.00	0.00	0.00	0.01	0.00	0.00	0.01
10-14	0.05	0.09	0.14	0.01	0.01	0.02	0.07	0.09	0.16
15-19	0.69	0.28	0.97	0.10	0.02	0.12	0.79	0.31	1.10
20-24	0.89	0.42	1.31	0.24	0.05	0.28	1.13	0.47	1.59
25-29	0.78	0.41	1.19	0.30	0.05	0.35	1.08	0.46	1.54
30-34	0.72	0.52	1.24	0.27	0.07	0.34	0.99	0.58	1.58
35-39	0.70	0.44	1.14	0.24	0.05	0.28	0.93	0.49	1.42
40-44	0.65	0.39	1.03	0.21	0.05	0.27	0.86	0.44	1.30
45-49	0.55	0.30	0.85	0.19	0.03	0.22	0.74	0.33	1.07
50-54	0.44	0.23	0.67	0.16	0.04	0.20	0.61	0.26	0.87
55-59	0.33	0.17	0.50	0.12	0.03	0.15	0.45	0.19	0.65
60+	0.49	0.16	0.66	0.09	0.03	0.12	0.59	0.19	0.78
Total	**6.30**	**3.40**	**9.69**	**1.93**	**0.42**	**2.36**	**8.23**	**3.82**	**12.05**

Source: ibid

Projected Age-Sex UPSS Labour Force of Jharkhand in 2012 (in million)

Age Group	Rural			Urban			Rural + Urban		
	Male	Female	Person	Male	Female	Person	Male	Female	Person
0-4	0.00	0.00	0.00	0.00	0.00	0.00	0.00	0.00	0.00
5-9	0.00	0.00	0.00	0.00	0.00	0.00	0.00	0.00	0.00
10-14	0.01	0.00	0.01	0.01	0.00	0.01	0.01	0.00	0.02
15-19	0.70	0.32	1.02	0.08	0.02	0.09	0.78	0.34	1.11
20-24	1.17	0.55	1.72	0.24	0.06	0.30	1.42	0.60	2.02
25-29	0.97	0.46	1.43	0.35	0.06	0.41	1.32	0.52	1.84
30-34	0.76	0.51	1.28	0.33	0.08	0.41	1.09	0.59	1.68
35-39	0.70	0.45	1.15	0.28	0.05	0.33	0.98	0.51	1.48
40-44	0.67	0.43	1.11	0.24	0.06	0.30	0.91	0.49	1.40
45-49	0.62	0.36	0.98	0.21	0.03	0.24	0.83	0.39	1.22
50-54	0.52	0.25	0.77	0.18	0.04	0.22	0.70	0.29	0.99
55-59	0.41	0.20	0.61	0.14	0.04	0.18	0.55	0.24	0.79
60+	0.63	0.20	0.83	0.11	0.04	0.15	0.74	0.24	0.98
Total	**7.17**	**3.73**	**10.91**	**2.15**	**0.48**	**2.63**	**9.33**	**4.21**	**13.54**

Source: ibid

Projected Age-Sex UPSS Labour Force of Jharkhand in 2017 (in million)

Age Group	Rural			Urban			Rural + Urban		
	Male	Female	Person	Male	Female	Person	Male	Female	Person
0-4	0.00	0.00	0.00	0.00	0.00	0.00	0.00	0.00	0.00
5-9	0.00	0.00	0.00	0.00	0.00	0.00	0.00	0.00	0.00
10-14	0.00	0.00	0.00	0.00	0.00	0.00	0.00	0.00	0.00
15-19	0.64	0.32	0.96	0.06	0.01	0.07	0.70	0.33	1.03
20-24	1.28	0.61	1.88	0.23	0.06	0.29	1.51	0.67	2.18
25-29	1.27	0.60	1.87	0.37	0.07	0.44	1.64	0.67	2.31
30-34	0.95	0.58	1.54	0.38	0.10	0.48	1.34	0.68	2.02
35-39	0.74	0.45	1.20	0.34	0.06	0.40	1.08	0.51	1.59
40-44	0.68	0.45	1.13	0.28	0.07	0.34	0.96	0.51	1.47
45-49	0.65	0.40	1.05	0.23	0.03	0.26	0.88	0.43	1.31
50-54	0.59	0.30	0.89	0.20	0.05	0.25	0.79	0.35	1.14
55-59	0.48	0.25	0.73	0.16	0.04	0.20	0.64	0.29	0.93
60+	0.79	0.25	1.03	0.13	0.05	0.18	0.92	0.29	1.21
Total	**8.08**	**4.20**	**12.28**	**2.37**	**0.54**	**2.91**	**10.45**	**4.74**	**15.19**

Source: ibid

Projected Age-Sex UPSS Labour Force of Karnataka in 2007 (in million)

Age Group	Rural			Urban			Rural + Urban		
	Male	Female	Person	Male	Female	Person	Male	Female	Person
0-4	0.00	0.00	0.00	0.00	0.00	0.00	0.00	0.00	0.00
5-9	0.00	0.00	0.00	0.00	0.00	0.00	0.00	0.00	0.00
10-14	0.17	0.18	0.36	0.01	0.01	0.02	0.19	0.19	0.38
15-19	1.19	0.79	1.98	0.44	0.14	0.58	1.63	0.93	2.56
20-24	1.67	0.93	2.60	0.83	0.32	1.15	2.50	1.25	3.75
25-29	1.49	0.97	2.46	1.00	0.33	1.33	2.49	1.30	3.79
30-34	1.28	1.08	2.36	0.92	0.29	1.21	2.20	1.38	3.58
35-39	1.16	1.07	2.23	0.80	0.30	1.10	1.96	1.37	3.33
40-44	1.11	0.99	2.10	0.70	0.23	0.94	1.81	1.23	3.03
45-49	0.98	0.75	1.73	0.61	0.17	0.78	1.59	0.92	2.51
50-54	0.80	0.53	1.33	0.47	0.13	0.59	1.27	0.65	1.92
55-59	0.60	0.39	0.98	0.30	0.08	0.39	0.90	0.47	1.37
60+	0.94	0.45	1.39	0.23	0.05	0.28	1.17	0.50	1.67
Total	**11.39**	**8.13**	**19.53**	**6.31**	**2.05**	**8.36**	**17.70**	**10.19**	**27.89**

Source: ibid

Projected Age-Sex UPSS Labour Force of Karnataka in 2012 (in million)

Age Group	Rural			Urban			Rural + Urban		
	Male	Female	Person	Male	Female	Person	Male	Female	Person
0-4	0.00	0.00	0.00	0.00	0.00	0.00	0.00	0.00	0.00
5-9	0.00	0.00	0.00	0.00	0.00	0.00	0.00	0.00	0.00
10-14	0.10	0.08	0.18	0.00	0.00	0.00	0.10	0.08	0.18
15-19	1.07	0.68	1.75	0.41	0.12	0.53	1.48	0.81	2.29
20-24	1.76	0.94	2.70	0.85	0.36	1.21	2.61	1.30	3.91
25-29	1.70	1.02	2.72	1.10	0.33	1.43	2.79	1.36	4.15
30-34	1.42	1.14	2.56	1.06	0.34	1.40	2.49	1.47	3.96
35-39	1.21	1.15	2.36	0.95	0.33	1.28	2.17	1.48	3.64
40-44	1.12	1.10	2.22	0.80	0.27	1.07	1.92	1.37	3.29
45-49	1.04	0.91	1.95	0.70	0.19	0.89	1.74	1.10	2.84
50-54	0.90	0.65	1.54	0.56	0.15	0.71	1.45	0.80	2.25
55-59	0.73	0.49	1.22	0.38	0.10	0.48	1.11	0.59	1.70
60+	1.10	0.54	1.65	0.26	0.05	0.31	1.37	0.59	1.96
Total	**12.15**	**8.71**	**20.85**	**7.09**	**2.23**	**9.32**	**19.23**	**10.94**	**30.17**

Source: ibid

Projected Age-Sex UPSS Labour Force of Karnataka in 2017 (in million)

Age Group	Rural			Urban			Rural + Urban		
	Male	Female	Person	Male	Female	Person	Male	Female	Person
0-4	0.00	0.00	0.00	0.00	0.00	0.00	0.00	0.00	0.00
5-9	0.00	0.00	0.00	0.00	0.00	0.00	0.00	0.00	0.00
10-14	0.03	0.00	0.03	0.00	0.00	0.00	0.03	0.00	0.03
15-19	0.92	0.56	1.49	0.39	0.10	0.50	1.32	0.67	1.98
20-24	1.61	0.85	2.45	0.87	0.38	1.25	2.48	1.22	3.70
25-29	1.80	1.11	2.91	1.15	0.38	1.53	2.96	1.49	4.44
30-34	1.64	1.27	2.91	1.15	0.36	1.51	2.78	1.63	4.42
35-39	1.35	1.22	2.58	1.09	0.37	1.46	2.45	1.59	4.04
40-44	1.18	1.20	2.38	0.94	0.31	1.25	2.12	1.51	3.63
45-49	1.05	1.01	2.06	0.80	0.22	1.02	1.85	1.23	3.08
50-54	0.95	0.78	1.73	0.64	0.19	0.82	1.59	0.97	2.56
55-59	0.82	0.62	1.44	0.45	0.12	0.57	1.27	0.75	2.02
60+	1.32	0.66	1.98	0.31	0.04	0.34	1.62	0.70	2.32
Total	**12.68**	**9.28**	**21.96**	**7.79**	**2.47**	**10.26**	**20.47**	**11.76**	**32.22**

Source: ibid

Projected Age-Sex UPSS Labour Force of Kerala in 2007 (in million)

Age Group	Rural			Urban			Rural + Urban		
	Male	Female	Person	Male	Female	Person	Male	Female	Person
0-4	0.00	0.00	0.00	0.00	0.00	0.00	0.00	0.00	0.00
5-9	0.00	0.00	0.00	0.00	0.00	0.00	0.00	0.00	0.00
10-14	0.00	0.00	0.00	0.00	0.00	0.00	0.00	0.00	0.00
15-19	0.35	0.15	0.50	0.13	0.06	0.19	0.48	0.21	0.69
20-24	0.98	0.49	1.47	0.29	0.18	0.48	1.27	0.67	1.94
25-29	1.02	0.53	1.55	0.35	0.18	0.53	1.36	0.71	2.08
30-34	0.95	0.58	1.53	0.33	0.18	0.51	1.28	0.76	2.04
35-39	0.87	0.58	1.44	0.31	0.17	0.49	1.18	0.75	1.93
40-44	0.79	0.51	1.30	0.30	0.16	0.45	1.09	0.67	1.75
45-49	0.69	0.42	1.12	0.27	0.12	0.39	0.96	0.54	1.51
50-54	0.59	0.30	0.89	0.23	0.12	0.34	0.82	0.42	1.24
55-59	0.44	0.23	0.67	0.18	0.04	0.22	0.62	0.27	0.89
60+	0.70	0.29	0.99	0.22	0.09	0.31	0.92	0.38	1.30
Total	**7.38**	**4.08**	**11.47**	**2.60**	**1.31**	**3.90**	**9.98**	**5.39**	**15.37**

Source: ibid

Projected Age-Sex UPSS Labour Force of Kerala in 2012 (in million)

Age Group	Rural			Urban			Rural + Urban		
	Male	Female	Person	Male	Female	Person	Male	Female	Person
0-4	0.00	0.00	0.00	0.00	0.00	0.00	0.00	0.00	0.00
5-9	0.00	0.00	0.00	0.00	0.00	0.00	0.00	0.00	0.00
10-14	0.00	0.00	0.00	0.00	0.00	0.00	0.00	0.00	0.00
15-19	0.29	0.10	0.39	0.11	0.06	0.17	0.40	0.16	0.56
20-24	0.96	0.44	1.39	0.27	0.18	0.45	1.23	0.61	1.84
25-29	1.07	0.50	1.57	0.34	0.18	0.52	1.41	0.68	2.09
30-34	1.02	0.58	1.61	0.34	0.18	0.53	1.37	0.77	2.13
35-39	0.93	0.60	1.53	0.33	0.18	0.51	1.26	0.78	2.04
40-44	0.84	0.55	1.39	0.31	0.17	0.48	1.15	0.71	1.87
45-49	0.75	0.47	1.22	0.29	0.13	0.42	1.04	0.60	1.65
50-54	0.65	0.33	0.98	0.24	0.14	0.38	0.89	0.46	1.36
55-59	0.51	0.26	0.77	0.20	0.04	0.24	0.71	0.30	1.01
60+	0.77	0.28	1.05	0.25	0.09	0.34	1.02	0.38	1.40
Total	7.79	4.11	11.90	2.69	1.34	4.03	10.48	5.45	15.93

Source: ibid

Projected Age-Sex UPSS Labour Force of Kerala in 2017 (in million)

Age Group	Rural			Urban			Rural + Urban		
	Male	Female	Person	Male	Female	Person	Male	Female	Person
0-4	0.00	0.00	0.00	0.00	0.00	0.00	0.00	0.00	0.00
5-9	0.00	0.00	0.00	0.00	0.00	0.00	0.00	0.00	0.00
10-14	0.00	0.00	0.00	0.00	0.00	0.00	0.00	0.00	0.00
15-19	0.25	0.06	0.31	0.11	0.05	0.16	0.36	0.11	0.47
20-24	0.91	0.42	1.33	0.25	0.16	0.41	1.16	0.58	1.74
25-29	1.05	0.48	1.53	0.32	0.17	0.49	1.37	0.64	2.02
30-34	1.07	0.58	1.65	0.34	0.17	0.52	1.41	0.75	2.17
35-39	1.01	0.63	1.63	0.34	0.18	0.52	1.35	0.81	2.16
40-44	0.90	0.59	1.49	0.33	0.18	0.51	1.23	0.76	2.00
45-49	0.80	0.52	1.32	0.31	0.15	0.46	1.11	0.66	1.78
50-54	0.71	0.39	1.10	0.27	0.15	0.42	0.98	0.54	1.52
55-59	0.56	0.31	0.88	0.22	0.03	0.25	0.78	0.35	1.13
60+	0.87	0.28	1.15	0.29	0.10	0.38	1.16	0.38	1.54
Total	8.14	4.25	12.39	2.77	1.35	4.12	10.92	5.59	16.51

Source: ibid

Projected Age-Sex UPSS Labour Force of Maharashtra in 2007 (in million)

Age Group	Rural			Urban			Rural + Urban		
	Male	Female	Person	Male	Female	Person	Male	Female	Person
0-4	0.00	0.00	0.00	0.00	0.00	0.00	0.00	0.00	0.00
5-9	0.00	0.01	0.01	0.00	0.00	0.00	0.00	0.01	0.01
10-14	0.22	0.24	0.45	0.04	0.04	0.08	0.26	0.27	0.54
15-19	1.59	1.07	2.66	0.92	0.30	1.22	2.51	1.37	3.88
20-24	2.56	1.71	4.27	2.10	0.54	2.63	4.65	2.25	6.90
25-29	2.26	1.56	3.83	2.55	0.58	3.13	4.81	2.15	6.96
30-34	1.99	1.70	3.68	2.31	0.62	2.93	4.30	2.32	6.61
35-39	1.85	1.68	3.54	1.99	0.62	2.61	3.85	2.31	6.15
40-44	1.73	1.52	3.24	1.70	0.52	2.22	3.43	2.04	5.47
45-49	1.50	1.20	2.69	1.41	0.40	1.80	2.90	1.59	4.50
50-54	1.18	0.86	2.04	1.09	0.26	1.35	2.27	1.12	3.39
55-59	0.89	0.62	1.50	0.69	0.16	0.85	1.58	0.78	2.36
60+	1.62	1.22	2.84	0.48	0.17	0.65	2.10	1.39	3.49
Total	**17.38**	**13.39**	**30.76**	**15.28**	**4.20**	**19.48**	**32.66**	**17.59**	**50.24**

Source: ibid

Projected Age-Sex UPSS Labour Force of Maharashtra in 2012 (in million)

Age Group	Rural			Urban			Rural + Urban		
	Male	Female	Person	Male	Female	Person	Male	Female	Person
0-4	0.00	0.00	0.00	0.00	0.00	0.00	0.00	0.00	0.00
5-9	0.00	0.00	0.00	0.00	0.00	0.00	0.00	0.00	0.00
10-14	0.07	0.09	0.16	0.02	0.03	0.05	0.09	0.12	0.21
15-19	1.33	0.85	2.17	0.90	0.30	1.21	2.23	1.15	3.38
20-24	2.64	1.73	4.37	2.29	0.64	2.93	4.93	2.38	7.30
25-29	2.63	1.64	4.27	2.87	0.71	3.58	5.50	2.36	7.86
30-34	2.23	1.68	3.91	2.65	0.72	3.37	4.88	2.40	7.28
35-39	1.95	1.73	3.68	2.33	0.75	3.08	4.28	2.48	6.76
40-44	1.80	1.63	3.43	1.98	0.62	2.60	3.78	2.26	6.03
45-49	1.66	1.45	3.11	1.65	0.46	2.11	3.32	1.91	5.23
50-54	1.40	1.06	2.46	1.33	0.34	1.67	2.73	1.40	4.13
55-59	1.08	0.77	1.85	0.88	0.20	1.08	1.96	0.97	2.93
60+	1.75	1.39	3.13	0.52	0.19	0.71	2.26	1.58	3.84
Total	**18.53**	**14.03**	**32.57**	**17.42**	**4.96**	**22.38**	**35.95**	**19.00**	**54.94**

Source: ibid

Projected Age-Sex UPSS Labour Force of Maharashtra in 2017 (in million)

Age Group	Rural			Urban			Rural + Urban		
	Male	Female	Person	Male	Female	Person	Male	Female	Person
0-4	0.00	0.00	0.00	0.00	0.00	0.00	0.00	0.00	0.00
5-9	0.00	0.00	0.00	0.00	0.00	0.00	0.00	0.00	0.00
10-14	0.00	0.00	0.00	0.00	0.03	0.03	0.00	0.03	0.03
15-19	1.09	0.63	1.71	0.91	0.31	1.22	2.00	0.94	2.93
20-24	2.31	1.54	3.85	2.48	0.70	3.18	4.80	2.24	7.03
25-29	2.78	1.76	4.54	3.13	0.82	3.95	5.91	2.58	8.49
30-34	2.69	1.96	4.64	2.89	0.78	3.67	5.58	2.73	8.31
35-39	2.26	1.79	4.05	2.61	0.79	3.40	4.87	2.58	7.45
40-44	1.94	1.71	3.64	2.27	0.69	2.96	4.21	2.39	6.60
45-49	1.76	1.59	3.35	1.90	0.53	2.43	3.66	2.12	5.78
50-54	1.58	1.26	2.84	1.56	0.41	1.97	3.14	1.67	4.81
55-59	1.30	0.94	2.24	1.08	0.25	1.33	2.37	1.20	3.57
60+	1.97	1.61	3.58	0.57	0.21	0.78	2.54	1.82	4.36
Total	**19.65**	**14.78**	**34.44**	**19.40**	**5.51**	**24.92**	**39.06**	**20.30**	**59.36**

Source: ibid

Projected Age-Sex UPSS Labour Force of Madhya Pradesh in 2007 (in million)

Age Group	Rural			Urban			Rural + Urban		
	Male	Female	Person	Male	Female	Person	Male	Female	Person
0-4	0.00	0.00	0.00	0.00	0.00	0.00	0.00	0.00	0.00
5-9	0.00	0.00	0.00	0.00	0.00	0.00	0.00	0.00	0.00
10-14	0.09	0.20	0.29	0.04	0.02	0.06	0.13	0.22	0.35
15-19	1.54	1.04	2.57	0.40	0.10	0.49	1.93	1.13	3.07
20-24	2.13	1.00	3.13	0.75	0.18	0.92	2.87	1.18	4.05
25-29	1.81	1.08	2.89	0.88	0.19	1.07	2.69	1.27	3.96
30-34	1.63	1.20	2.83	0.76	0.19	0.95	2.39	1.39	3.78
35-39	1.51	1.16	2.67	0.67	0.20	0.87	2.19	1.36	3.55
40-44	1.35	1.00	2.35	0.60	0.16	0.76	1.95	1.16	3.11
45-49	1.11	0.71	1.82	0.51	0.13	0.64	1.62	0.85	2.46
50-54	0.84	0.54	1.38	0.39	0.09	0.49	1.23	0.63	1.87
55-59	0.64	0.39	1.03	0.26	0.05	0.31	0.90	0.44	1.33
60+	1.07	0.50	1.57	0.28	0.08	0.36	1.35	0.58	1.93
Total	**13.73**	**8.81**	**22.55**	**5.53**	**1.39**	**6.92**	**19.26**	**10.21**	**29.47**

Source: ibid

Projected Age-Sex UPSS Labour Force of Madhya Pradesh in 2012 (in million)

Age Group	Rural			Urban			Rural + Urban		
	Male	Female	Person	Male	Female	Person	Male	Female	Person
0-4	0.00	0.00	0.00	0.00	0.00	0.00	0.00	0.00	0.00
5-9	0.00	0.00	0.00	0.00	0.00	0.00	0.00	0.00	0.00
10-14	0.00	0.04	0.04	0.02	0.02	0.04	0.02	0.05	0.08
15-19	1.48	1.02	2.49	0.40	0.11	0.51	1.87	1.13	3.00
20-24	2.53	1.14	3.67	0.81	0.22	1.03	3.34	1.37	4.70
25-29	2.15	1.13	3.28	1.05	0.23	1.28	3.20	1.36	4.56
30-34	1.74	1.19	2.93	0.93	0.21	1.15	2.67	1.40	4.08
35-39	1.56	1.22	2.78	0.79	0.22	1.01	2.35	1.44	3.79
40-44	1.45	1.15	2.60	0.67	0.18	0.84	2.12	1.33	3.45
45-49	1.31	0.87	2.18	0.59	0.15	0.74	1.90	1.02	2.92
50-54	1.03	0.66	1.68	0.50	0.11	0.62	1.53	0.77	2.30
55-59	0.77	0.44	1.22	0.33	0.06	0.39	1.10	0.50	1.60
60+	1.20	0.57	1.77	0.33	0.10	0.43	1.53	0.66	2.19
Total	**15.22**	**9.42**	**24.64**	**6.41**	**1.62**	**8.03**	**21.63**	**11.04**	**32.67**

Source: ibid

Projected Age-Sex UPSS Labour Force of Madhya Pradesh in 2017 (in million)

Age Group	Rural			Urban			Rural + Urban		
	Male	Female	Person	Male	Female	Person	Male	Female	Person
0-4	0.00	0.00	0.00	0.00	0.00	0.00	0.00	0.00	0.00
5-9	0.00	0.00	0.00	0.00	0.00	0.00	0.00	0.00	0.00
10-14	0.00	0.00	0.00	0.01	0.01	0.02	0.01	0.01	0.02
15-19	1.33	0.90	2.23	0.39	0.11	0.50	1.72	1.01	2.73
20-24	2.65	1.15	3.81	0.80	0.24	1.04	3.45	1.39	4.85
25-29	2.61	1.37	3.98	1.15	0.27	1.42	3.77	1.64	5.41
30-34	2.08	1.30	3.39	1.10	0.25	1.35	3.18	1.55	4.73
35-39	1.68	1.22	2.90	0.95	0.25	1.20	2.63	1.47	4.10
40-44	1.52	1.21	2.73	0.77	0.19	0.95	2.28	1.40	3.68
45-49	1.42	0.99	2.41	0.65	0.16	0.81	2.07	1.16	3.22
50-54	1.22	0.81	2.03	0.59	0.14	0.73	1.81	0.95	2.76
55-59	0.95	0.53	1.49	0.40	0.07	0.47	1.35	0.61	1.96
60+	1.39	0.65	2.04	0.40	0.12	0.52	1.79	0.77	2.56
Total	**16.85**	**10.15**	**27.00**	**7.21**	**1.81**	**9.02**	**24.06**	**11.96**	**36.02**

Source: ibid

Projected Age-Sex UPSS Labour Force of Other NE States in 2007 (in million)

Age Group	Rural			Urban			Rural + Urban		
	Male	Female	Person	Male	Female	Person	Male	Female	Person
0-4	0.00	0.00	0.00	0.00	0.00	0.00	0.00	0.00	0.00
5-9	0.00	0.00	0.00	0.00	0.00	0.00	0.00	0.00	0.00
10-14	0.04	0.02	0.06	0.00	0.01	0.01	0.04	0.02	0.07
15-19	0.25	0.16	0.40	0.02	0.02	0.05	0.27	0.18	0.45
20-24	0.42	0.28	0.69	0.08	0.05	0.13	0.50	0.33	0.83
25-29	0.43	0.24	0.67	0.13	0.06	0.19	0.56	0.30	0.86
30-34	0.37	0.23	0.60	0.13	0.05	0.18	0.50	0.28	0.78
35-39	0.34	0.18	0.52	0.12	0.05	0.16	0.46	0.23	0.68
40-44	0.30	0.16	0.47	0.11	0.04	0.14	0.41	0.20	0.61
45-49	0.25	0.14	0.40	0.09	0.03	0.12	0.34	0.18	0.52
50-54	0.20	0.11	0.31	0.07	0.02	0.09	0.27	0.13	0.40
55-59	0.15	0.08	0.23	0.05	0.02	0.06	0.20	0.10	0.29
60+	0.24	0.11	0.35	0.03	0.01	0.04	0.27	0.12	0.39
Total	**2.99**	**1.71**	**4.70**	**0.83**	**0.35**	**1.18**	**3.82**	**2.06**	**5.88**

Source: ibid

Projected Age-Sex UPSS Labour Force of Other NE States in 2012 (in million)

Age Group	Rural			Urban			Rural + Urban		
	Male	Female	Person	Male	Female	Person	Male	Female	Person
0-4	0.00	0.00	0.00	0.00	0.00	0.00	0.00	0.00	0.00
5-9	0.00	0.00	0.00	0.00	0.00	0.00	0.00	0.00	0.00
10-14	0.05	0.01	0.05	0.00	0.01	0.01	0.05	0.01	0.06
15-19	0.25	0.15	0.40	0.02	0.02	0.05	0.27	0.17	0.44
20-24	0.48	0.33	0.81	0.09	0.05	0.14	0.57	0.38	0.95
25-29	0.52	0.29	0.81	0.15	0.07	0.22	0.67	0.36	1.03
30-34	0.43	0.27	0.70	0.15	0.06	0.21	0.58	0.33	0.91
35-39	0.37	0.22	0.58	0.13	0.05	0.19	0.50	0.27	0.77
40-44	0.33	0.20	0.53	0.12	0.04	0.16	0.45	0.24	0.69
45-49	0.29	0.18	0.48	0.10	0.04	0.14	0.39	0.22	0.62
50-54	0.24	0.15	0.39	0.08	0.03	0.11	0.32	0.18	0.50
55-59	0.19	0.11	0.30	0.06	0.02	0.08	0.25	0.13	0.38
60+	0.31	0.15	0.46	0.04	0.02	0.05	0.34	0.17	0.51
Total	**3.44**	**2.06**	**5.50**	**0.94**	**0.41**	**1.36**	**4.39**	**2.47**	**6.86**

Source: ibid

Projected Age-Sex UPSS Labour Force of Other NE States in 2017 (in million)

Age Group	Rural			Urban			Rural + Urban		
	Male	Female	Person	Male	Female	Person	Male	Female	Person
0-4	0.00	0.00	0.00	0.00	0.00	0.00	0.00	0.00	0.00
5-9	0.00	0.00	0.00	0.00	0.00	0.00	0.00	0.00	0.00
10-14	0.04	0.00	0.04	0.00	0.01	0.01	0.04	0.01	0.05
15-19	0.23	0.14	0.37	0.02	0.03	0.05	0.26	0.16	0.42
20-24	0.47	0.33	0.80	0.09	0.06	0.15	0.56	0.39	0.95
25-29	0.59	0.34	0.93	0.16	0.08	0.24	0.75	0.42	1.17
30-34	0.51	0.33	0.84	0.17	0.07	0.24	0.68	0.39	1.08
35-39	0.42	0.25	0.67	0.15	0.06	0.22	0.58	0.31	0.89
40-44	0.36	0.23	0.59	0.13	0.05	0.18	0.49	0.28	0.78
45-49	0.32	0.22	0.54	0.12	0.05	0.16	0.43	0.27	0.70
50-54	0.28	0.19	0.47	0.10	0.04	0.14	0.38	0.23	0.60
55-59	0.22	0.16	0.38	0.07	0.03	0.10	0.30	0.18	0.48
60+	0.40	0.21	0.60	0.04	0.03	0.07	0.44	0.24	0.67
Total	**3.85**	**2.40**	**6.25**	**1.06**	**0.49**	**1.54**	**4.90**	**2.89**	**7.79**

Source: ibid

Projected Age-Sex UPSS Labour Force of Orissa in 2007 (in million)

Age Group	Rural			Urban			Rural + Urban		
	Male	Female	Person	Male	Female	Person	Male	Female	Person
0-4	0.00	0.00	0.00	0.00	0.00	0.00	0.00	0.00	0.00
5-9	0.01	0.00	0.01	0.00	0.00	0.00	0.01	0.00	0.01
10-14	0.16	0.14	0.30	0.01	0.01	0.02	0.17	0.15	0.32
15-19	1.13	0.75	1.89	0.12	0.05	0.16	1.25	0.80	2.05
20-24	1.34	0.67	2.01	0.25	0.07	0.32	1.59	0.74	2.33
25-29	1.26	0.70	1.96	0.32	0.09	0.41	1.58	0.79	2.37
30-34	1.19	0.74	1.93	0.29	0.08	0.36	1.47	0.82	2.29
35-39	1.12	0.73	1.84	0.26	0.06	0.32	1.38	0.79	2.16
40-44	1.03	0.65	1.68	0.23	0.08	0.31	1.27	0.73	1.99
45-49	0.88	0.51	1.39	0.20	0.05	0.25	1.08	0.56	1.63
50-54	0.69	0.37	1.06	0.16	0.04	0.19	0.85	0.41	1.26
55-59	0.51	0.21	0.72	0.08	0.02	0.10	0.59	0.23	0.82
60+	0.79	0.32	1.10	0.06	0.03	0.09	0.85	0.34	1.19
Total	**10.11**	**5.80**	**15.90**	**1.97**	**0.57**	**2.54**	**12.07**	**6.37**	**18.44**

Source: ibid

Projected Age-Sex UPSS Labour Force of Orissa in 2012 (in million

Age Group	Rural			Urban			Rural + Urban		
	Male	Female	Person	Male	Female	Person	Male	Female	Person
0-4	0.00	0.00	0.00	0.00	0.00	0.00	0.00	0.00	0.00
5-9	0.00	0.00	0.00	0.00	0.00	0.00	0.00	0.00	0.00
10-14	0.06	0.08	0.14	0.01	0.00	0.01	0.07	0.08	0.15
15-19	1.11	0.76	1.88	0.11	0.05	0.16	1.22	0.81	2.03
20-24	1.54	0.75	2.29	0.27	0.09	0.36	1.80	0.85	2.65
25-29	1.39	0.75	2.13	0.36	0.13	0.48	1.74	0.87	2.61
30-34	1.22	0.79	2.01	0.33	0.10	0.43	1.55	0.89	2.44
35-39	1.13	0.79	1.93	0.30	0.07	0.37	1.44	0.87	2.30
40-44	1.07	0.76	1.83	0.26	0.10	0.37	1.34	0.86	2.20
45-49	0.98	0.63	1.61	0.23	0.07	0.30	1.21	0.69	1.91
50-54	0.82	0.46	1.28	0.19	0.05	0.24	1.00	0.51	1.52
55-59	0.61	0.25	0.86	0.09	0.02	0.12	0.70	0.27	0.98
60+	0.86	0.37	1.22	0.06	0.04	0.10	0.92	0.41	1.33
Total	**10.80**	**6.39**	**17.18**	**2.21**	**0.73**	**2.93**	**13.00**	**7.11**	**20.12**

Source: ibid

Projected Age-Sex UPSS Labour Force of Orissa in 2017 (in million)

Age Group	Rural			Urban			Rural + Urban		
	Male	Female	Person	Male	Female	Person	Male	Female	Person
0-4	0.00	0.00	0.00	0.00	0.00	0.00	0.00	0.00	0.00
5-9	0.00	0.00	0.00	0.00	0.00	0.00	0.00	0.00	0.00
10-14	0.00	0.01	0.01	0.00	0.00	0.00	0.00	0.01	0.02
15-19	1.01	0.71	1.72	0.10	0.05	0.15	1.10	0.76	1.87
20-24	1.55	0.73	2.27	0.27	0.10	0.37	1.82	0.82	2.64
25-29	1.59	0.83	2.41	0.38	0.14	0.52	1.97	0.97	2.94
30-34	1.35	0.87	2.22	0.37	0.11	0.48	1.71	0.99	2.70
35-39	1.17	0.85	2.02	0.34	0.08	0.42	1.52	0.93	2.45
40-44	1.10	0.84	1.94	0.30	0.13	0.43	1.40	0.97	2.37
45-49	1.03	0.74	1.76	0.26	0.07	0.33	1.28	0.81	2.09
50-54	0.92	0.57	1.50	0.22	0.06	0.28	1.14	0.64	1.77
55-59	0.73	0.30	1.03	0.10	0.03	0.13	0.83	0.33	1.16
60+	0.97	0.44	1.41	0.06	0.05	0.12	1.04	0.49	1.53
Total	**11.42**	**6.90**	**18.31**	**2.40**	**0.83**	**3.23**	**13.82**	**7.73**	**21.55**

Source: ibid

Projected Age-Sex UPSS Labour Force of Other States in 2007 (in million)

Age Group	Rural			Urban			Rural + Urban		
	Male	Female	Person	Male	Female	Person	Male	Female	Person
0-4	0.00	0.00	0.00	0.00	0.00	0.00	0.00	0.00	0.00
5-9	0.00	0.00	0.00	0.00	0.00	0.00	0.00	0.00	0.00
10-14	0.00	0.00	0.00	0.01	0.00	0.01	0.01	0.00	0.01
15-19	0.05	0.03	0.08	0.27	0.04	0.31	0.32	0.07	0.39
20-24	0.17	0.05	0.22	0.90	0.12	1.02	1.07	0.17	1.24
25-29	0.16	0.05	0.21	0.96	0.17	1.13	1.12	0.22	1.34
30-34	0.13	0.04	0.17	0.83	0.16	0.99	0.96	0.20	1.16
35-39	0.11	0.02	0.14	0.80	0.15	0.95	0.91	0.18	1.09
40-44	0.08	0.02	0.11	0.66	0.15	0.81	0.75	0.17	0.91
45-49	0.07	0.02	0.08	0.50	0.08	0.58	0.57	0.09	0.66
50-54	0.05	0.02	0.07	0.35	0.02	0.37	0.40	0.04	0.44
55-59	0.03	0.01	0.04	0.20	0.02	0.22	0.23	0.02	0.26
60+	0.04	0.03	0.07	0.19	0.01	0.20	0.23	0.04	0.27
Total	**0.89**	**0.29**	**1.18**	**5.67**	**0.92**	**6.59**	**6.56**	**1.21**	**7.77**

Source: ibid

Projected Age-Sex UPSS Labour Force of Other States in 2012 (in million)

Age Group	Rural			Urban			Rural + Urban		
	Male	Female	Person	Male	Female	Person	Male	Female	Person
0-4	0.00	0.00	0.00	0.00	0.00	0.00	0.00	0.00	0.00
5-9	0.00	0.00	0.00	0.00	0.00	0.00	0.00	0.00	0.00
10-14	0.00	0.00	0.00	0.00	0.00	0.00	0.00	0.00	0.00
15-19	0.05	0.04	0.09	0.29	0.04	0.33	0.34	0.08	0.42
20-24	0.21	0.07	0.27	1.10	0.15	1.25	1.30	0.22	1.52
25-29	0.18	0.06	0.24	1.17	0.20	1.37	1.35	0.26	1.62
30-34	0.14	0.04	0.18	1.02	0.16	1.18	1.17	0.20	1.37
35-39	0.12	0.02	0.14	1.01	0.19	1.20	1.13	0.21	1.34
40-44	0.09	0.03	0.12	0.85	0.20	1.04	0.94	0.22	1.16
45-49	0.07	0.02	0.09	0.65	0.09	0.74	0.72	0.11	0.83
50-54	0.05	0.03	0.08	0.44	0.02	0.46	0.49	0.05	0.53
55-59	0.03	0.01	0.04	0.23	0.02	0.25	0.26	0.02	0.29
60+	0.04	0.02	0.07	0.19	0.00	0.20	0.24	0.03	0.26
Total	**0.99**	**0.33**	**1.32**	**6.95**	**1.07**	**8.01**	**7.94**	**1.40**	**9.34**

Source: ibid

Projected Age-Sex UPSS Labour Force of Other States in 2017 (in million)

Age Group	Rural			Urban			Rural + Urban		
	Male	Female	Person	Male	Female	Person	Male	Female	Person
0-4	0.00	0.00	0.00	0.00	0.00	0.00	0.00	0.00	0.00
5-9	0.00	0.00	0.00	0.00	0.00	0.00	0.00	0.00	0.00
10-14	0.00	0.00	0.00	0.00	0.00	0.00	0.00	0.00	0.00
15-19	0.04	0.04	0.08	0.27	0.04	0.31	0.31	0.07	0.39
20-24	0.24	0.07	0.31	1.26	0.16	1.43	1.50	0.23	1.73
25-29	0.20	0.06	0.26	1.33	0.22	1.55	1.53	0.28	1.81
30-34	0.15	0.04	0.20	1.16	0.18	1.35	1.31	0.23	1.54
35-39	0.13	0.02	0.15	1.17	0.23	1.40	1.30	0.25	1.55
40-44	0.10	0.02	0.12	1.00	0.23	1.23	1.10	0.25	1.35
45-49	0.08	0.02	0.10	0.77	0.10	0.87	0.85	0.12	0.96
50-54	0.05	0.02	0.08	0.51	0.01	0.52	0.56	0.04	0.60
55-59	0.04	0.00	0.04	0.27	0.02	0.29	0.30	0.02	0.33
60+	0.04	0.03	0.07	0.25	0.00	0.25	0.29	0.03	0.32
Total	**1.08**	**0.33**	**1.41**	**7.98**	**1.18**	**9.16**	**9.06**	**1.51**	**10.57**

Source: ibid

Projected Age-Sex UPSS Labour Force of Punjab in 2007 (in million)

Age Group	Rural			Urban			Rural + Urban		
	Male	Female	Person	Male	Female	Person	Male	Female	Person
0-4	0.00	0.00	0.00	0.00	0.00	0.00	0.00	0.00	0.00
5-9	0.00	0.00	0.00	0.00	0.00	0.00	0.00	0.00	0.00
10-14	0.02	0.01	0.03	0.02	0.00	0.02	0.04	0.01	0.05
15-19	0.50	0.22	0.72	0.21	0.04	0.24	0.70	0.26	0.96
20-24	0.79	0.34	1.14	0.50	0.11	0.61	1.29	0.45	1.74
25-29	0.70	0.31	1.01	0.52	0.12	0.64	1.22	0.43	1.65
30-34	0.60	0.34	0.93	0.44	0.10	0.54	1.04	0.43	1.47
35-39	0.54	0.35	0.89	0.38	0.09	0.47	0.92	0.44	1.35
40-44	0.50	0.31	0.81	0.34	0.09	0.43	0.84	0.40	1.24
45-49	0.44	0.25	0.69	0.30	0.05	0.35	0.74	0.30	1.04
50-54	0.35	0.17	0.52	0.23	0.06	0.29	0.59	0.23	0.81
55-59	0.27	0.14	0.40	0.16	0.03	0.19	0.43	0.16	0.59
60+	0.50	0.20	0.70	0.15	0.03	0.18	0.65	0.23	0.88
Total	5.19	2.64	7.83	3.25	0.71	3.96	8.45	3.35	11.79

Source: ibid

Projected Age-Sex UPSS Labour Force of Punjab in 2012 (in million)

Age Group	Rural			Urban			Rural + Urban		
	Male	Female	Person	Male	Female	Person	Male	Female	Person
0-4	0.00	0.00	0.00	0.00	0.00	0.00	0.00	0.00	0.00
5-9	0.00	0.00	0.00	0.00	0.00	0.00	0.00	0.00	0.00
10-14	0.00	0.00	0.00	0.01	0.00	0.01	0.01	0.00	0.01
15-19	0.41	0.17	0.58	0.19	0.03	0.22	0.59	0.21	0.80
20-24	0.80	0.34	1.14	0.54	0.13	0.67	1.34	0.47	1.81
25-29	0.76	0.32	1.08	0.62	0.15	0.77	1.38	0.47	1.85
30-34	0.67	0.35	1.02	0.55	0.12	0.67	1.23	0.47	1.70
35-39	0.56	0.37	0.93	0.47	0.10	0.57	1.03	0.47	1.50
40-44	0.51	0.34	0.84	0.39	0.10	0.49	0.90	0.43	1.33
45-49	0.48	0.29	0.77	0.34	0.06	0.40	0.82	0.35	1.17
50-54	0.41	0.21	0.63	0.28	0.07	0.35	0.69	0.28	0.97
55-59	0.32	0.17	0.50	0.21	0.04	0.25	0.54	0.21	0.75
60+	0.54	0.23	0.78	0.17	0.03	0.20	0.71	0.27	0.98
Total	5.46	2.80	8.26	3.78	0.83	4.61	9.24	3.63	12.87

Source: ibid

Projected Age-Sex UPSS Labour Force of Punjab in 2017 (in million)

Age Group	Rural			Urban			Rural + Urban		
	Male	Female	Person	Male	Female	Person	Male	Female	Person
0-4	0.00	0.00	0.00	0.00	0.00	0.00	0.00	0.00	0.00
5-9	0.00	0.00	0.00	0.00	0.00	0.00	0.00	0.00	0.00
10-14	0.00	0.00	0.00	0.01	0.00	0.01	0.01	0.00	0.01
15-19	0.30	0.13	0.43	0.17	0.03	0.20	0.47	0.15	0.62
20-24	0.71	0.28	0.99	0.58	0.14	0.71	1.29	0.42	1.71
25-29	0.78	0.31	1.09	0.69	0.17	0.86	1.47	0.48	1.95
30-34	0.76	0.38	1.14	0.64	0.13	0.77	1.40	0.52	1.92
35-39	0.65	0.39	1.04	0.57	0.12	0.69	1.22	0.51	1.73
40-44	0.54	0.36	0.90	0.47	0.11	0.57	1.01	0.46	1.47
45-49	0.49	0.32	0.81	0.38	0.07	0.44	0.87	0.38	1.25
50-54	0.45	0.25	0.71	0.31	0.08	0.39	0.77	0.33	1.10
55-59	0.38	0.21	0.59	0.25	0.05	0.30	0.63	0.26	0.89
60+	0.61	0.28	0.89	0.20	0.04	0.24	0.81	0.32	1.13
Total	5.68	2.91	8.59	4.26	0.93	5.19	9.94	3.84	13.78

Source: ibid

Projected Age-Sex UPSS Labour Force of Rajasthan in 2007 (in million)

Age Group	Rural			Urban			Rural + Urban		
	Male	Female	Person	Male	Female	Person	Male	Female	Person
0-4	0.00	0.00	0.00	0.00	0.00	0.00	0.00	0.00	0.00
5-9	0.00	0.00	0.00	0.00	0.00	0.00	0.00	0.00	0.00
10-14	0.14	0.32	0.46	0.07	0.02	0.09	0.21	0.34	0.55
15-19	1.38	1.22	2.60	0.31	0.13	0.45	1.70	1.35	3.04
20-24	2.10	1.33	3.43	0.65	0.19	0.84	2.75	1.52	4.28
25-29	1.77	1.22	2.99	0.70	0.19	0.89	2.47	1.41	3.88
30-34	1.54	1.17	2.71	0.61	0.19	0.80	2.15	1.36	3.52
35-39	1.40	1.12	2.52	0.53	0.18	0.70	1.93	1.29	3.22
40-44	1.25	0.93	2.19	0.47	0.15	0.62	1.72	1.09	2.81
45-49	1.05	0.75	1.80	0.40	0.12	0.51	1.45	0.87	2.32
50-54	0.84	0.55	1.38	0.31	0.07	0.38	1.14	0.62	1.76
55-59	0.62	0.37	0.99	0.20	0.05	0.25	0.83	0.41	1.24
60+	0.96	0.45	1.41	0.17	0.05	0.22	1.13	0.50	1.62
Total	**13.06**	**9.42**	**22.48**	**4.42**	**1.34**	**5.76**	**17.48**	**10.76**	**28.24**

Source: ibid

Projected Age-Sex UPSS Labour Force of Rajasthan in 2012 (in million)

Age Group	Rural			Urban			Rural + Urban		
	Male	Female	Person	Male	Female	Person	Male	Female	Person
0-4	0.00	0.00	0.00	0.00	0.00	0.00	0.00	0.00	0.00
5-9	0.00	0.00	0.00	0.00	0.00	0.00	0.00	0.00	0.00
10-14	0.00	0.09	0.09	0.06	0.00	0.06	0.06	0.10	0.16
15-19	1.33	1.23	2.56	0.30	0.12	0.42	1.63	1.35	2.99
20-24	2.56	1.60	4.16	0.72	0.22	0.94	3.27	1.83	5.10
25-29	2.16	1.34	3.50	0.81	0.22	1.03	2.97	1.56	4.53
30-34	1.72	1.24	2.97	0.74	0.24	0.97	2.46	1.48	3.94
35-39	1.50	1.22	2.72	0.62	0.20	0.81	2.11	1.42	3.53
40-44	1.36	1.06	2.42	0.53	0.17	0.70	1.88	1.23	3.12
45-49	1.21	0.91	2.12	0.46	0.14	0.59	1.67	1.05	2.71
50-54	1.00	0.67	1.66	0.38	0.09	0.47	1.38	0.76	2.13
55-59	0.76	0.44	1.20	0.27	0.07	0.34	1.03	0.51	1.54
60+	1.12	0.52	1.64	0.19	0.05	0.24	1.30	0.57	1.88
Total	**14.72**	**10.33**	**25.04**	**5.06**	**1.53**	**6.59**	**19.77**	**11.86**	**31.63**

Source: ibid

Projected Age-Sex UPSS Labour Force of Rajasthan in 2017 (in million)

Age Group	Rural			Urban			Rural + Urban		
	Male	Female	Person	Male	Female	Person	Male	Female	Person
0-4	0.00	0.00	0.00	0.00	0.00	0.00	0.00	0.00	0.00
5-9	0.00	0.00	0.00	0.00	0.00	0.00	0.00	0.00	0.00
10-14	0.00	0.00	0.00	0.06	0.00	0.06	0.06	0.00	0.06
15-19	1.17	1.12	2.28	0.28	0.11	0.39	1.45	1.22	2.67
20-24	2.79	1.79	4.58	0.73	0.24	0.97	3.52	2.02	5.55
25-29	2.69	1.69	4.38	0.89	0.25	1.14	3.58	1.94	5.52
30-34	2.12	1.43	3.55	0.85	0.27	1.12	2.97	1.70	4.67
35-39	1.69	1.30	2.98	0.73	0.22	0.96	2.42	1.52	3.94
40-44	1.45	1.15	2.60	0.61	0.19	0.80	2.07	1.34	3.41
45-49	1.31	1.04	2.36	0.51	0.16	0.66	1.82	1.20	3.02
50-54	1.15	0.81	1.96	0.43	0.11	0.54	1.58	0.92	2.50
55-59	0.91	0.54	1.44	0.33	0.09	0.42	1.23	0.63	1.86
60+	1.32	0.60	1.92	0.21	0.06	0.27	1.52	0.66	2.19
Total	16.61	11.45	28.06	5.61	1.71	7.32	22.22	13.16	35.38

Source: ibid

Projected Age-Sex UPSS Labour Force of Tamil Nadu in 2007 (in million)

Age Group	Rural			Urban			Rural + Urban		
	Male	Female	Person	Male	Female	Person	Male	Female	Person
0-4	0.00	0.00	0.00	0.00	0.00	0.00	0.00	0.00	0.00
5-9	0.00	0.00	0.00	0.00	0.00	0.00	0.00	0.00	0.00
10-14	0.00	0.01	0.01	0.02	0.03	0.06	0.02	0.04	0.06
15-19	0.67	0.65	1.31	0.59	0.29	0.88	1.25	0.94	2.19
20-24	1.22	0.76	1.98	1.46	0.57	2.03	2.68	1.33	4.01
25-29	1.25	0.76	2.02	1.57	0.59	2.17	2.83	1.36	4.18
30-34	1.19	0.94	2.13	1.44	0.64	2.08	2.63	1.58	4.21
35-39	1.09	0.93	2.02	1.32	0.55	1.87	2.41	1.47	3.89
40-44	1.05	0.94	1.99	1.16	0.44	1.60	2.21	1.38	3.59
45-49	0.95	0.80	1.75	1.00	0.37	1.38	1.96	1.17	3.13
50-54	0.82	0.61	1.43	0.82	0.29	1.11	1.63	0.90	2.54
55-59	0.63	0.47	1.10	0.56	0.17	0.73	1.19	0.64	1.83
60+	1.04	0.65	1.69	0.49	0.19	0.69	1.54	0.84	2.38
Total	9.91	7.51	17.43	10.44	4.15	14.59	20.36	11.66	32.02

Source: ibid

Projected Age-Sex UPSS Labour Force of Tamil Nadu in 2012 (in million)

Age Group	Rural			Urban			Rural + Urban		
	Male	Female	Person	Male	Female	Person	Male	Female	Person
0-4	0.00	0.00	0.00	0.00	0.00	0.00	0.00	0.00	0.00
5-9	0.00	0.00	0.00	0.00	0.00	0.00	0.00	0.00	0.00
10-14	0.00	0.00	0.00	0.00	0.01	0.01	0.00	0.01	0.01
15-19	0.45	0.47	0.92	0.55	0.28	0.83	1.00	0.75	1.75
20-24	0.89	0.54	1.42	1.64	0.67	2.30	2.52	1.20	3.73
25-29	1.10	0.49	1.60	1.83	0.69	2.52	2.93	1.18	4.12
30-34	1.15	0.83	1.98	1.66	0.77	2.42	2.81	1.60	4.41
35-39	1.04	0.92	1.95	1.54	0.69	2.23	2.58	1.60	4.18
40-44	0.99	0.96	1.95	1.34	0.50	1.84	2.33	1.46	3.79
45-49	0.96	0.90	1.85	1.18	0.46	1.64	2.14	1.36	3.49
50-54	0.87	0.70	1.57	0.95	0.35	1.30	1.82	1.05	2.87
55-59	0.71	0.54	1.26	0.69	0.20	0.89	1.40	0.75	2.15
60+	1.14	0.78	1.92	0.56	0.22	0.77	1.69	0.99	2.69
Total	**9.30**	**7.13**	**16.42**	**11.93**	**4.83**	**16.77**	**21.23**	**11.96**	**33.19**

Source: ibid

Projected Age-Sex UPSS Labour Force of Tamil Nadu in 2017 (in million)

Age Group	Rural			Urban			Rural + Urban		
	Male	Female	Person	Male	Female	Person	Male	Female	Person
0-4	0.00	0.00	0.00	0.00	0.00	0.00	0.00	0.00	0.00
5-9	0.00	0.00	0.00	0.00	0.00	0.00	0.00	0.00	0.00
10-14	0.00	0.00	0.00	0.00	0.00	0.00	0.00	0.00	0.00
15-19	0.25	0.31	0.56	0.51	0.28	0.79	0.77	0.58	1.35
20-24	0.46	0.28	0.75	1.87	0.75	2.61	2.33	1.03	3.36
25-29	0.86	0.21	1.08	2.02	0.80	2.82	2.89	1.01	3.90
30-34	1.08	0.65	1.74	1.83	0.83	2.66	2.91	1.48	4.39
35-39	1.03	0.88	1.90	1.74	0.76	2.49	2.76	1.63	4.39
40-44	0.97	0.99	1.96	1.52	0.57	2.09	2.50	1.56	4.06
45-49	0.92	0.93	1.85	1.34	0.53	1.86	2.26	1.46	3.71
50-54	0.88	0.78	1.66	1.10	0.41	1.51	1.98	1.19	3.17
55-59	0.77	0.61	1.38	0.80	0.24	1.04	1.57	0.85	2.42
60+	1.26	0.93	2.19	0.63	0.24	0.88	1.89	1.18	3.07
Total	**8.50**	**6.57**	**15.07**	**13.36**	**5.39**	**18.75**	**21.85**	**11.97**	**33.82**

Source: ibid

Projected Age-Sex UPSS Labour Force of Uttar Pradesh in 2007 (in million)

Age Group	Rural			Urban			Rural + Urban		
	Male	Female	Person	Male	Female	Person	Male	Female	Person
0-4	0.00	0.00	0.00	0.00	0.00	0.00	0.00	0.00	0.00
5-9	0.02	0.02	0.04	0.02	0.01	0.04	0.04	0.03	0.07
10-14	0.68	0.51	1.18	0.24	0.09	0.33	0.92	0.60	1.52
15-19	4.52	1.96	6.48	1.02	0.23	1.25	5.54	2.19	7.73
20-24	5.98	1.48	7.46	1.79	0.23	2.02	7.77	1.71	9.48
25-29	5.11	1.72	6.83	1.79	0.28	2.07	6.90	2.00	8.90
30-34	4.40	2.08	6.49	1.53	0.23	1.76	5.93	2.31	8.24
35-39	4.05	2.09	6.14	1.30	0.24	1.54	5.35	2.33	7.68
40-44	3.67	1.87	5.54	1.17	0.26	1.43	4.85	2.12	6.97
45-49	3.12	1.51	4.63	1.02	0.22	1.23	4.14	1.72	5.87
50-54	2.54	1.14	3.68	0.85	0.16	1.01	3.38	1.30	4.68
55-59	1.97	0.83	2.79	0.56	0.11	0.67	2.53	0.94	3.47
60+	3.84	1.46	5.30	0.56	0.13	0.68	4.39	1.59	5.98
Total	**39.89**	**16.67**	**56.56**	**11.85**	**2.17**	**14.03**	**51.74**	**18.84**	**70.58**

Source: ibid

Projected Age-Sex UPSS Labour Force of Uttar Pradesh in 2012 (in million)

Age Group	Rural			Urban			Rural + Urban		
	Male	Female	Person	Male	Female	Person	Male	Female	Person
0-4	0.00	0.00	0.00	0.00	0.00	0.00	0.00	0.00	0.00
5-9	0.00	0.00	0.00	0.03	0.01	0.04	0.03	0.01	0.04
10-14	0.30	0.26	0.56	0.21	0.03	0.24	0.50	0.30	0.80
15-19	4.40	2.16	6.56	0.91	0.24	1.16	5.31	2.41	7.72
20-24	7.44	1.89	9.34	1.94	0.30	2.24	9.39	2.19	11.58
25-29	6.36	1.92	8.28	2.16	0.34	2.50	8.52	2.27	10.78
30-34	4.90	2.14	7.05	1.96	0.28	2.24	6.86	2.43	9.29
35-39	4.20	2.27	6.47	1.58	0.27	1.85	5.78	2.54	8.32
40-44	3.85	2.18	6.03	1.30	0.29	1.59	5.15	2.47	7.62
45-49	3.51	1.88	5.39	1.13	0.23	1.36	4.64	2.11	6.74
50-54	2.93	1.44	4.37	1.01	0.19	1.20	3.93	1.63	5.57
55-59	2.30	1.05	3.35	0.71	0.15	0.86	3.01	1.20	4.21
60+	4.38	1.81	6.19	0.64	0.16	0.81	5.02	1.98	7.00
Total	**44.57**	**19.02**	**63.59**	**13.57**	**2.51**	**16.08**	**58.14**	**21.53**	**79.67**

Source: ibid

Projected Age-Sex UPSS Labour Force of Uttar Pradesh in 2017 (in million)

Age Group	Rural			Urban			Rural + Urban		
	Male	Female	Person	Male	Female	Person	Male	Female	Person
0-4	0.00	0.00	0.00	0.00	0.00	0.00	0.00	0.00	0.00
5-9	0.00	0.00	0.00	0.04	0.00	0.04	0.04	0.00	0.04
10-14	0.00	0.02	0.02	0.22	0.00	0.22	0.22	0.02	0.24
15-19	3.79	2.11	5.90	0.81	0.23	1.04	4.60	2.34	6.93
20-24	7.80	2.15	9.96	1.86	0.30	2.16	9.67	2.45	12.12
25-29	8.11	2.54	10.65	2.35	0.39	2.74	10.46	2.93	13.39
30-34	6.15	2.44	8.59	2.37	0.34	2.71	8.52	2.78	11.30
35-39	4.69	2.33	7.02	1.98	0.32	2.30	6.68	2.64	9.32
40-44	4.03	2.30	6.33	1.56	0.32	1.88	5.58	2.62	8.21
45-49	3.69	2.15	5.84	1.23	0.25	1.49	4.93	2.40	7.33
50-54	3.30	1.72	5.02	1.12	0.22	1.34	4.42	1.94	6.36
55-59	2.68	1.26	3.94	0.84	0.18	1.02	3.51	1.45	4.96
60+	5.07	2.26	7.33	0.75	0.20	0.95	5.82	2.46	8.29
Total	**49.32**	**21.28**	**70.60**	**15.12**	**2.76**	**17.89**	**64.45**	**24.04**	**88.49**

Source: ibid

Projected Age-Sex UPSS Labour Force of Uttarakhand in 2007 (in million)

Age Group	Rural			Urban			Rural + Urban		
	Male	Female	Person	Male	Female	Person	Male	Female	Person
0-4	0.00	0.00	0.00	0.00	0.00	0.00	0.00	0.00	0.00
5-9	0.00	0.00	0.00	0.00	0.00	0.00	0.00	0.00	0.00
10-14	0.03	0.01	0.04	0.00	0.00	0.00	0.03	0.01	0.04
15-19	0.20	0.16	0.36	0.05	0.01	0.06	0.25	0.17	0.41
20-24	0.30	0.22	0.52	0.11	0.02	0.13	0.41	0.24	0.66
25-29	0.25	0.19	0.44	0.12	0.02	0.14	0.37	0.22	0.58
30-34	0.20	0.17	0.37	0.11	0.02	0.13	0.31	0.20	0.51
35-39	0.18	0.15	0.33	0.10	0.02	0.12	0.28	0.18	0.45
40-44	0.16	0.13	0.29	0.09	0.01	0.10	0.25	0.14	0.39
45-49	0.14	0.11	0.26	0.07	0.02	0.09	0.22	0.13	0.35
50-54	0.12	0.10	0.22	0.06	0.01	0.07	0.18	0.11	0.29
55-59	0.09	0.09	0.18	0.04	0.01	0.05	0.14	0.10	0.23
60+	0.20	0.16	0.36	0.03	0.01	0.04	0.23	0.17	0.40
Total	**1.88**	**1.50**	**3.38**	**0.79**	**0.17**	**0.96**	**2.67**	**1.67**	**4.33**

Source: ibid

Projected Age-Sex UPSS Labour Force of Uttarakhand in 2012 (in million)

Age Group	Rural			Urban			Rural + Urban		
	Male	Female	Person	Male	Female	Person	Male	Female	Person
0-4	0.00	0.00	0.00	0.00	0.00	0.00	0.00	0.00	0.00
5-9	0.00	0.00	0.00	0.00	0.00	0.00	0.00	0.00	0.00
10-14	0.01	0.00	0.01	0.00	0.00	0.00	0.01	0.00	0.02
15-19	0.18	0.15	0.33	0.04	0.01	0.05	0.22	0.16	0.39
20-24	0.35	0.24	0.59	0.12	0.03	0.14	0.46	0.27	0.73
25-29	0.32	0.22	0.53	0.14	0.03	0.17	0.46	0.25	0.70
30-34	0.24	0.20	0.43	0.14	0.03	0.16	0.37	0.22	0.60
35-39	0.19	0.17	0.36	0.11	0.03	0.14	0.30	0.20	0.50
40-44	0.17	0.14	0.31	0.10	0.01	0.11	0.27	0.16	0.43
45-49	0.16	0.13	0.29	0.08	0.02	0.11	0.24	0.15	0.39
50-54	0.13	0.12	0.25	0.07	0.01	0.09	0.21	0.13	0.34
55-59	0.11	0.10	0.21	0.05	0.01	0.07	0.16	0.11	0.28
60+	0.22	0.18	0.40	0.05	0.01	0.06	0.27	0.19	0.47
Total	**2.07**	**1.65**	**3.73**	**0.91**	**0.20**	**1.11**	**2.99**	**1.85**	**4.84**

Source: ibid

Projected Age-Sex UPSS Labour Force of Uttarakhand in 2017 (in million)

Age Group	Rural			Urban			Rural + Urban		
	Male	Female	Person	Male	Female	Person	Male	Female	Person
0-4	0.00	0.00	0.00	0.00	0.00	0.00	0.00	0.00	0.00
5-9	0.00	0.00	0.00	0.00	0.00	0.00	0.00	0.00	0.00
10-14	0.00	0.00	0.00	0.00	0.00	0.00	0.00	0.00	0.00
15-19	0.15	0.14	0.29	0.04	0.01	0.05	0.19	0.15	0.34
20-24	0.34	0.23	0.58	0.12	0.03	0.14	0.46	0.26	0.72
25-29	0.37	0.24	0.61	0.15	0.03	0.18	0.51	0.27	0.79
30-34	0.31	0.23	0.53	0.16	0.03	0.19	0.46	0.26	0.72
35-39	0.23	0.19	0.42	0.14	0.03	0.17	0.37	0.23	0.60
40-44	0.18	0.16	0.34	0.11	0.02	0.13	0.30	0.17	0.47
45-49	0.16	0.14	0.31	0.09	0.03	0.12	0.26	0.17	0.43
50-54	0.15	0.13	0.28	0.08	0.02	0.10	0.23	0.15	0.38
55-59	0.12	0.12	0.24	0.07	0.01	0.08	0.19	0.13	0.32
60+	0.25	0.21	0.46	0.08	0.02	0.09	0.33	0.23	0.56
Total	**2.26**	**1.79**	**4.05**	**1.03**	**0.22**	**1.25**	**3.29**	**2.01**	**5.30**

Source: ibid

Projected Age-Sex UPSS Labour Force of West Bengal in 2007 (in million)

Age Group	Rural			Urban			Rural + Urban		
	Male	Female	Person	Male	Female	Person	Male	Female	Person
0-4	0.00	0.00	0.00	0.00	0.00	0.00	0.00	0.00	0.00
5-9	0.00	0.00	0.00	0.00	0.02	0.02	0.00	0.02	0.02
10-14	0.22	0.18	0.40	0.10	0.06	0.16	0.32	0.24	0.55
15-19	1.94	0.63	2.57	0.42	0.19	0.61	2.36	0.82	3.17
20-24	2.68	0.63	3.31	0.94	0.33	1.27	3.62	0.96	4.58
25-29	2.47	0.75	3.22	1.12	0.27	1.39	3.59	1.03	4.61
30-34	2.32	0.89	3.21	1.09	0.25	1.34	3.41	1.14	4.55
35-39	2.21	0.80	3.01	1.03	0.26	1.28	3.24	1.06	4.30
40-44	2.01	0.60	2.61	0.96	0.21	1.17	2.97	0.81	3.78
45-49	1.67	0.45	2.12	0.87	0.11	0.98	2.53	0.57	3.10
50-54	1.25	0.30	1.55	0.72	0.10	0.82	1.97	0.40	2.37
55-59	0.89	0.09	0.98	0.53	0.07	0.60	1.41	0.16	1.58
60+	1.22	0.17	1.39	0.38	0.03	0.41	1.59	0.21	1.80
Total	**18.86**	**5.49**	**24.36**	**8.16**	**1.91**	**10.07**	**27.02**	**7.40**	**34.42**

Source: ibid

Projected Age-Sex UPSS Labour Force of West Bengal in 2012 (in million)

Age Group	Rural			Urban			Rural + Urban		
	Male	Female	Person	Male	Female	Person	Male	Female	Person
0-4	0.00	0.00	0.00	0.00	0.00	0.00	0.00	0.00	0.00
5-9	0.00	0.00	0.00	0.00	0.02	0.03	0.00	0.02	0.03
10-14	0.09	0.13	0.22	0.08	0.05	0.13	0.18	0.18	0.35
15-19	1.87	0.60	2.47	0.36	0.17	0.53	2.22	0.78	3.00
20-24	3.11	0.69	3.80	0.93	0.37	1.31	4.04	1.06	5.11
25-29	2.83	0.77	3.60	1.19	0.30	1.49	4.02	1.08	5.09
30-34	2.42	0.90	3.33	1.17	0.28	1.45	3.59	1.19	4.78
35-39	2.27	0.86	3.13	1.10	0.27	1.37	3.36	1.13	4.49
40-44	2.15	0.66	2.82	1.02	0.24	1.26	3.17	0.90	4.07
45-49	1.93	0.56	2.50	0.94	0.13	1.07	2.88	0.69	3.57
50-54	1.55	0.34	1.89	0.82	0.12	0.94	2.37	0.46	2.83
55-59	1.14	0.06	1.19	0.65	0.09	0.74	1.78	0.15	1.93
60+	1.45	0.18	1.63	0.41	0.02	0.43	1.86	0.20	2.07
Total	**20.81**	**5.77**	**26.58**	**8.67**	**2.07**	**10.74**	**29.48**	**7.84**	**37.32**

Source: ibid

Projected Age-Sex UPSS Labour Force of West Bengal in 2017 (in million)

Age Group	Rural			Urban			Rural + Urban		
	Male	Female	Person	Male	Female	Person	Male	Female	Person
0-4	0.00	0.00	0.00	0.00	0.00	0.00	0.00	0.00	0.00
5-9	0.00	0.00	0.00	0.01	0.02	0.03	0.01	0.02	0.03
10-14	0.00	0.08	0.08	0.08	0.04	0.12	0.08	0.12	0.20
15-19	1.68	0.53	2.21	0.30	0.16	0.46	1.97	0.69	2.67
20-24	3.12	0.66	3.78	0.86	0.36	1.22	3.98	1.02	5.00
25-29	3.30	0.89	4.19	1.20	0.32	1.52	4.50	1.21	5.71
30-34	2.79	0.97	3.76	1.23	0.30	1.53	4.02	1.27	5.29
35-39	2.38	0.86	3.24	1.17	0.28	1.45	3.55	1.14	4.69
40-44	2.22	0.74	2.96	1.08	0.25	1.34	3.30	0.99	4.29
45-49	2.08	0.66	2.74	1.00	0.13	1.13	3.08	0.79	3.87
50-54	1.81	0.39	2.20	0.90	0.14	1.03	2.71	0.53	3.23
55-59	1.42	0.00	1.42	0.74	0.11	0.86	2.16	0.11	2.27
60+	1.79	0.19	1.98	0.45	0.00	0.45	2.23	0.20	2.43
Total	**22.59**	**5.97**	**28.56**	**9.01**	**2.12**	**11.13**	**31.60**	**8.09**	**39.69**

Source: ibid

Projected Age-Sex UPSS Labour Force of India in 2007 (in million)

Age Group	Rural			Urban			Rural + Urban		
	Male	Female	Person	Male	Female	Person	Male	Female	Person
0-4	0.00	0.00	0.00	0.00	0.00	0.00	0.00	0.00	0.00
5-9	0.04	0.05	0.09	0.04	0.04	0.08	0.08	0.08	0.17
10-14	2.55	2.63	5.19	0.83	0.40	1.23	3.38	3.04	6.42
15-19	23.69	13.10	36.79	6.67	2.12	8.79	30.37	15.21	45.58
20-24	33.67	15.24	48.91	14.11	3.69	17.80	47.77	18.93	66.70
25-29	30.10	15.57	45.67	15.91	3.87	19.78	46.01	19.43	65.45
30-34	26.93	17.01	43.95	14.33	3.92	18.25	41.26	20.94	62.20
35-39	25.00	16.49	41.49	12.74	3.73	16.48	37.74	20.23	57.96
40-44	22.88	14.51	37.39	11.27	3.28	14.54	34.15	17.79	51.94
45-49	19.51	11.46	30.97	9.62	2.42	12.04	29.13	13.88	43.01
50-54	15.59	8.41	24.00	7.57	1.80	9.36	23.16	10.20	33.36
55-59	11.70	5.86	17.56	4.97	1.10	6.06	16.67	6.96	23.62
60+	19.16	8.11	27.27	4.26	1.18	5.44	23.42	9.29	32.71
Total	**230.84**	**128.44**	**359.27**	**102.31**	**27.55**	**129.86**	**333.15**	**155.98**	**489.13**

Source: ibid

Projected Age-Sex UPSS Labour Force of India in 2012 (in million)

Age Group	Rural			Urban			Rural + Urban		
	Male	Female	Person	Male	Female	Person	Male	Female	Person
0-4	0.00	0.00	0.00	0.00	0.00	0.00	0.00	0.00	0.00
5-9	0.00	0.00	0.01	0.04	0.03	0.08	0.05	0.04	0.08
10-14	0.83	1.10	1.94	0.57	0.23	0.80	1.41	1.33	2.74
15-19	22.38	12.37	34.76	6.24	2.03	8.26	28.62	14.40	43.02
20-24	38.74	16.65	55.39	15.25	4.30	19.55	53.99	20.95	74.94
25-29	35.05	16.27	51.32	18.21	4.54	22.76	53.26	20.82	74.08
30-34	29.17	17.36	46.53	16.85	4.58	21.43	46.02	21.94	67.96
35-39	25.89	17.54	43.44	14.86	4.37	19.24	40.76	21.91	62.67
40-44	23.97	16.25	40.22	12.78	3.75	16.53	36.75	20.00	56.75
45-49	21.85	13.73	35.58	11.09	2.82	13.91	32.93	16.55	49.49
50-54	18.20	10.16	28.36	9.05	2.19	11.24	27.25	12.35	39.60
55-59	14.08	7.04	21.11	6.25	1.37	7.62	20.33	8.40	28.73
60+	21.83	9.53	31.35	4.87	1.31	6.18	26.70	10.83	37.53
Total	**251.99**	**138.01**	**390.00**	**116.08**	**31.51**	**147.58**	**368.06**	**169.52**	**537.58**

Source: ibid

Projected Age-Sex UPSS Labour Force of India in 2017 (in million)

Age Group	Rural			Urban			Rural + Urban		
	Male	Female	Person	Male	Female	Person	Male	Female	Person
0-4	0.00	0.00	0.00	0.00	0.00	0.00	0.00	0.00	0.00
5-9	0.00	0.00	0.00	0.05	0.03	0.08	0.05	0.03	0.08
10-14	0.10	0.21	0.32	0.48	0.14	0.62	0.58	0.35	0.93
15-19	19.55	10.71	30.26	5.84	1.92	7.76	25.39	12.62	38.02
20-24	38.88	16.45	55.33	15.76	4.49	20.25	54.64	20.94	75.58
25-29	40.99	18.54	59.52	19.70	5.08	24.78	60.69	23.62	84.30
30-34	34.34	18.98	53.32	18.95	5.04	23.99	53.28	24.03	77.31
35-39	28.26	18.13	46.39	17.20	4.80	22.00	45.46	22.93	68.39
40-44	25.05	17.38	42.43	14.67	4.18	18.85	39.71	21.57	61.28
45-49	23.05	15.43	38.48	12.39	3.18	15.57	35.44	18.61	54.05
50-54	20.52	12.11	32.63	10.32	2.58	12.91	30.85	14.69	45.54
55-59	16.58	8.42	25.00	7.40	1.69	9.08	23.98	10.11	34.09
60+	25.40	11.33	36.73	5.66	1.52	7.17	31.06	12.85	43.91
Total	**272.72**	**147.68**	**420.40**	**128.41**	**34.64**	**163.04**	**401.12**	**182.32**	**583.44**

Source: ibid

Annex 5.3: State-wise MCWS Labour Force by Sector and Sex as on 1st April of 2007, 2012 and 2017.

Table 1: State-wise MCWS Labour Force Projections for 2007

State/Union Territory	Rural			Urban			Total		
	Male	Female	Persons	Male	Female	Persons	Male	Female	Persons
Andhra Pradesh	17.70	12.12	29.82	6.77	2.45	9.22	24.47	14.57	39.04
Assam	7.00	1.64	8.64	1.31	0.19	1.50	8.31	1.83	10.14
Bihar	21.45	4.36	25.81	2.59	0.34	2.93	24.04	4.70	28.73
Gujarat	10.25	5.79	16.04	7.01	1.50	8.51	17.26	7.29	24.55
Haryana	4.48	2.22	6.69	2.31	0.42	2.73	6.79	2.64	9.43
Himachal Pradesh	1.66	1.25	2.91	0.24	0.07	0.32	1.90	1.32	3.22
Jammu & Kashmir	2.36	0.80	3.16	0.95	0.16	1.11	3.31	0.95	4.26
Karnataka	10.96	6.76	17.72	6.21	1.77	7.98	17.17	8.53	25.69
Kerala	6.94	3.17	10.11	2.43	1.13	3.56	9.38	4.30	13.67
Madhya Pradesh	13.21	6.39	19.60	5.44	1.15	6.60	18.65	7.54	26.20
Maharashtra	16.66	10.24	26.90	15.14	4.11	19.26	31.80	14.35	46.15
Orissa	9.53	3.65	13.18	1.92	0.45	2.37	11.46	4.10	15.55
Punjab	5.13	2.79	7.92	3.24	0.63	3.87	8.37	3.42	11.79
Rajasthan	12.84	7.78	20.62	4.38	1.11	5.49	17.22	8.88	26.11
Tamil Nadu	9.67	7.08	16.75	10.31	3.75	14.06	19.98	10.83	30.81
Uttar Pradesh	38.28	13.44	51.72	11.69	1.84	13.52	49.97	15.27	65.24
West Bengal	18.28	4.01	22.29	8.04	1.66	9.71	26.32	5.67	31.99
Jharkhand	6.05	1.97	8.01	1.87	0.35	2.22	7.92	2.31	10.23
Chhattisgarh	4.83	3.84	8.67	1.47	0.36	1.84	6.30	4.21	10.51
Uttarakhand	1.73	1.13	2.86	0.79	0.15	0.93	2.51	1.28	3.80
Other NE States	2.91	1.50	4.41	0.82	0.33	1.15	3.73	1.84	5.56
Other states	0.88	0.20	1.08	5.66	0.89	6.55	6.54	1.09	7.63
Total	222.79	102.11	324.91	100.61	24.80	125.41	323.40	126.91	450.32

Source: ibid

Table 2: State-wise MCWS Labour Force Projections for 2012

State/Union	Rural			Urban			Total		
Territory	Male	Female	Persons	Male	Female	Persons	Male	Female	Persons
Andhra Pradesh	19.10	13.21	32.31	7.28	2.83	10.11	26.38	16.04	42.42
Assam	7.82	1.96	9.78	1.54	0.24	1.79	9.36	2.20	11.56
Bihar	24.23	4.55	28.77	2.93	0.39	3.31	27.15	4.93	32.08
Gujarat	11.22	6.49	17.71	8.06	1.72	9.78	19.28	8.21	27.49
Haryana	4.94	2.79	7.73	2.76	0.52	3.28	7.70	3.31	11.01
Himachal Pradesh	1.78	1.38	3.17	0.28	0.09	0.37	2.06	1.47	3.53
Jammu & Kashmir	2.54	0.84	3.38	1.10	0.16	1.26	3.64	1.00	4.63
Karnataka	11.74	7.45	19.19	7.02	2.00	9.02	18.76	9.45	28.21
Kerala	7.36	3.41	10.78	2.53	1.23	3.76	9.90	4.64	14.54
Madhya Pradesh	14.70	6.79	21.49	6.34	1.36	7.70	21.04	8.15	29.19
Maharashtra	17.92	11.25	29.17	17.31	4.97	22.27	35.23	16.22	51.45
Orissa	10.10	3.97	14.07	2.15	0.56	2.71	12.25	4.53	16.78
Punjab	5.41	3.40	8.81	3.77	0.76	4.53	9.18	4.16	13.35
Rajasthan	14.54	8.64	23.18	5.03	1.31	6.35	19.57	9.96	29.53
Tamil Nadu	9.09	7.12	16.21	11.81	4.54	16.36	20.90	11.66	32.57
Uttar Pradesh	43.01	16.02	59.04	13.44	2.16	15.60	56.46	18.18	74.64
West Bengal	20.21	4.56	24.77	8.55	1.79	10.34	28.76	6.35	35.11
Jharkhand	6.87	2.25	9.12	2.08	0.40	2.47	8.94	2.65	11.59
Chhattisgarh	5.26	4.09	9.35	1.72	0.45	2.17	6.98	4.54	11.52
Uttarakhand	1.90	1.26	3.17	0.91	0.17	1.08	2.81	1.44	4.25
Other NE States	3.35	1.81	5.17	0.93	0.39	1.32	4.29	2.20	6.49
Other states	0.99	0.26	1.25	6.94	1.04	7.99	7.93	1.31	9.24
Total	244.08	113.52	357.61	114.49	29.08	143.57	358.57	142.60	501.17

Source: ibid

Table 3: State-wise MCWS Labour Force Projections for 2017

State/Union Territory	Rural			Urban			Total		
	Male	Female	Persons	Male	Female	Persons	Male	Female	Persons
Andhra Pradesh	20.25	13.95	34.20	7.66	3.15	10.81	27.91	17.10	45.01
Assam	8.63	2.28	10.91	1.75	0.27	2.03	10.38	2.56	12.94
Bihar	27.11	4.78	31.89	3.21	0.44	3.65	30.32	5.22	35.54
Gujarat	12.06	7.22	19.28	8.98	1.94	10.92	21.04	9.15	30.20
Haryana	5.34	3.40	8.74	3.21	0.61	3.82	8.55	4.01	12.57
Himachal Pradesh	1.91	1.47	3.38	0.31	0.09	0.41	2.22	1.57	3.79
Jammu & Kashmir	2.78	0.91	3.69	1.22	0.17	1.39	4.00	1.08	5.07
Karnataka	12.25	8.13	20.38	7.71	2.20	9.92	19.97	10.33	30.29
Kerala	7.68	3.51	11.19	2.60	1.31	3.91	10.28	4.82	15.10
Madhya Pradesh	16.28	7.29	23.57	7.15	1.52	8.67	23.43	8.81	32.24
Maharashtra	19.04	12.17	31.20	19.28	5.83	25.12	38.32	18.00	56.32
Orissa	10.76	4.25	15.00	2.35	0.64	2.99	13.11	4.89	18.00
Punjab	5.64	4.02	9.66	4.24	0.84	5.09	9.88	4.86	14.74
Rajasthan	16.44	9.59	26.03	5.59	1.46	7.05	22.03	11.05	33.08
Tamil Nadu	8.36	7.00	15.36	13.23	5.07	18.29	21.59	12.07	33.65
Uttar Pradesh	47.97	18.81	66.78	15.03	2.35	17.38	63.00	21.17	84.16
West Bengal	21.94	4.99	26.93	8.88	1.84	10.72	30.83	6.83	37.65
Jharkhand	7.71	4.07	11.78	2.28	0.54	2.82	10.00	4.61	14.60
Chhattisgarh	5.68	4.40	10.07	1.99	0.52	2.51	7.67	4.91	12.58
Uttarakhand	2.10	1.75	3.85	1.02	0.20	1.22	3.12	1.95	5.07
Other NE States	3.75	2.13	5.88	1.04	0.46	1.50	4.80	2.59	7.39
Other states	1.08	0.32	1.40	7.98	1.16	9.14	9.06	1.48	10.54
Total	**264.75**	**126.42**	**391.18**	**126.74**	**32.60**	**159.35**	**391.50**	**159.03**	**550.53**

Source: ibid

Table 4: Growth Rate in MCWS Labour Force Between 2007 and 2012

State/Union	Rural			Urban			Total		
Territory	Male	Female	Persons	Male	Female	Persons	Male	Female	Persons
Andhra Pradesh	1.54	1.73	1.62	1.45	2.90	1.84	1.51	1.93	1.67
Assam	2.25	3.59	2.51	3.30	5.13	3.54	2.42	3.75	2.67
Bihar	2.47	0.85	2.20	2.46	2.75	2.49	2.47	0.99	2.23
Gujarat	1.81	2.32	2.00	2.84	2.78	2.83	2.23	2.42	2.29
Haryana	1.99	4.70	2.92	3.58	4.32	3.69	2.54	4.64	3.15
Himachal Pradesh	1.46	2.06	1.72	2.84	3.40	2.97	1.64	2.14	1.84
Jammu & Kashmir	1.48	0.99	1.36	2.92	0.35	2.58	1.90	0.89	1.68
Karnataka	1.39	1.97	1.61	2.49	2.54	2.50	1.79	2.09	1.89
Kerala	1.18	1.51	1.28	0.81	1.69	1.09	1.08	1.56	1.23
Madhya Pradesh	2.16	1.23	1.86	3.08	3.35	3.13	2.43	1.57	2.19
Maharashtra	1.47	1.91	1.64	2.71	3.84	2.95	2.07	2.48	2.20
Orissa	1.16	1.72	1.32	2.22	4.56	2.68	1.34	2.05	1.53
Punjab	1.05	4.05	2.15	3.10	3.93	3.24	1.86	4.03	2.51
Rajasthan	2.52	2.13	2.37	2.80	3.53	2.95	2.59	2.31	2.49
Tamil Nadu	-1.23	0.10	-0.66	2.77	3.92	3.08	0.91	1.49	1.11
Uttar Pradesh	2.36	3.58	2.68	2.84	3.32	2.90	2.47	3.55	2.73
West Bengal	2.03	2.62	2.14	1.23	1.50	1.28	1.79	2.30	1.88
Jharkhand	2.57	2.77	2.62	2.16	2.55	2.22	2.47	2.73	2.53
Chhattisgarh	1.71	1.25	1.51	3.19	4.23	3.40	2.07	1.52	1.85
Uttarakhand	1.96	2.20	2.06	2.92	3.39	3.00	2.27	2.34	2.29
Other NE States	2.89	3.78	3.20	2.71	3.15	2.84	2.85	3.67	3.12
Other states	2.36	5.15	2.91	4.18	3.27	4.06	3.94	3.63	3.90
Total	**1.84**	**2.14**	**1.94**	**2.62**	**3.24**	**2.74**	**2.09**	**2.36**	**2.16**

Source: ibid

Table 5: Growth Rate in MCWS Labour Force Between 2012 and 2017

State/Union	Rural			Urban			Total		
Territory	Male	Female	Persons	Male	Female	Persons	Male	Female	Persons
Andhra Pradesh	1.18	1.09	1.14	1.03	2.17	1.36	1.14	1.29	1.19
Assam	1.99	3.09	2.22	2.58	2.50	2.57	2.09	3.03	2.27
Bihar	2.28	0.99	2.08	1.86	2.82	1.97	2.23	1.14	2.07
Gujarat	1.47	2.14	1.72	2.18	2.41	2.22	1.77	2.20	1.90
Haryana	1.58	4.03	2.49	3.08	3.42	3.13	2.13	3.94	2.68
Himachal Pradesh	1.34	1.28	1.31	2.32	1.39	2.10	1.47	1.29	1.40
Jammu & Kashmir	1.81	1.73	1.79	2.08	0.88	1.94	1.89	1.60	1.83
Karnataka	0.86	1.75	1.21	1.91	1.90	1.90	1.26	1.78	1.43
Kerala	0.83	0.57	0.75	0.54	1.25	0.78	0.76	0.75	0.76
Madhya Pradesh	2.06	1.42	1.86	2.46	2.20	2.41	2.18	1.55	2.01
Maharashtra	1.22	1.58	1.36	2.19	3.27	2.43	1.70	2.11	1.83
Orissa	1.28	1.34	1.30	1.80	2.73	2.00	1.37	1.52	1.41
Punjab	0.83	3.39	1.85	2.38	2.07	2.33	1.48	3.16	2.01
Rajasthan	2.48	2.10	2.34	2.15	2.07	2.13	2.40	2.10	2.30
Tamil Nadu	-1.66	-0.32	-1.06	2.29	2.19	2.26	0.64	0.69	0.66
Uttar Pradesh	2.20	3.26	2.50	2.26	1.73	2.18	2.22	3.08	2.43
West Bengal	1.66	1.81	1.69	0.77	0.50	0.72	1.40	1.44	1.41
Jharkhand	2.35	12.54	5.25	1.90	6.37	2.67	2.25	11.70	4.72
Chhattisgarh	1.55	1.45	1.51	2.94	2.94	2.94	1.90	1.60	1.78
Uttarakhand	1.96	6.73	3.96	2.37	2.47	2.39	2.09	6.24	3.57
Other NE States	2.28	3.27	2.63	2.26	3.33	2.58	2.28	3.28	2.62
Other states	1.76	4.21	2.29	2.81	2.20	2.73	2.68	2.61	2.68
Total	**1.64**	**2.18**	**1.81**	**2.05**	**2.31**	**2.11**	**1.77**	**2.20**	**1.90**

Source: ibid

Annex 5.4: State and Age Group-wise MCWS Labour Force by Sector and Sex as on 1st April of 2007, 2012 and 2017.

Projected Age-Sex MCWS Labour Force of Andhra Pradesh in 2007 (in million)

Age Group	Rural			Urban			Rural + Urban		
	Male	Female	Person	Male	Female	Person	Male	Female	Person
0-4	0.00	0.00	0.00	0.00	0.00	0.00	0.00	0.00	0.00
5-9	0.01	0.01	0.02	0.00	0.00	0.00	0.01	0.01	0.02
10-14	0.25	0.42	0.67	0.06	0.05	0.11	0.31	0.47	0.78
15-19	1.96	1.51	3.47	0.50	0.20	0.69	2.46	1.71	4.16
20-24	2.56	1.37	3.93	0.91	0.33	1.24	3.47	1.70	5.17
25-29	2.33	1.53	3.86	1.03	0.34	1.37	3.36	1.86	5.23
30-34	2.12	1.61	3.73	0.95	0.31	1.26	3.08	1.92	5.00
35-39	1.96	1.49	3.45	0.84	0.37	1.21	2.81	1.86	4.67
40-44	1.78	1.24	3.03	0.76	0.30	1.06	2.54	1.55	4.08
45-49	1.53	1.02	2.54	0.66	0.19	0.85	2.19	1.21	3.40
50-54	1.20	0.74	1.94	0.52	0.16	0.67	1.72	0.90	2.62
55-59	0.87	0.61	1.48	0.32	0.09	0.41	1.19	0.70	1.89
60+	1.12	0.58	1.69	0.22	0.11	0.34	1.34	0.69	2.03
Total	17.70	12.12	29.82	6.77	2.45	9.22	24.47	14.57	39.04

Source: ibid

Projected Age-Sex MCWS Labour Force of Andhra Pradesh in 2012 (in million)

Age Group	Rural			Urban			Rural + Urban		
	Male	Female	Person	Male	Female	Person	Male	Female	Person
0-4	0.00	0.00	0.00	0.00	0.00	0.00	0.00	0.00	0.00
5-9	0.00	0.00	0.00	0.00	0.00	0.00	0.00	0.00	0.00
10-14	0.02	0.27	0.29	0.02	0.04	0.06	0.04	0.31	0.35
15-19	1.84	1.45	3.29	0.43	0.18	0.61	2.27	1.63	3.90
20-24	2.90	1.53	4.43	0.89	0.36	1.25	3.80	1.88	5.68
25-29	2.64	1.61	4.26	1.08	0.38	1.46	3.73	1.99	5.72
30-34	2.31	1.72	4.02	1.06	0.38	1.44	3.37	2.10	5.47
35-39	2.09	1.67	3.76	0.94	0.46	1.40	3.03	2.13	5.15
40-44	1.89	1.45	3.33	0.82	0.37	1.19	2.71	1.82	4.53
45-49	1.71	1.20	2.92	0.75	0.22	0.97	2.47	1.43	3.89
50-54	1.39	0.87	2.26	0.62	0.19	0.81	2.01	1.06	3.07
55-59	1.05	0.74	1.79	0.40	0.11	0.51	1.45	0.85	2.31
60+	1.26	0.70	1.95	0.26	0.14	0.40	1.51	0.84	2.35
Total	19.10	13.21	32.31	7.28	2.83	10.11	26.38	16.04	42.42

Source: ibid

Projected Age-Sex MCWS Labour Force of Andhra Pradesh in 2017 (in million)

Age Group	Rural			Urban			Rural + Urban		
	Male	Female	Person	Male	Female	Person	Male	Female	Person
0-4	0.00	0.00	0.00	0.00	0.00	0.00	0.00	0.00	0.00
5-9	0.00	0.00	0.00	0.00	0.00	0.00	0.00	0.00	0.00
10-14	0.00	0.14	0.14	0.00	0.04	0.04	0.00	0.18	0.18
15-19	1.55	1.31	2.86	0.37	0.16	0.53	1.92	1.47	3.39
20-24	2.87	1.54	4.41	0.81	0.36	1.16	3.68	1.89	5.57
25-29	2.99	1.81	4.80	1.09	0.41	1.49	4.08	2.22	6.30
30-34	2.60	1.77	4.37	1.14	0.39	1.53	3.74	2.16	5.90
35-39	2.25	1.69	3.94	1.05	0.54	1.59	3.29	2.23	5.53
40-44	1.99	1.55	3.54	0.92	0.45	1.37	2.91	2.00	4.91
45-49	1.80	1.34	3.15	0.82	0.26	1.08	2.63	1.60	4.22
50-54	1.54	1.03	2.57	0.70	0.23	0.93	2.24	1.26	3.50
55-59	1.21	0.92	2.14	0.47	0.14	0.61	1.69	1.06	2.75
60+	1.44	0.84	2.29	0.29	0.18	0.48	1.74	1.02	2.76
Total	20.25	13.95	34.20	7.66	3.15	10.81	27.91	17.10	45.01

Source: ibid

Projected Age-Sex MCWS Labour Force of Assam in 2007 (in million)

Age Group	Rural			Urban			Rural + Urban		
	Male	Female	Person	Male	Female	Person	Male	Female	Person
0-4	0.00	0.00	0.00	0.00	0.00	0.00	0.00	0.00	0.00
5-9	0.00	0.00	0.01	0.00	0.00	0.00	0.00	0.00	0.01
10-14	0.09	0.02	0.11	0.00	0.00	0.00	0.09	0.02	0.11
15-19	0.64	0.21	0.85	0.06	0.01	0.07	0.70	0.22	0.92
20-24	0.97	0.24	1.21	0.14	0.04	0.18	1.11	0.28	1.39
25-29	0.95	0.20	1.15	0.20	0.03	0.23	1.15	0.23	1.38
30-34	0.87	0.22	1.09	0.20	0.03	0.23	1.07	0.25	1.32
35-39	0.82	0.22	1.04	0.19	0.03	0.22	1.01	0.25	1.26
40-44	0.75	0.21	0.96	0.17	0.02	0.18	0.92	0.22	1.14
45-49	0.62	0.14	0.75	0.14	0.02	0.16	0.75	0.15	0.91
50-54	0.48	0.10	0.58	0.11	0.01	0.12	0.59	0.11	0.70
55-59	0.33	0.04	0.37	0.07	0.00	0.07	0.40	0.05	0.45
60+	0.47	0.04	0.51	0.04	0.00	0.04	0.51	0.04	0.56
Total	7.00	1.64	8.64	1.31	0.19	1.50	8.31	1.83	10.14

Source: ibid

Projected Age-Sex MCWS Labour Force of Assam in 2012 (in million)

Age Group	Rural			Urban			Rural + Urban		
	Male	Female	Person	Male	Female	Person	Male	Female	Person
0-4	0.00	0.00	0.00	0.00	0.00	0.00	0.00	0.00	0.00
5-9	0.00	0.00	0.00	0.00	0.00	0.00	0.00	0.00	0.00
10-14	0.08	0.01	0.09	0.00	0.00	0.00	0.08	0.01	0.09
15-19	0.65	0.21	0.87	0.06	0.00	0.07	0.72	0.22	0.94
20-24	1.16	0.31	1.46	0.17	0.05	0.22	1.32	0.36	1.68
25-29	1.10	0.22	1.32	0.23	0.05	0.27	1.32	0.27	1.59
30-34	0.91	0.24	1.15	0.23	0.04	0.27	1.15	0.27	1.42
35-39	0.83	0.26	1.09	0.22	0.04	0.26	1.06	0.29	1.35
40-44	0.79	0.27	1.06	0.19	0.02	0.21	0.98	0.29	1.27
45-49	0.71	0.19	0.90	0.16	0.03	0.19	0.87	0.22	1.09
50-54	0.59	0.15	0.74	0.14	0.01	0.15	0.73	0.15	0.88
55-59	0.42	0.05	0.48	0.09	0.01	0.10	0.52	0.06	0.58
60+	0.58	0.05	0.63	0.05	0.00	0.05	0.62	0.06	0.68
Total	**7.82**	**1.96**	**9.78**	**1.54**	**0.24**	**1.79**	**9.36**	**2.20**	**11.56**

Source: ibid

Projected Age-Sex MCWS Labour Force of Assam in 2017 (in million)

Age Group	Rural			Urban			Rural + Urban		
	Male	Female	Person	Male	Female	Person	Male	Female	Person
0-4	0.00	0.00	0.00	0.00	0.00	0.00	0.00	0.00	0.00
5-9	0.00	0.00	0.00	0.00	0.00	0.00	0.00	0.00	0.00
10-14	0.07	0.01	0.08	0.00	0.00	0.00	0.07	0.01	0.08
15-19	0.62	0.21	0.83	0.06	0.00	0.06	0.68	0.21	0.89
20-24	1.19	0.35	1.54	0.18	0.06	0.24	1.37	0.40	1.78
25-29	1.30	0.27	1.56	0.26	0.05	0.32	1.56	0.32	1.88
30-34	1.05	0.26	1.31	0.27	0.04	0.31	1.32	0.30	1.62
35-39	0.87	0.28	1.15	0.26	0.04	0.29	1.13	0.32	1.45
40-44	0.81	0.32	1.13	0.21	0.02	0.23	1.02	0.34	1.37
45-49	0.75	0.24	0.99	0.18	0.03	0.22	0.93	0.28	1.21
50-54	0.70	0.21	0.91	0.16	0.01	0.17	0.86	0.22	1.08
55-59	0.53	0.07	0.60	0.11	0.01	0.12	0.65	0.08	0.72
60+	0.73	0.07	0.80	0.05	0.00	0.05	0.78	0.08	0.86
Total	**8.63**	**2.28**	**10.91**	**1.75**	**0.27**	**2.03**	**10.38**	**2.56**	**12.94**

Source: ibid

Projected Age-Sex MCWS Labour Force of Bihar in 2007 (in million)

Age Group	Rural			Urban			Rural + Urban		
	Male	Female	Person	Male	Female	Person	Male	Female	Person
0-4	0.00	0.00	0.00	0.00	0.00	0.00	0.00	0.00	0.00
5-9	0.00	0.00	0.00	0.00	0.00	0.00	0.00	0.00	0.00
10-14	0.20	0.04	0.24	0.02	0.01	0.03	0.22	0.05	0.27
15-19	2.34	0.26	2.60	0.15	0.01	0.16	2.49	0.27	2.76
20-24	3.07	0.38	3.45	0.33	0.04	0.38	3.40	0.43	3.83
25-29	2.67	0.51	3.18	0.40	0.04	0.44	3.06	0.55	3.61
30-34	2.41	0.62	3.03	0.35	0.04	0.39	2.76	0.66	3.42
35-39	2.31	0.68	2.99	0.32	0.05	0.36	2.62	0.73	3.35
40-44	2.15	0.60	2.75	0.29	0.04	0.33	2.44	0.64	3.08
45-49	1.84	0.42	2.26	0.25	0.02	0.28	2.09	0.45	2.53
50-54	1.49	0.32	1.81	0.20	0.03	0.23	1.70	0.35	2.04
55-59	1.15	0.23	1.38	0.15	0.02	0.17	1.30	0.25	1.55
60+	1.82	0.30	2.12	0.13	0.03	0.16	1.95	0.33	2.28
Total	**21.45**	**4.36**	**25.81**	**2.59**	**0.34**	**2.93**	**24.04**	**4.70**	**28.73**

Source: ibid

Projected Age-Sex MCWS Labour Force of Bihar in 2012 (in million)

Age Group	Rural			Urban			Rural + Urban		
	Male	Female	Person	Male	Female	Person	Male	Female	Person
0-4	0.00	0.00	0.00	0.00	0.00	0.00	0.00	0.00	0.00
5-9	0.00	0.00	0.00	0.00	0.00	0.00	0.00	0.00	0.00
10-14	0.06	0.00	0.06	0.01	0.00	0.01	0.07	0.00	0.07
15-19	2.41	0.18	2.60	0.12	0.00	0.12	2.54	0.18	2.72
20-24	4.06	0.45	4.51	0.36	0.05	0.41	4.42	0.50	4.92
25-29	3.32	0.53	3.85	0.48	0.05	0.52	3.80	0.58	4.38
30-34	2.58	0.59	3.16	0.43	0.04	0.47	3.00	0.63	3.64
35-39	2.34	0.69	3.03	0.37	0.05	0.42	2.70	0.74	3.44
40-44	2.23	0.65	2.88	0.32	0.05	0.37	2.55	0.70	3.25
45-49	2.05	0.47	2.52	0.28	0.03	0.31	2.33	0.50	2.82
50-54	1.73	0.35	2.09	0.23	0.04	0.27	1.97	0.39	2.36
55-59	1.37	0.28	1.65	0.18	0.04	0.22	1.56	0.31	1.87
60+	2.08	0.36	2.43	0.14	0.04	0.18	2.22	0.40	2.62
Total	**24.23**	**4.55**	**28.77**	**2.93**	**0.39**	**3.31**	**27.15**	**4.93**	**32.08**

Source: ibid

Projected Age-Sex MCWS Labour Force of Bihar in 2017 (in million)

Age Group	Rural			Urban			Rural + Urban		
	Male	Female	Person	Male	Female	Person	Male	Female	Person
0-4	0.00	0.00	0.00	0.00	0.00	0.00	0.00	0.00	0.00
5-9	0.00	0.00	0.00	0.00	0.00	0.00	0.00	0.00	0.00
10-14	0.00	0.00	0.00	0.00	0.00	0.00	0.00	0.00	0.00
15-19	2.25	0.07	2.32	0.10	0.00	0.10	2.34	0.07	2.42
20-24	4.47	0.45	4.92	0.33	0.05	0.39	4.80	0.51	5.31
25-29	4.41	0.67	5.08	0.52	0.05	0.57	4.92	0.73	5.65
30-34	3.23	0.62	3.85	0.51	0.06	0.57	3.74	0.68	4.42
35-39	2.50	0.67	3.16	0.44	0.06	0.50	2.94	0.72	3.66
40-44	2.25	0.66	2.91	0.37	0.05	0.42	2.62	0.72	3.33
45-49	2.12	0.48	2.61	0.30	0.03	0.33	2.43	0.52	2.94
50-54	1.94	0.39	2.33	0.26	0.04	0.30	2.19	0.43	2.62
55-59	1.60	0.33	1.93	0.21	0.04	0.25	1.81	0.37	2.18
60+	2.36	0.43	2.79	0.16	0.05	0.21	2.52	0.48	3.00
Total	**27.11**	**4.78**	**31.89**	**3.21**	**0.44**	**3.65**	**30.32**	**5.22**	**35.54**

Source: ibid

Projected Age-Sex MCWS Labour Force of Chhattisgarh in 2007 (in million)

Age Group	Rural			Urban			Rural + Urban		
	Male	Female	Person	Male	Female	Person	Male	Female	Person
0-4	0.00	0.00	0.00	0.00	0.00	0.00	0.00	0.00	0.00
5-9	0.00	0.00	0.00	0.00	0.00	0.00	0.00	0.00	0.00
10-14	0.06	0.04	0.10	0.02	0.00	0.02	0.08	0.05	0.13
15-19	0.48	0.30	0.78	0.09	0.03	0.12	0.57	0.33	0.90
20-24	0.70	0.51	1.20	0.19	0.04	0.23	0.89	0.54	1.43
25-29	0.60	0.46	1.06	0.24	0.05	0.28	0.83	0.51	1.34
30-34	0.56	0.53	1.08	0.22	0.05	0.26	0.77	0.57	1.35
35-39	0.54	0.49	1.03	0.19	0.05	0.25	0.74	0.54	1.28
40-44	0.50	0.48	0.98	0.17	0.05	0.21	0.66	0.53	1.19
45-49	0.42	0.37	0.78	0.14	0.04	0.18	0.55	0.41	0.96
50-54	0.33	0.27	0.60	0.10	0.02	0.12	0.43	0.29	0.72
55-59	0.26	0.19	0.45	0.07	0.01	0.09	0.33	0.21	0.53
60+	0.39	0.21	0.60	0.06	0.01	0.07	0.45	0.23	0.67
Total	**4.83**	**3.84**	**8.67**	**1.47**	**0.36**	**1.84**	**6.30**	**4.21**	**10.51**

Source: ibid

Projected Age-Sex MCWS Labour Force of Chhattisgarh in 2012 (in million)

Age Group	Rural			Urban			Rural + Urban		
	Male	Female	Person	Male	Female	Person	Male	Female	Person
0-4	0.00	0.00	0.00	0.00	0.00	0.00	0.00	0.00	0.00
5-9	0.00	0.00	0.00	0.00	0.00	0.00	0.00	0.00	0.00
10-14	0.04	0.00	0.04	0.02	0.00	0.02	0.06	0.00	0.06
15-19	0.48	0.27	0.75	0.09	0.04	0.12	0.56	0.31	0.87
20-24	0.83	0.59	1.42	0.20	0.05	0.25	1.03	0.64	1.67
25-29	0.70	0.49	1.19	0.29	0.07	0.35	0.98	0.56	1.54
30-34	0.56	0.52	1.07	0.26	0.06	0.32	0.82	0.57	1.39
35-39	0.53	0.50	1.02	0.23	0.06	0.29	0.76	0.56	1.32
40-44	0.52	0.53	1.05	0.19	0.05	0.24	0.71	0.59	1.30
45-49	0.48	0.44	0.91	0.16	0.05	0.21	0.64	0.48	1.13
50-54	0.40	0.31	0.71	0.13	0.03	0.16	0.52	0.34	0.86
55-59	0.30	0.22	0.52	0.09	0.02	0.11	0.39	0.24	0.63
60+	0.44	0.24	0.69	0.07	0.02	0.08	0.51	0.26	0.77
Total	**5.26**	**4.11**	**9.36**	**1.72**	**0.45**	**2.17**	**6.98**	**4.55**	**11.53**

Source: ibid

Projected Age-Sex MCWS Labour Force of Chhattisgarh in 2017 (in million)

Age Group	Rural			Urban			Rural + Urban		
	Male	Female	Person	Male	Female	Person	Male	Female	Person
0-4	0.00	0.00	0.00	0.00	0.00	0.00	0.00	0.00	0.00
5-9	0.00	0.00	0.00	0.00	0.00	0.00	0.00	0.00	0.00
10-14	0.00	0.00	0.00	0.02	0.00	0.02	0.02	0.00	0.02
15-19	0.45	0.22	0.67	0.09	0.04	0.13	0.54	0.26	0.80
20-24	0.85	0.60	1.44	0.22	0.05	0.28	1.07	0.65	1.72
25-29	0.84	0.58	1.41	0.33	0.08	0.41	1.16	0.66	1.82
30-34	0.65	0.57	1.22	0.32	0.07	0.39	0.97	0.64	1.61
35-39	0.53	0.49	1.02	0.27	0.07	0.35	0.80	0.56	1.37
40-44	0.52	0.54	1.06	0.22	0.06	0.28	0.74	0.60	1.34
45-49	0.50	0.49	0.99	0.19	0.05	0.24	0.69	0.54	1.23
50-54	0.46	0.37	0.83	0.15	0.04	0.19	0.61	0.41	1.02
55-59	0.36	0.26	0.62	0.11	0.02	0.13	0.47	0.29	0.75
60+	0.52	0.28	0.80	0.08	0.02	0.10	0.60	0.30	0.90
Total	**5.68**	**4.40**	**10.07**	**1.99**	**0.52**	**2.51**	**7.67**	**4.91**	**12.58**

Source: ibid

Projected Age-Sex MCWS Labour Force of Gujarat in 2007 (in million)

Age Group	Rural			Urban			Rural + Urban		
	Male	Female	Person	Male	Female	Person	Male	Female	Person
0-4	0.00	0.00	0.00	0.00	0.00	0.00	0.00	0.00	0.00
5-9	0.00	0.00	0.00	0.01	0.00	0.01	0.01	0.00	0.01
10-14	0.08	0.07	0.14	0.03	0.01	0.05	0.11	0.08	0.19
15-19	1.18	0.60	1.78	0.50	0.12	0.62	1.68	0.72	2.40
20-24	1.46	0.68	2.15	1.01	0.22	1.23	2.47	0.90	3.38
25-29	1.35	0.65	2.00	1.12	0.18	1.31	2.48	0.83	3.30
30-34	1.22	0.70	1.92	1.00	0.21	1.21	2.22	0.91	3.13
35-39	1.16	0.78	1.94	0.87	0.23	1.10	2.03	1.01	3.04
40-44	1.05	0.71	1.76	0.75	0.19	0.95	1.81	0.90	2.71
45-49	0.87	0.62	1.49	0.66	0.16	0.81	1.53	0.78	2.30
50-54	0.68	0.44	1.12	0.49	0.09	0.58	1.17	0.53	1.70
55-59	0.50	0.28	0.78	0.30	0.07	0.38	0.80	0.36	1.15
60+	0.71	0.26	0.96	0.25	0.02	0.27	0.95	0.28	1.23
Total	**10.25**	**5.79**	**16.04**	**7.01**	**1.50**	**8.51**	**17.26**	**7.29**	**24.55**

Source: ibid

Projected Age-Sex MCWS Labour Force of Gujarat in 2012 (in million)

Age Group	Rural			Urban			Rural + Urban		
	Male	Female	Person	Male	Female	Person	Male	Female	Person
0-4	0.00	0.00	0.00	0.00	0.00	0.00	0.00	0.00	0.00
5-9	0.00	0.00	0.00	0.01	0.00	0.01	0.01	0.00	0.01
10-14	0.02	0.00	0.02	0.02	0.01	0.03	0.05	0.01	0.06
15-19	1.17	0.59	1.76	0.51	0.12	0.63	1.68	0.71	2.39
20-24	1.56	0.71	2.27	1.10	0.26	1.36	2.66	0.97	3.63
25-29	1.50	0.70	2.19	1.27	0.22	1.49	2.76	0.92	3.68
30-34	1.32	0.77	2.09	1.19	0.23	1.42	2.51	1.00	3.51
35-39	1.21	0.85	2.07	1.01	0.27	1.29	2.23	1.13	3.35
40-44	1.13	0.83	1.96	0.87	0.20	1.06	2.00	1.03	3.02
45-49	1.01	0.78	1.78	0.77	0.20	0.96	1.77	0.97	2.75
50-54	0.82	0.58	1.40	0.60	0.11	0.70	1.42	0.69	2.10
55-59	0.62	0.37	0.99	0.42	0.10	0.51	1.03	0.47	1.50
60+	0.86	0.32	1.18	0.31	0.01	0.31	1.16	0.33	1.49
Total	11.22	6.49	17.71	8.06	1.72	9.78	19.28	8.21	27.49

Source: ibid

Projected Age-Sex MCWS Labour Force of Gujarat in 2017 (in million

Age Group	Rural			Urban			Rural + Urban		
	Male	Female	Person	Male	Female	Person	Male	Female	Person
0-4	0.00	0.00	0.00	0.00	0.00	0.00	0.00	0.00	0.00
5-9	0.00	0.00	0.00	0.01	0.00	0.01	0.01	0.00	0.01
10-14	0.00	0.00	0.00	0.00	0.01	0.01	0.00	0.01	0.01
15-19	1.09	0.54	1.64	0.54	0.12	0.65	1.63	0.66	2.29
20-24	1.52	0.69	2.21	1.16	0.30	1.45	2.67	0.99	3.66
25-29	1.60	0.73	2.32	1.37	0.26	1.63	2.97	0.98	3.95
30-34	1.48	0.84	2.32	1.32	0.25	1.57	2.80	1.09	3.89
35-39	1.34	0.95	2.29	1.17	0.32	1.49	2.51	1.27	3.78
40-44	1.20	0.92	2.12	0.98	0.22	1.20	2.18	1.14	3.32
45-49	1.09	0.91	2.00	0.85	0.24	1.09	1.94	1.15	3.09
50-54	0.95	0.74	1.69	0.69	0.13	0.81	1.64	0.87	2.51
55-59	0.74	0.48	1.22	0.51	0.12	0.63	1.25	0.60	1.85
60+	1.07	0.40	1.47	0.39	0.01	0.40	1.45	0.41	1.87
Total	**12.06**	**7.22**	**19.28**	**8.98**	**1.96**	**10.94**	**21.04**	**9.18**	**30.23**

Source: ibid

Projected Age-Sex MCWS Labour Force of Haryana in 2007 (in million)

Age Group	Rural			Urban			Rural + Urban		
	Male	Female	Person	Male	Female	Person	Male	Female	Person
0-4	0.00	0.00	0.00	0.00	0.00	0.00	0.00	0.00	0.00
5-9	0.00	0.00	0.00	0.00	0.00	0.00	0.00	0.00	0.00
10-14	0.01	0.03	0.04	0.00	0.00	0.01	0.02	0.03	0.05
15-19	0.34	0.20	0.55	0.13	0.04	0.18	0.48	0.25	0.72
20-24	0.78	0.30	1.09	0.36	0.06	0.42	1.14	0.36	1.50
25-29	0.69	0.27	0.96	0.39	0.05	0.44	1.08	0.32	1.40
30-34	0.60	0.33	0.92	0.34	0.06	0.40	0.93	0.39	1.32
35-39	0.50	0.30	0.79	0.29	0.07	0.36	0.79	0.36	1.15
40-44	0.45	0.29	0.74	0.25	0.07	0.32	0.70	0.36	1.06
45-49	0.36	0.22	0.58	0.22	0.03	0.25	0.57	0.25	0.82
50-54	0.27	0.11	0.37	0.16	0.02	0.18	0.43	0.12	0.55
55-59	0.19	0.08	0.27	0.10	0.01	0.10	0.28	0.09	0.37
60+	0.29	0.10	0.39	0.07	0.01	0.08	0.36	0.11	0.47
Total	**4.48**	**2.22**	**6.69**	**2.31**	**0.42**	**2.73**	**6.79**	**2.64**	**9.43**

Source: ibid

Projected Age-Sex MCWS Labour Force of Haryana in 2012 (in million)

Age Group	Rural			Urban			Rural + Urban		
	Male	Female	Person	Male	Female	Person	Male	Female	Person
0-4	0.00	0.00	0.00	0.00	0.00	0.00	0.00	0.00	0.00
5-9	0.00	0.00	0.00	0.00	0.00	0.00	0.00	0.00	0.00
10-14	0.00	0.02	0.02	0.00	0.00	0.00	0.00	0.02	0.02
15-19	0.27	0.21	0.48	0.11	0.04	0.16	0.38	0.25	0.64
20-24	0.83	0.39	1.22	0.41	0.07	0.48	1.24	0.46	1.70
25-29	0.81	0.34	1.15	0.49	0.07	0.56	1.29	0.42	1.71
30-34	0.68	0.39	1.07	0.43	0.08	0.51	1.11	0.48	1.58
35-39	0.56	0.35	0.91	0.37	0.08	0.45	0.93	0.43	1.36
40-44	0.49	0.37	0.86	0.30	0.08	0.38	0.79	0.45	1.24
45-49	0.43	0.31	0.74	0.25	0.04	0.29	0.68	0.35	1.03
50-54	0.34	0.16	0.49	0.20	0.03	0.23	0.54	0.18	0.72
55-59	0.24	0.12	0.36	0.13	0.01	0.14	0.37	0.13	0.50
60+	0.30	0.13	0.43	0.08	0.01	0.08	0.38	0.14	0.51
Total	**4.94**	**2.79**	**7.73**	**2.76**	**0.52**	**3.28**	**7.70**	**3.31**	**11.01**

Source: ibid

Projected Age-Sex MCWS Labour Force of Haryana in 2017 (in million)

Age Group	Rural			Urban			Rural + Urban		
	Male	Female	Person	Male	Female	Person	Male	Female	Person
0-4	0.00	0.00	0.00	0.00	0.00	0.00	0.00	0.00	0.00
5-9	0.00	0.00	0.00	0.00	0.00	0.00	0.00	0.00	0.00
10-14	0.00	0.00	0.00	0.00	0.00	0.00	0.00	0.00	0.00
15-19	0.19	0.20	0.39	0.09	0.05	0.14	0.28	0.25	0.53
20-24	0.79	0.40	1.19	0.47	0.08	0.55	1.26	0.48	1.74
25-29	0.87	0.42	1.29	0.58	0.10	0.67	1.45	0.52	1.97
30-34	0.80	0.53	1.33	0.52	0.11	0.63	1.32	0.64	1.96
35-39	0.65	0.42	1.07	0.45	0.09	0.55	1.11	0.51	1.62
40-44	0.55	0.45	1.00	0.36	0.09	0.45	0.91	0.54	1.45
45-49	0.47	0.41	0.88	0.29	0.04	0.33	0.76	0.45	1.21
50-54	0.40	0.22	0.62	0.23	0.03	0.26	0.63	0.25	0.88
55-59	0.30	0.18	0.48	0.15	0.02	0.17	0.45	0.19	0.64
60+	0.32	0.17	0.50	0.08	0.01	0.09	0.40	0.18	0.58
Total	**5.34**	**3.40**	8.74	**3.23**	**0.61**	**3.84**	**8.57**	**4.01**	12.58

Source: ibid

Projected Age-Sex MCWS Labour Force of Himachal Pradesh in 2007 (in million)

Age Group	Rural			Urban			Rural + Urban		
	Male	Female	Person	Male	Female	Person	Male	Female	Person
0-4	0.00	0.00	0.00	0.00	0.00	0.00	0.00	0.00	0.00
5-9	0.00	0.00	0.00	0.00	0.00	0.00	0.00	0.00	0.00
10-14	0.00	0.00	0.01	0.00	0.00	0.00	0.00	0.00	0.01
15-19	0.07	0.06	0.13	0.01	0.00	0.01	0.08	0.06	0.15
20-24	0.21	0.17	0.38	0.03	0.01	0.03	0.24	0.17	0.41
25-29	0.24	0.18	0.41	0.04	0.01	0.05	0.28	0.19	0.47
30-34	0.22	0.17	0.39	0.04	0.01	0.05	0.26	0.18	0.44
35-39	0.19	0.15	0.34	0.03	0.01	0.04	0.22	0.16	0.38
40-44	0.16	0.14	0.31	0.03	0.01	0.04	0.19	0.15	0.34
45-49	0.14	0.11	0.25	0.02	0.01	0.03	0.17	0.11	0.28
50-54	0.12	0.09	0.21	0.02	0.01	0.03	0.14	0.09	0.24
55-59	0.10	0.07	0.17	0.01	0.00	0.02	0.11	0.07	0.19
60+	0.19	0.12	0.31	0.01	0.00	0.01	0.20	0.12	0.32
Total	**1.66**	**1.25**	**2.91**	**0.24**	**0.07**	**0.32**	**1.90**	**1.32**	**3.22**

Source: ibid

Projected Age-Sex MCWS Labour Force of Himachal Pradesh in 2012 (in million)

Age Group	Rural			Urban			Rural + Urban		
	Male	Female	Person	Male	Female	Person	Male	Female	Person
0-4	0.00	0.00	0.00	0.00	0.00	0.00	0.00	0.00	0.00
5-9	0.00	0.00	0.00	0.00	0.00	0.00	0.00	0.00	0.00
10-14	0.00	0.00	0.00	0.00	0.00	0.00	0.00	0.00	0.00
15-19	0.05	0.04	0.09	0.01	0.00	0.01	0.06	0.05	0.11
20-24	0.21	0.17	0.38	0.03	0.01	0.04	0.24	0.18	0.42
25-29	0.26	0.19	0.45	0.04	0.02	0.06	0.31	0.21	0.51
30-34	0.25	0.18	0.43	0.04	0.01	0.06	0.29	0.20	0.49
35-39	0.21	0.17	0.39	0.04	0.01	0.05	0.25	0.18	0.44
40-44	0.18	0.16	0.34	0.03	0.01	0.05	0.21	0.17	0.38
45-49	0.16	0.13	0.29	0.03	0.01	0.04	0.19	0.14	0.33
50-54	0.14	0.10	0.24	0.02	0.01	0.03	0.16	0.11	0.27
55-59	0.11	0.08	0.20	0.02	0.01	0.02	0.13	0.09	0.22
60+	0.21	0.15	0.36	0.01	0.00	0.02	0.22	0.15	0.37
Total	**1.78**	**1.38**	**3.17**	**0.28**	**0.09**	**0.37**	**2.06**	**1.47**	**3.53**

Source: ibid

Projected Age-Sex MCWS Labour Force of Himachal Pradesh in 2017 (in million)

Age Group	Rural			Urban			Rural + Urban		
	Male	Female	Person	Male	Female	Person	Male	Female	Person
0-4	0.00	0.00	0.00	0.00	0.00	0.00	0.00	0.00	0.00
5-9	0.00	0.00	0.00	0.00	0.00	0.00	0.00	0.00	0.00
10-14	0.00	0.00	0.00	0.00	0.00	0.00	0.00	0.00	0.00
15-19	0.03	0.03	0.06	0.01	0.00	0.01	0.04	0.03	0.08
20-24	0.18	0.15	0.34	0.04	0.01	0.04	0.22	0.16	0.38
25-29	0.27	0.19	0.46	0.04	0.02	0.06	0.32	0.21	0.53
30-34	0.28	0.20	0.47	0.04	0.01	0.06	0.32	0.21	0.53
35-39	0.24	0.19	0.43	0.04	0.01	0.05	0.29	0.20	0.48
40-44	0.20	0.18	0.38	0.04	0.01	0.05	0.24	0.19	0.43
45-49	0.18	0.14	0.32	0.03	0.01	0.04	0.21	0.15	0.36
50-54	0.15	0.12	0.27	0.03	0.01	0.04	0.18	0.13	0.31
55-59	0.13	0.10	0.22	0.02	0.01	0.03	0.15	0.10	0.25
60+	0.23	0.19	0.42	0.02	0.00	0.02	0.25	0.19	0.44
Total	**1.91**	**1.47**	**3.38**	**0.31**	**0.09**	**0.41**	**2.22**	**1.57**	**3.79**

Source: ibid

Projected Age-Sex MCWS Labour Force of Jammu & Kashmir in 2007 (in million)

Age Group	Rural			Urban			Rural + Urban		
	Male	Female	Person	Male	Female	Person	Male	Female	Person
0-4	0.00	0.00	0.00	0.00	0.00	0.00	0.00	0.00	0.00
5-9	0.00	0.00	0.00	0.00	0.00	0.00	0.00	0.00	0.00
10-14	0.01	0.01	0.03	0.00	0.02	0.02	0.01	0.03	0.04
15-19	0.23	0.10	0.33	0.01	0.01	0.03	0.25	0.12	0.36
20-24	0.36	0.14	0.50	0.12	0.02	0.14	0.48	0.17	0.65
25-29	0.33	0.11	0.44	0.15	0.03	0.17	0.47	0.14	0.61
30-34	0.27	0.10	0.37	0.14	0.02	0.16	0.42	0.11	0.53
35-39	0.25	0.09	0.34	0.13	0.02	0.15	0.38	0.11	0.49
40-44	0.22	0.07	0.30	0.12	0.01	0.13	0.34	0.09	0.43
45-49	0.19	0.05	0.25	0.10	0.01	0.11	0.29	0.07	0.36
50-54	0.15	0.04	0.19	0.08	0.01	0.08	0.23	0.04	0.28
55-59	0.11	0.03	0.15	0.05	0.00	0.05	0.16	0.04	0.20
60+	0.23	0.04	0.27	0.05	0.00	0.06	0.28	0.04	0.33
Total	**2.36**	**0.80**	**3.16**	**0.95**	**0.16**	**1.11**	**3.31**	**0.95**	**4.26**

Source: ibid

Projected Age-Sex MCWS Labour Force of Jammu & Kashmir in 2012 (in million)

Age Group	Rural			Urban			Rural + Urban		
	Male	Female	Person	Male	Female	Person	Male	Female	Person
0-4	0.00	0.00	0.00	0.00	0.00	0.00	0.00	0.00	0.00
5-9	0.00	0.00	0.00	0.00	0.00	0.00	0.00	0.00	0.00
10-14	0.00	0.00	0.00	0.00	0.01	0.01	0.00	0.01	0.01
15-19	0.18	0.10	0.27	0.00	0.01	0.01	0.18	0.11	0.29
20-24	0.38	0.17	0.55	0.13	0.03	0.16	0.51	0.19	0.71
25-29	0.39	0.13	0.52	0.17	0.03	0.20	0.56	0.16	0.72
30-34	0.31	0.10	0.42	0.16	0.02	0.18	0.47	0.12	0.60
35-39	0.26	0.09	0.35	0.15	0.02	0.17	0.41	0.11	0.51
40-44	0.23	0.07	0.30	0.14	0.01	0.15	0.37	0.08	0.45
45-49	0.21	0.06	0.27	0.12	0.02	0.13	0.33	0.07	0.40
50-54	0.17	0.04	0.22	0.10	0.01	0.10	0.27	0.05	0.32
55-59	0.13	0.04	0.17	0.07	0.00	0.07	0.20	0.04	0.25
60+	0.27	0.04	0.31	0.07	0.00	0.07	0.34	0.05	0.38
Total	**2.54**	**0.84**	**3.38**	**1.10**	**0.16**	**1.26**	**3.64**	**1.00**	**4.63**

Source: ibid

Projected Age-Sex MCWS Labour Force of Jammu & Kashmir in 2017 (in million)

Age Group	Rural			Urban			Rural + Urban		
	Male	Female	Person	Male	Female	Person	Male	Female	Person
0-4	0.00	0.00	0.00	0.00	0.00	0.00	0.00	0.00	0.00
5-9	0.00	0.00	0.00	0.00	0.00	0.00	0.00	0.00	0.00
10-14	0.00	0.00	0.00	0.00	0.01	0.01	0.00	0.01	0.01
15-19	0.16	0.08	0.25	0.00	0.01	0.01	0.16	0.10	0.26
20-24	0.36	0.16	0.52	0.13	0.02	0.15	0.49	0.18	0.67
25-29	0.45	0.15	0.59	0.18	0.03	0.21	0.63	0.17	0.80
30-34	0.38	0.13	0.51	0.18	0.02	0.20	0.56	0.15	0.71
35-39	0.29	0.10	0.40	0.17	0.02	0.19	0.46	0.12	0.59
40-44	0.25	0.07	0.32	0.15	0.01	0.17	0.40	0.09	0.49
45-49	0.22	0.06	0.28	0.13	0.02	0.15	0.35	0.08	0.43
50-54	0.19	0.05	0.24	0.11	0.01	0.12	0.31	0.06	0.37
55-59	0.16	0.05	0.21	0.08	0.01	0.09	0.24	0.06	0.29
60+	0.32	0.05	0.37	0.09	0.00	0.09	0.41	0.06	0.47
Total	**2.78**	**0.91**	**3.69**	**1.23**	**0.17**	**1.40**	**4.01**	**1.08**	**5.08**

Source: ibid

Projected Age-Sex MCWS Labour Force of Jharkhand in 2007 (in million)

Age Group	Rural			Urban			Rural + Urban		
	Male	Female	Person	Male	Female	Person	Male	Female	Person
0-4	0.00	0.00	0.00	0.00	0.00	0.00	0.00	0.00	0.00
5-9	0.00	0.00	0.00	0.00	0.00	0.00	0.00	0.00	0.00
10-14	0.05	0.07	0.12	0.01	0.01	0.02	0.06	0.08	0.14
15-19	0.62	0.15	0.77	0.07	0.02	0.09	0.69	0.18	0.86
20-24	0.87	0.25	1.12	0.22	0.05	0.27	1.09	0.30	1.39
25-29	0.76	0.22	0.97	0.31	0.02	0.33	1.07	0.24	1.30
30-34	0.71	0.28	0.98	0.27	0.05	0.32	0.97	0.33	1.30
35-39	0.69	0.24	0.93	0.24	0.04	0.28	0.93	0.28	1.21
40-44	0.64	0.24	0.88	0.21	0.05	0.26	0.85	0.29	1.14
45-49	0.54	0.19	0.73	0.19	0.02	0.21	0.73	0.21	0.94
50-54	0.43	0.13	0.56	0.16	0.03	0.19	0.59	0.16	0.75
55-59	0.32	0.09	0.42	0.12	0.03	0.14	0.44	0.12	0.56
60+	0.43	0.10	0.53	0.07	0.03	0.10	0.50	0.13	0.63
Total	**6.05**	**1.97**	**8.01**	**1.87**	**0.35**	**2.22**	**7.92**	**2.31**	**10.23**

Source: ibid

Projected Age-Sex MCWS Labour Force of Jharkhand in 2012 (in million)

Age Group	Rural			Urban			Rural + Urban		
	Male	Female	Person	Male	Female	Person	Male	Female	Person
0-4	0.00	0.00	0.00	0.00	0.00	0.00	0.00	0.00	0.00
5-9	0.00	0.00	0.00	0.00	0.00	0.00	0.00	0.00	0.00
10-14	0.01	0.06	0.06	0.01	0.00	0.01	0.01	0.06	0.07
15-19	0.63	0.16	0.79	0.05	0.01	0.06	0.67	0.18	0.85
20-24	1.15	0.34	1.49	0.23	0.06	0.28	1.38	0.40	1.77
25-29	0.94	0.25	1.19	0.36	0.03	0.39	1.30	0.28	1.58
30-34	0.75	0.29	1.04	0.32	0.06	0.38	1.07	0.34	1.41
35-39	0.69	0.25	0.94	0.28	0.05	0.33	0.97	0.30	1.27
40-44	0.66	0.28	0.94	0.23	0.06	0.29	0.90	0.33	1.23
45-49	0.61	0.23	0.84	0.21	0.02	0.23	0.82	0.26	1.07
50-54	0.50	0.16	0.66	0.17	0.04	0.21	0.68	0.20	0.87
55-59	0.39	0.12	0.50	0.14	0.04	0.18	0.53	0.15	0.68
60+	0.53	0.12	0.66	0.08	0.04	0.12	0.62	0.16	0.78
Total	**6.87**	**2.25**	**9.12**	**2.08**	**0.40**	**2.47**	**8.94**	**2.65**	**11.59**

Source: ibid

Projected Age-Sex MCWS Labour Force of Jharkhand in 2017 (in million)

Age Group	Rural			Urban			Rural + Urban		
	Male	Female	Person	Male	Female	Person	Male	Female	Person
0-4	0.00	0.00	0.00	0.00	0.00	0.00	0.00	0.00	0.00
5-9	0.00	0.00	0.00	0.00	0.00	0.00	0.00	0.00	0.00
10-14	0.00	0.04	0.04	0.00	0.00	0.00	0.00	0.04	0.04
15-19	0.57	0.15	0.72	0.02	0.01	0.03	0.59	0.16	0.75
20-24	1.25	0.61	1.86	0.22	0.06	0.27	1.47	0.67	2.14
25-29	1.23	0.60	1.83	0.38	0.07	0.46	1.61	0.67	2.29
30-34	0.94	0.58	1.52	0.38	0.10	0.47	1.31	0.68	1.99
35-39	0.73	0.45	1.19	0.34	0.06	0.40	1.08	0.51	1.59
40-44	0.67	0.45	1.12	0.27	0.07	0.34	0.94	0.51	1.46
45-49	0.64	0.40	1.03	0.23	0.03	0.26	0.87	0.43	1.30
50-54	0.57	0.30	0.87	0.19	0.05	0.24	0.76	0.35	1.11
55-59	0.46	0.25	0.70	0.16	0.04	0.20	0.62	0.29	0.91
60+	0.66	0.25	0.90	0.09	0.05	0.13	0.75	0.29	1.04
Total	**7.71**	**4.07**	**11.78**	**2.28**	**0.54**	**2.82**	**10.00**	**4.61**	**14.60**

Source: ibid

Projected Age-Sex MCWS Labour Force of Karnataka in 2007 (in million)

Age Group	Rural			Urban			Rural + Urban		
	Male	Female	Person	Male	Female	Person	Male	Female	Person
0-4	0.00	0.00	0.00	0.00	0.00	0.00	0.00	0.00	0.00
5-9	0.00	0.00	0.00	0.00	0.00	0.00	0.00	0.00	0.00
10-14	0.16	0.16	0.31	0.01	0.00	0.01	0.17	0.16	0.33
15-19	1.12	0.66	1.78	0.44	0.12	0.56	1.56	0.78	2.34
20-24	1.60	0.71	2.31	0.81	0.34	1.14	2.41	1.04	3.45
25-29	1.45	0.80	2.25	0.99	0.22	1.21	2.44	1.02	3.45
30-34	1.25	0.91	2.16	0.91	0.26	1.17	2.16	1.17	3.33
35-39	1.14	0.91	2.05	0.80	0.25	1.04	1.94	1.16	3.09
40-44	1.07	0.87	1.94	0.69	0.21	0.90	1.77	1.07	2.84
45-49	0.96	0.65	1.60	0.60	0.15	0.74	1.55	0.79	2.34
50-54	0.77	0.43	1.20	0.45	0.11	0.57	1.22	0.54	1.76
55-59	0.57	0.32	0.89	0.28	0.07	0.35	0.85	0.39	1.24
60+	0.87	0.36	1.23	0.23	0.05	0.28	1.10	0.41	1.50
Total	**10.96**	**6.76**	**17.72**	**6.21**	**1.77**	**7.98**	**17.17**	**8.53**	**25.69**

Source: ibid

Projected Age-Sex MCWS Labour Force of Karnataka in 2012 (in million)

Age Group	Rural			Urban			Rural + Urban		
	Male	Female	Person	Male	Female	Person	Male	Female	Person
0-4	0.00	0.00	0.00	0.00	0.00	0.00	0.00	0.00	0.00
5-9	0.00	0.00	0.00	0.00	0.00	0.00	0.00	0.00	0.00
10-14	0.10	0.08	0.17	0.00	0.00	0.00	0.10	0.08	0.17
15-19	1.02	0.59	1.61	0.41	0.11	0.52	1.43	0.70	2.13
20-24	1.68	0.73	2.41	0.84	0.40	1.24	2.52	1.13	3.65
25-29	1.65	0.87	2.52	1.09	0.22	1.32	2.74	1.09	3.84
30-34	1.39	0.98	2.37	1.06	0.31	1.37	2.45	1.29	3.74
35-39	1.19	1.01	2.20	0.95	0.28	1.23	2.14	1.29	3.43
40-44	1.09	1.00	2.09	0.80	0.24	1.04	1.89	1.24	3.13
45-49	1.02	0.80	1.82	0.69	0.17	0.86	1.70	0.97	2.67
50-54	0.86	0.54	1.40	0.55	0.14	0.69	1.41	0.68	2.08
55-59	0.70	0.42	1.12	0.36	0.09	0.45	1.06	0.50	1.57
60+	1.04	0.44	1.48	0.27	0.05	0.32	1.31	0.49	1.80
Total	**11.74**	**7.45**	**19.19**	**7.02**	**2.00**	**9.02**	**18.76**	**9.45**	**28.21**

Source: ibid

Projected Age-Sex MCWS Labour Force of Karnataka in 2017 (in million)

Age Group	Rural			Urban			Rural + Urban		
	Male	Female	Person	Male	Female	Person	Male	Female	Person
0-4	0.00	0.00	0.00	0.00	0.00	0.00	0.00	0.00	0.00
5-9	0.00	0.00	0.00	0.00	0.00	0.00	0.00	0.00	0.00
10-14	0.04	0.00	0.04	0.00	0.00	0.00	0.04	0.00	0.04
15-19	0.89	0.51	1.40	0.39	0.10	0.49	1.29	0.60	1.89
20-24	1.54	0.65	2.19	0.85	0.45	1.30	2.39	1.10	3.49
25-29	1.75	0.96	2.71	1.15	0.22	1.37	2.90	1.18	4.08
30-34	1.60	1.11	2.71	1.14	0.33	1.47	2.74	1.44	4.18
35-39	1.33	1.09	2.43	1.09	0.31	1.40	2.42	1.41	3.83
40-44	1.14	1.12	2.27	0.93	0.28	1.21	2.08	1.40	3.48
45-49	1.02	0.92	1.94	0.78	0.19	0.98	1.81	1.11	2.92
50-54	0.91	0.66	1.57	0.62	0.17	0.79	1.53	0.83	2.36
55-59	0.79	0.54	1.33	0.43	0.11	0.53	1.21	0.65	1.86
60+	1.23	0.55	1.78	0.33	0.04	0.36	1.56	0.59	2.15
Total	12.25	8.13	20.38	7.71	2.20	9.92	19.97	10.33	30.29

Source: ibid

Projected Age-Sex MCWS Labour Force of Kerala in 2007 (in million)

Age Group	Rural			Urban			Rural + Urban		
	Male	Female	Person	Male	Female	Person	Male	Female	Person
0-4	0.00	0.00	0.00	0.00	0.00	0.00	0.00	0.00	0.00
5-9	0.00	0.00	0.00	0.00	0.00	0.00	0.00	0.00	0.00
10-14	0.01	0.00	0.01	0.00	0.00	0.00	0.01	0.00	0.01
15-19	0.32	0.16	0.48	0.12	0.05	0.17	0.44	0.21	0.65
20-24	0.95	0.44	1.38	0.28	0.17	0.45	1.23	0.60	1.83
25-29	0.99	0.43	1.42	0.33	0.20	0.53	1.32	0.63	1.95
30-34	0.91	0.43	1.34	0.33	0.17	0.49	1.24	0.60	1.84
35-39	0.83	0.42	1.25	0.30	0.15	0.45	1.13	0.57	1.70
40-44	0.76	0.38	1.13	0.29	0.11	0.40	1.04	0.49	1.53
45-49	0.67	0.31	0.97	0.25	0.11	0.36	0.92	0.41	1.33
50-54	0.55	0.22	0.77	0.21	0.09	0.31	0.77	0.31	1.08
55-59	0.40	0.17	0.56	0.15	0.03	0.18	0.54	0.20	0.74
60+	0.56	0.22	0.79	0.17	0.05	0.22	0.73	0.27	1.00
Total	**6.94**	**3.17**	**10.11**	**2.43**	**1.13**	**3.56**	**9.38**	**4.30**	**13.67**

Source: ibid

Projected Age-Sex MCWS Labour Force of Kerala in 2012 (in million)

Age Group	Rural			Urban			Rural + Urban		
	Male	Female	Person	Male	Female	Person	Male	Female	Person
0-4	0.00	0.00	0.00	0.00	0.00	0.00	0.00	0.00	0.00
5-9	0.00	0.00	0.00	0.00	0.00	0.00	0.00	0.00	0.00
10-14	0.00	0.00	0.00	0.00	0.00	0.00	0.00	0.00	0.00
15-19	0.27	0.13	0.40	0.11	0.04	0.15	0.38	0.18	0.55
20-24	0.93	0.42	1.35	0.26	0.16	0.42	1.19	0.59	1.78
25-29	1.04	0.44	1.47	0.34	0.21	0.55	1.37	0.65	2.02
30-34	0.99	0.46	1.45	0.34	0.18	0.52	1.33	0.64	1.97
35-39	0.90	0.45	1.35	0.32	0.17	0.49	1.22	0.62	1.84
40-44	0.82	0.42	1.24	0.30	0.12	0.43	1.12	0.54	1.66
45-49	0.73	0.36	1.09	0.27	0.13	0.40	1.00	0.49	1.49
50-54	0.62	0.26	0.88	0.23	0.12	0.35	0.85	0.38	1.23
55-59	0.46	0.21	0.67	0.17	0.04	0.20	0.63	0.25	0.88
60+	0.62	0.25	0.88	0.19	0.06	0.25	0.82	0.31	1.13
Total	**7.36**	**3.41**	**10.78**	**2.53**	**1.23**	**3.76**	**9.90**	**4.64**	**14.54**

Source: ibid

Projected Age-Sex MCWS Labour Force of Kerala in 2017 (in million)

Age Group	Rural			Urban			Rural + Urban		
	Male	Female	Person	Male	Female	Person	Male	Female	Person
0-4	0.00	0.00	0.00	0.00	0.00	0.00	0.00	0.00	0.00
5-9	0.00	0.00	0.00	0.00	0.00	0.00	0.00	0.00	0.00
10-14	0.00	0.00	0.00	0.00	0.00	0.00	0.00	0.00	0.00
15-19	0.23	0.14	0.37	0.10	0.04	0.14	0.33	0.18	0.51
20-24	0.88	0.39	1.27	0.24	0.16	0.40	1.12	0.55	1.67
25-29	1.02	0.40	1.42	0.32	0.22	0.53	1.33	0.62	1.95
30-34	1.04	0.45	1.48	0.34	0.19	0.53	1.37	0.63	2.01
35-39	0.97	0.47	1.44	0.33	0.18	0.51	1.30	0.64	1.95
40-44	0.87	0.45	1.32	0.32	0.13	0.45	1.19	0.58	1.77
45-49	0.78	0.39	1.17	0.29	0.14	0.44	1.07	0.54	1.61
50-54	0.67	0.30	0.97	0.26	0.14	0.40	0.92	0.44	1.37
55-59	0.51	0.24	0.75	0.18	0.04	0.23	0.69	0.28	0.97
60+	0.71	0.29	1.01	0.22	0.06	0.29	0.94	0.36	1.29
Total	**7.68**	**3.51**	**11.19**	**2.60**	**1.31**	**3.91**	**10.28**	**4.82**	**15.10**

Source: ibid

Projected Age-Sex MCWS Labour Force of Maharashtra in 2007 (in million)

Age Group	Rural			Urban			Rural + Urban		
	Male	Female	Person	Male	Female	Person	Male	Female	Person
0-4	0.00	0.00	0.00	0.00	0.00	0.00	0.00	0.00	0.00
5-9	0.00	0.01	0.01	0.00	0.00	0.00	0.00	0.01	0.01
10-14	0.18	0.18	0.36	0.05	0.04	0.08	0.23	0.21	0.44
15-19	1.48	0.87	2.36	0.92	0.28	1.20	2.40	1.15	3.56
20-24	2.45	1.21	3.66	2.07	0.51	2.58	4.52	1.72	6.24
25-29	2.20	1.22	3.42	2.53	0.57	3.10	4.72	1.79	6.52
30-34	1.93	0.42	2.35	2.30	0.61	2.90	4.23	1.02	5.25
35-39	1.79	1.53	3.32	1.98	0.68	2.66	3.77	2.21	5.98
40-44	1.66	1.32	2.98	1.68	0.53	2.21	3.35	1.85	5.20
45-49	1.43	1.12	2.56	1.40	0.34	1.74	2.83	1.46	4.29
50-54	1.15	0.74	1.89	1.08	0.26	1.34	2.23	1.00	3.23
55-59	0.84	0.59	1.42	0.68	0.14	0.81	1.51	0.73	2.24
60+	1.54	1.02	2.57	0.47	0.17	0.63	2.01	1.19	3.20
Total	**16.66**	**10.24**	**26.90**	**15.14**	**4.11**	**19.26**	**31.80**	**14.35**	**46.15**

Source: ibid

Projected Age-Sex MCWS Labour Force of Maharashtra in 2012 (in million)

Age Group	Rural			Urban			Rural + Urban		
	Male	Female	Person	Male	Female	Person	Male	Female	Person
0-4	0.00	0.00	0.00	0.00	0.00	0.00	0.00	0.00	0.00
5-9	0.00	0.00	0.00	0.00	0.00	0.00	0.00	0.00	0.00
10-14	0.06	0.08	0.14	0.02	0.03	0.05	0.08	0.12	0.20
15-19	1.24	0.75	1.99	0.92	0.30	1.22	2.16	1.05	3.20
20-24	2.54	1.30	3.84	2.26	0.64	2.90	4.80	1.94	6.74
25-29	2.58	1.31	3.89	2.85	0.71	3.56	5.43	2.02	7.45
30-34	2.18	0.40	2.58	2.64	0.70	3.35	4.82	1.10	5.93
35-39	1.89	1.62	3.51	2.32	0.83	3.14	4.21	2.45	6.65
40-44	1.75	1.47	3.22	1.95	0.63	2.59	3.70	2.11	5.81
45-49	1.60	1.40	3.00	1.64	0.41	2.06	3.24	1.81	5.05
50-54	1.37	0.96	2.33	1.31	0.34	1.65	2.68	1.30	3.98
55-59	1.03	0.75	1.78	0.87	0.18	1.05	1.90	0.93	2.83
60+	1.69	1.20	2.89	0.51	0.20	0.71	2.21	1.39	3.60
Total	**17.92**	**11.25**	**29.17**	**17.31**	**4.97**	**22.27**	**35.23**	**16.22**	**51.45**

Source: ibid

Projected Age-Sex MCWS Labour Force of Maharashtra in 2017 (in million)

Age Group	Rural			Urban			Rural + Urban		
	Male	Female	Person	Male	Female	Person	Male	Female	Person
0-4	0.00	0.00	0.00	0.00	0.00	0.00	0.00	0.00	0.00
5-9	0.00	0.00	0.00	0.00	0.00	0.00	0.00	0.00	0.00
10-14	0.00	0.00	0.00	0.00	0.03	0.03	0.00	0.03	0.03
15-19	1.02	0.63	1.64	0.94	0.32	1.26	1.96	0.95	2.91
20-24	2.22	1.13	3.35	2.45	0.76	3.21	4.68	1.89	6.56
25-29	2.72	1.40	4.12	3.10	0.85	3.96	5.82	2.26	8.08
30-34	2.62	0.48	3.11	2.88	0.81	3.69	5.50	1.30	6.80
35-39	2.18	1.73	3.91	2.60	0.95	3.55	4.78	2.68	7.47
40-44	1.88	1.56	3.44	2.25	0.72	2.97	4.12	2.29	6.41
45-49	1.68	1.61	3.30	1.89	0.47	2.36	3.57	2.09	5.66
50-54	1.54	1.20	2.74	1.54	0.44	1.98	3.08	1.64	4.72
55-59	1.23	0.99	2.22	1.06	0.22	1.29	2.29	1.22	3.51
60+	1.94	1.42	3.36	0.57	0.24	0.81	2.51	1.66	4.17
Total	**19.04**	**12.17**	**31.20**	**19.28**	**5.83**	**25.12**	**38.32**	**18.00**	**56.32**

Source: ibid

Projected Age-Sex MCWS Labour Force of Madhya Pradesh in 2007 (in million)

Age Group	Rural			Urban			Rural + Urban		
	Male	Female	Person	Male	Female	Person	Male	Female	Person
0-4	0.00	0.00	0.00	0.00	0.00	0.00	0.00	0.00	0.00
5-9	0.00	0.00	0.01	0.00	0.00	0.00	0.00	0.00	0.01
10-14	0.08	0.13	0.21	0.04	0.02	0.05	0.11	0.15	0.27
15-19	1.46	0.72	2.18	0.38	0.07	0.45	1.83	0.79	2.62
20-24	2.05	0.61	2.66	0.74	0.14	0.88	2.79	0.76	3.55
25-29	1.76	0.75	2.52	0.87	0.15	1.02	2.63	0.91	3.54
30-34	1.58	0.89	2.47	0.76	0.15	0.91	2.34	1.04	3.38
35-39	1.48	0.90	2.38	0.67	0.17	0.84	2.15	1.07	3.22
40-44	1.32	0.76	2.08	0.59	0.14	0.73	1.91	0.90	2.81
45-49	1.07	0.53	1.61	0.50	0.11	0.61	1.57	0.64	2.22
50-54	0.81	0.40	1.21	0.39	0.08	0.47	1.20	0.48	1.68
55-59	0.61	0.29	0.90	0.24	0.05	0.29	0.85	0.34	1.19
60+	0.99	0.39	1.38	0.27	0.07	0.34	1.26	0.46	1.72
Total	**13.21**	**6.39**	**19.60**	**5.44**	**1.15**	**6.60**	**18.65**	**7.55**	**26.20**

Source: ibid

Projected Age-Sex MCWS Labour Force of Madhya Pradesh in 2012 (in million)

Age Group	Rural			Urban			Rural + Urban		
	Male	Female	Person	Male	Female	Person	Male	Female	Person
0-4	0.00	0.00	0.00	0.00	0.00	0.00	0.00	0.00	0.00
5-9	0.00	0.00	0.00	0.00	0.00	0.00	0.00	0.00	0.00
10-14	0.00	0.03	0.03	0.03	0.01	0.04	0.03	0.04	0.07
15-19	1.41	0.70	2.11	0.38	0.08	0.45	1.79	0.77	2.56
20-24	2.45	0.67	3.11	0.81	0.19	0.99	3.25	0.85	4.11
25-29	2.10	0.78	2.88	1.03	0.19	1.23	3.13	0.98	4.11
30-34	1.70	0.87	2.57	0.93	0.17	1.10	2.62	1.04	3.66
35-39	1.52	0.95	2.47	0.79	0.20	0.98	2.31	1.14	3.45
40-44	1.43	0.87	2.29	0.66	0.15	0.82	2.09	1.02	3.11
45-49	1.27	0.65	1.92	0.58	0.13	0.71	1.85	0.78	2.63
50-54	0.99	0.49	1.48	0.50	0.10	0.60	1.49	0.59	2.07
55-59	0.73	0.34	1.08	0.31	0.06	0.37	1.05	0.40	1.45
60+	1.11	0.46	1.57	0.32	0.08	0.41	1.43	0.54	1.97
Total	**14.70**	**6.79**	**21.49**	**6.34**	**1.36**	**7.70**	**21.04**	**8.15**	**29.19**

Source: ibid

Projected Age-Sex MCWS Labour Force of Madhya Pradesh in 2017 (in million)

Age Group	Rural			Urban			Rural + Urban		
	Male	Female	Person	Male	Female	Person	Male	Female	Person
0-4	0.00	0.00	0.00	0.00	0.00	0.00	0.00	0.00	0.00
5-9	0.00	0.00	0.00	0.00	0.00	0.00	0.00	0.00	0.00
10-14	0.00	0.00	0.00	0.02	0.01	0.03	0.02	0.01	0.03
15-19	1.28	0.61	1.89	0.37	0.08	0.45	1.66	0.69	2.34
20-24	2.56	0.63	3.19	0.81	0.20	1.01	3.37	0.83	4.20
25-29	2.54	0.94	3.48	1.14	0.22	1.36	3.68	1.16	4.84
30-34	2.03	0.94	2.97	1.09	0.20	1.29	3.12	1.14	4.26
35-39	1.64	0.95	2.59	0.95	0.22	1.17	2.59	1.17	3.76
40-44	1.48	0.92	2.40	0.77	0.16	0.93	2.25	1.08	3.33
45-49	1.37	0.74	2.11	0.64	0.14	0.78	2.01	0.88	2.89
50-54	1.17	0.60	1.78	0.59	0.11	0.71	1.77	0.72	2.48
55-59	0.90	0.42	1.32	0.38	0.08	0.46	1.29	0.49	1.78
60+	1.29	0.54	1.83	0.40	0.10	0.50	1.68	0.64	2.33
Total	**16.28**	**7.29**	**23.57**	**7.15**	**1.52**	**8.67**	**23.43**	**8.81**	**32.24**

Source: ibid

Projected Age-Sex MCWS Labour Force of Other NE States in 2007 (in million)

Age Group	Rural			Urban			Rural + Urban		
	Male	Female	Person	Male	Female	Person	Male	Female	Person
0-4	0.00	0.00	0.00	0.00	0.00	0.00	0.00	0.00	0.00
5-9	0.00	0.00	0.00	0.00	0.00	0.00	0.00	0.00	0.00
10-14	0.03	0.01	0.04	0.00	0.01	0.01	0.03	0.02	0.05
15-19	0.22	0.12	0.34	0.02	0.02	0.04	0.24	0.14	0.38
20-24	0.40	0.24	0.64	0.08	0.05	0.13	0.48	0.29	0.77
25-29	0.42	0.22	0.64	0.13	0.05	0.18	0.55	0.27	0.82
30-34	0.37	0.20	0.58	0.13	0.05	0.18	0.50	0.25	0.75
35-39	0.34	0.16	0.50	0.12	0.04	0.16	0.45	0.20	0.66
40-44	0.30	0.15	0.45	0.10	0.03	0.14	0.41	0.19	0.59
45-49	0.25	0.13	0.38	0.09	0.03	0.12	0.34	0.16	0.50
50-54	0.20	0.09	0.29	0.07	0.02	0.09	0.27	0.12	0.38
55-59	0.15	0.08	0.22	0.05	0.01	0.06	0.19	0.09	0.28
60+	0.23	0.10	0.33	0.03	0.01	0.04	0.26	0.11	0.37
Total	**2.91**	**1.50**	**4.41**	**0.82**	**0.33**	**1.15**	**3.73**	**1.84**	**5.56**

Source: ibid

Projected Age-Sex MCWS Labour Force of Other NE States in 2012 (in million)

Age Group	Rural			Urban			Rural + Urban		
	Male	Female	Person	Male	Female	Person	Male	Female	Person
0-4	0.00	0.00	0.00	0.00	0.00	0.00	0.00	0.00	0.00
5-9	0.00	0.00	0.00	0.00	0.00	0.00	0.00	0.00	0.00
10-14	0.03	0.01	0.04	0.00	0.01	0.01	0.04	0.01	0.05
15-19	0.22	0.11	0.33	0.02	0.02	0.04	0.24	0.13	0.37
20-24	0.46	0.28	0.75	0.09	0.05	0.14	0.55	0.33	0.88
25-29	0.51	0.26	0.77	0.15	0.06	0.21	0.66	0.33	0.98
30-34	0.43	0.24	0.67	0.15	0.06	0.20	0.58	0.29	0.87
35-39	0.37	0.19	0.56	0.13	0.05	0.18	0.50	0.24	0.74
40-44	0.33	0.18	0.51	0.12	0.04	0.16	0.45	0.22	0.67
45-49	0.29	0.16	0.45	0.10	0.04	0.14	0.39	0.20	0.59
50-54	0.24	0.13	0.37	0.08	0.03	0.11	0.32	0.16	0.48
55-59	0.18	0.11	0.29	0.06	0.02	0.08	0.24	0.12	0.37
60+	0.29	0.14	0.43	0.03	0.02	0.05	0.33	0.16	0.48
Total	**3.35**	**1.81**	**5.17**	**0.93**	**0.39**	**1.32**	**4.29**	**2.20**	**6.49**

Source: ibid

Projected Age-Sex MCWS Labour Force of Other NE States in 2017 (in million)

Age Group	Rural			Urban			Rural + Urban		
	Male	Female	Person	Male	Female	Person	Male	Female	Person
0-4	0.00	0.00	0.00	0.00	0.00	0.00	0.00	0.00	0.00
5-9	0.00	0.00	0.00	0.00	0.00	0.00	0.00	0.00	0.00
10-14	0.03	0.00	0.03	0.00	0.01	0.01	0.03	0.01	0.04
15-19	0.21	0.11	0.32	0.02	0.02	0.04	0.23	0.13	0.36
20-24	0.45	0.29	0.74	0.09	0.05	0.14	0.54	0.34	0.88
25-29	0.58	0.31	0.89	0.16	0.07	0.23	0.74	0.38	1.12
30-34	0.51	0.29	0.80	0.17	0.06	0.23	0.68	0.35	1.03
35-39	0.42	0.22	0.64	0.15	0.06	0.21	0.57	0.28	0.85
40-44	0.36	0.22	0.58	0.13	0.05	0.18	0.49	0.26	0.76
45-49	0.31	0.20	0.51	0.12	0.05	0.16	0.43	0.24	0.67
50-54	0.28	0.17	0.44	0.10	0.04	0.13	0.37	0.20	0.58
55-59	0.22	0.15	0.37	0.07	0.03	0.10	0.29	0.17	0.47
60+	0.38	0.19	0.57	0.04	0.03	0.07	0.42	0.22	0.63
Total	3.75	2.13	5.88	1.04	0.46	1.50	4.80	2.59	7.39

Source: ibid

Projected Age-Sex MCWS Labour Force of Orissa in 2007 (in million)

Age Group	Rural			Urban			Rural + Urban		
	Male	Female	Person	Male	Female	Person	Male	Female	Person
0-4	0.00	0.00	0.00	0.00	0.00	0.00	0.00	0.00	0.00
5-9	0.00	0.00	0.00	0.00	0.00	0.00	0.00	0.00	0.00
10-14	0.10	0.08	0.18	0.01	0.01	0.02	0.11	0.09	0.19
15-19	1.05	0.48	1.54	0.11	0.04	0.15	1.17	0.52	1.69
20-24	1.27	0.40	1.67	0.24	0.06	0.30	1.51	0.46	1.97
25-29	1.21	0.47	1.67	0.31	0.07	0.38	1.52	0.54	2.06
30-34	1.14	0.44	1.58	0.28	0.06	0.35	1.42	0.51	1.93
35-39	1.08	0.45	1.53	0.26	0.05	0.31	1.34	0.50	1.84
40-44	0.99	0.44	1.43	0.23	0.06	0.29	1.22	0.50	1.72
45-49	0.85	0.32	1.17	0.20	0.04	0.23	1.04	0.36	1.40
50-54	0.66	0.24	0.90	0.15	0.03	0.18	0.82	0.26	1.08
55-59	0.49	0.12	0.61	0.07	0.02	0.09	0.56	0.14	0.70
60+	0.70	0.20	0.90	0.05	0.02	0.07	0.76	0.22	0.97
Total	9.53	3.65	13.18	1.92	0.45	2.37	11.46	4.10	15.55

Source: ibid

Projected Age-Sex MCWS Labour Force of Orissa in 2012 (in million)

Age Group	Rural			Urban			Rural + Urban		
	Male	Female	Person	Male	Female	Person	Male	Female	Person
0-4	0.00	0.00	0.00	0.00	0.00	0.00	0.00	0.00	0.00
5-9	0.00	0.00	0.00	0.00	0.00	0.00	0.00	0.00	0.00
10-14	0.00	0.02	0.02	0.01	0.00	0.01	0.01	0.03	0.03
15-19	1.02	0.48	1.50	0.11	0.04	0.15	1.13	0.51	1.65
20-24	1.43	0.45	1.89	0.25	0.08	0.33	1.68	0.53	2.21
25-29	1.31	0.50	1.81	0.34	0.10	0.44	1.65	0.60	2.25
30-34	1.16	0.46	1.62	0.33	0.08	0.41	1.48	0.54	2.02
35-39	1.09	0.49	1.58	0.30	0.05	0.35	1.39	0.54	1.94
40-44	1.02	0.51	1.53	0.26	0.08	0.34	1.28	0.59	1.87
45-49	0.94	0.40	1.33	0.23	0.05	0.27	1.16	0.44	1.60
50-54	0.78	0.30	1.07	0.19	0.04	0.23	0.96	0.34	1.30
55-59	0.58	0.14	0.72	0.09	0.02	0.10	0.67	0.16	0.83
60+	0.77	0.23	0.99	0.05	0.03	0.08	0.82	0.25	1.07
Total	10.10	3.97	14.08	2.15	0.56	2.71	12.25	4.53	16.78

Source: ibid

Projected Age-Sex MCWS Labour Force of Orissa in 2017 (in million)

Age Group	Rural			Urban			Rural + Urban		
	Male	Female	Person	Male	Female	Person	Male	Female	Person
0-4	0.00	0.00	0.00	0.00	0.00	0.00	0.00	0.00	0.00
5-9	0.00	0.00	0.00	0.00	0.00	0.00	0.00	0.00	0.00
10-14	0.00	0.00	0.00	0.00	0.00	0.00	0.00	0.00	0.00
15-19	0.92	0.43	1.35	0.11	0.04	0.15	1.02	0.47	1.50
20-24	1.45	0.44	1.89	0.25	0.08	0.33	1.70	0.52	2.22
25-29	1.51	0.55	2.06	0.37	0.12	0.48	1.87	0.67	2.55
30-34	1.28	0.50	1.78	0.36	0.09	0.45	1.64	0.59	2.23
35-39	1.13	0.52	1.65	0.34	0.06	0.40	1.47	0.58	2.05
40-44	1.05	0.56	1.61	0.29	0.10	0.40	1.35	0.66	2.01
45-49	0.98	0.46	1.44	0.25	0.05	0.30	1.23	0.51	1.75
50-54	0.88	0.37	1.25	0.22	0.05	0.26	1.09	0.42	1.51
55-59	0.70	0.16	0.86	0.10	0.02	0.12	0.79	0.18	0.98
60+	0.87	0.26	1.14	0.05	0.03	0.08	0.92	0.30	1.22
Total	**10.76**	**4.27**	**15.03**	**2.35**	**0.64**	**2.99**	**13.11**	**4.91**	**18.02**

Source: ibid

Projected Age-Sex MCWS Labour Force of Other States in 2007 (in million)

Age Group	Rural			Urban			Rural + Urban		
	Male	Female	Person	Male	Female	Person	Male	Female	Person
0-4	0.00	0.00	0.00	0.00	0.00	0.00	0.00	0.00	0.00
5-9	0.00	0.00	0.00	0.00	0.00	0.00	0.00	0.00	0.00
10-14	0.00	0.00	0.00	0.01	0.00	0.01	0.01	0.00	0.01
15-19	0.05	0.03	0.08	0.27	0.04	0.31	0.32	0.07	0.39
20-24	0.16	0.03	0.20	0.90	0.12	1.02	1.06	0.16	1.22
25-29	0.16	0.03	0.19	0.96	0.16	1.12	1.12	0.19	1.31
30-34	0.13	0.03	0.15	0.84	0.16	0.99	0.97	0.18	1.15
35-39	0.11	0.01	0.13	0.80	0.14	0.94	0.91	0.16	1.07
40-44	0.08	0.02	0.10	0.65	0.14	0.79	0.74	0.15	0.89
45-49	0.07	0.02	0.08	0.50	0.08	0.58	0.57	0.09	0.66
50-54	0.05	0.01	0.06	0.35	0.02	0.37	0.40	0.03	0.43
55-59	0.03	0.01	0.04	0.20	0.01	0.21	0.23	0.02	0.25
60+	0.04	0.02	0.06	0.18	0.01	0.19	0.22	0.03	0.25
Total	**0.88**	**0.20**	**1.08**	**5.66**	**0.89**	**6.55**	**6.54**	**1.09**	**7.63**

Source: ibid

Projected Age-Sex MCWS Labour Force of Other States in 2012 (in million)

Age Group	Rural			Urban			Rural + Urban		
	Male	Female	Person	Male	Female	Person	Male	Female	Person
0-4	0.00	0.00	0.00	0.00	0.00	0.00	0.00	0.00	0.00
5-9	0.00	0.00	0.00	0.00	0.00	0.00	0.00	0.00	0.00
10-14	0.00	0.00	0.00	0.00	0.00	0.00	0.00	0.00	0.00
15-19	0.05	0.03	0.08	0.29	0.04	0.34	0.34	0.08	0.42
20-24	0.20	0.05	0.26	1.09	0.15	1.24	1.30	0.20	1.50
25-29	0.18	0.05	0.23	1.17	0.18	1.36	1.35	0.23	1.58
30-34	0.14	0.03	0.17	1.03	0.15	1.18	1.17	0.18	1.35
35-39	0.12	0.01	0.14	1.01	0.18	1.19	1.13	0.20	1.33
40-44	0.09	0.03	0.12	0.84	0.19	1.03	0.93	0.22	1.15
45-49	0.07	0.02	0.09	0.65	0.10	0.75	0.72	0.12	0.84
50-54	0.05	0.02	0.07	0.44	0.02	0.47	0.49	0.04	0.53
55-59	0.03	0.01	0.04	0.23	0.01	0.24	0.26	0.02	0.28
60+	0.05	0.02	0.07	0.19	0.00	0.19	0.24	0.02	0.26
Total	**0.99**	**0.26**	**1.25**	**6.94**	**1.04**	**7.99**	**7.93**	**1.31**	**9.24**

Source: ibid

Projected Age-Sex MCWS Labour Force of Other States in 2017 (in million)

Age Group	Rural			Urban			Rural + Urban		
	Male	Female	Person	Male	Female	Person	Male	Female	Person
0-4	0.00	0.00	0.00	0.00	0.00	0.00	0.00	0.00	0.00
5-9	0.00	0.00	0.00	0.00	0.00	0.00	0.00	0.00	0.00
10-14	0.00	0.00	0.00	0.00	0.00	0.00	0.00	0.00	0.00
15-19	0.04	0.04	0.08	0.28	0.05	0.32	0.32	0.08	0.40
20-24	0.24	0.07	0.31	1.26	0.17	1.42	1.50	0.23	1.73
25-29	0.20	0.06	0.26	1.33	0.20	1.53	1.53	0.26	1.79
30-34	0.15	0.04	0.20	1.17	0.18	1.35	1.32	0.22	1.54
35-39	0.13	0.02	0.15	1.17	0.22	1.39	1.30	0.24	1.54
40-44	0.10	0.03	0.12	0.99	0.22	1.21	1.09	0.25	1.34
45-49	0.08	0.02	0.09	0.77	0.11	0.88	0.84	0.13	0.97
50-54	0.05	0.01	0.07	0.51	0.02	0.53	0.56	0.04	0.60
55-59	0.03	0.01	0.04	0.27	0.01	0.27	0.30	0.02	0.31
60+	0.06	0.02	0.08	0.24	0.00	0.24	0.29	0.02	0.32
Total	**1.08**	**0.32**	**1.40**	**7.98**	**1.17**	**9.15**	**9.06**	**1.49**	**10.55**

Source: ibid

Projected Age-Sex MCWS Labour Force of Punjab in 2007 (in million)

Age Group	Rural			Urban			Rural + Urban		
	Male	Female	Person	Male	Female	Person	Male	Female	Person
0-4	0.00	0.00	0.00	0.00	0.00	0.00	0.00	0.00	0.00
5-9	0.00	0.00	0.00	0.00	0.00	0.00	0.00	0.00	0.00
10-14	0.03	0.02	0.06	0.02	0.00	0.02	0.05	0.02	0.07
15-19	0.50	0.25	0.74	0.21	0.04	0.24	0.70	0.28	0.99
20-24	0.78	0.34	1.12	0.49	0.10	0.59	1.27	0.44	1.72
25-29	0.69	0.33	1.02	0.52	0.11	0.63	1.21	0.44	1.65
30-34	0.59	0.34	0.93	0.44	0.08	0.53	1.03	0.42	1.46
35-39	0.53	0.38	0.91	0.38	0.08	0.46	0.91	0.46	1.37
40-44	0.49	0.33	0.83	0.34	0.07	0.41	0.83	0.41	1.24
45-49	0.43	0.26	0.69	0.30	0.04	0.34	0.73	0.30	1.03
50-54	0.34	0.19	0.53	0.23	0.05	0.28	0.57	0.24	0.81
55-59	0.26	0.15	0.41	0.16	0.02	0.18	0.42	0.17	0.59
60+	0.49	0.21	0.69	0.15	0.02	0.17	0.64	0.23	0.86
Total	5.13	2.79	7.92	3.24	0.63	3.87	8.37	3.42	11.79

Source: ibid

Projected Age-Sex MCWS Labour Force of Punjab in 2012 (in million)

Age Group	Rural			Urban			Rural + Urban		
	Male	Female	Person	Male	Female	Person	Male	Female	Person
0-4	0.00	0.00	0.00	0.00	0.00	0.00	0.00	0.00	0.00
5-9	0.00	0.00	0.00	0.00	0.00	0.00	0.00	0.00	0.00
10-14	0.00	0.00	0.00	0.01	0.00	0.01	0.01	0.00	0.01
15-19	0.42	0.25	0.67	0.19	0.03	0.22	0.61	0.29	0.90
20-24	0.79	0.40	1.18	0.54	0.12	0.66	1.33	0.52	1.85
25-29	0.75	0.39	1.13	0.62	0.14	0.76	1.37	0.53	1.90
30-34	0.67	0.41	1.07	0.55	0.11	0.66	1.22	0.51	1.73
35-39	0.55	0.45	1.00	0.47	0.10	0.57	1.02	0.55	1.57
40-44	0.50	0.42	0.91	0.39	0.08	0.47	0.89	0.50	1.38
45-49	0.47	0.35	0.83	0.34	0.05	0.39	0.81	0.41	1.22
50-54	0.40	0.27	0.67	0.28	0.06	0.34	0.68	0.33	1.02
55-59	0.32	0.21	0.53	0.21	0.04	0.25	0.53	0.25	0.78
60+	0.54	0.26	0.80	0.17	0.03	0.20	0.71	0.29	1.00
Total	5.41	3.40	8.81	3.77	0.76	4.54	9.18	4.16	13.35

Source: ibid

Projected Age-Sex MCWS Labour Force of Punjab in 2017 (in million)

Age Group	Rural			Urban			Rural + Urban		
	Male	Female	Person	Male	Female	Person	Male	Female	Person
0-4	0.00	0.00	0.00	0.00	0.00	0.00	0.00	0.00	0.00
5-9	0.00	0.00	0.00	0.00	0.00	0.00	0.00	0.00	0.00
10-14	0.00	0.00	0.00	0.00	0.00	0.00	0.00	0.00	0.00
15-19	0.32	0.24	0.56	0.17	0.03	0.20	0.49	0.27	0.76
20-24	0.70	0.37	1.07	0.58	0.12	0.70	1.27	0.50	1.77
25-29	0.77	0.43	1.20	0.68	0.16	0.85	1.46	0.59	2.05
30-34	0.75	0.50	1.25	0.64	0.12	0.76	1.39	0.62	2.01
35-39	0.64	0.54	1.18	0.57	0.12	0.68	1.20	0.66	1.86
40-44	0.53	0.49	1.03	0.46	0.09	0.55	1.00	0.58	1.58
45-49	0.48	0.44	0.92	0.38	0.06	0.43	0.86	0.50	1.36
50-54	0.44	0.36	0.81	0.31	0.07	0.38	0.76	0.44	1.19
55-59	0.38	0.30	0.68	0.25	0.04	0.29	0.63	0.34	0.97
60+	0.62	0.34	0.96	0.20	0.03	0.23	0.82	0.37	1.19
Total	**5.64**	**4.02**	**9.66**	**4.25**	**0.84**	**5.09**	**9.89**	**4.87**	**14.75**

Source: ibid

Projected Age-Sex MCWS Labour Force of Rajasthan in 2007 (in million)

Age Group	Rural			Urban			Rural + Urban		
	Male	Female	Person	Male	Female	Person	Male	Female	Person
0-4	0.00	0.00	0.00	0.00	0.00	0.00	0.00	0.00	0.00
5-9	0.00	0.00	0.00	0.00	0.00	0.00	0.00	0.00	0.00
10-14	0.14	0.29	0.42	0.07	0.01	0.08	0.21	0.30	0.51
15-19	1.34	0.99	2.34	0.32	0.13	0.45	1.66	1.12	2.78
20-24	2.07	1.04	3.11	0.64	0.15	0.79	2.71	1.19	3.90
25-29	1.75	0.99	2.74	0.69	0.14	0.84	2.45	1.13	3.58
30-34	1.52	0.96	2.48	0.61	0.16	0.77	2.13	1.12	3.24
35-39	1.38	0.94	2.32	0.52	0.15	0.67	1.90	1.08	2.99
40-44	1.24	0.77	2.01	0.47	0.13	0.60	1.71	0.90	2.61
45-49	1.03	0.63	1.66	0.39	0.09	0.49	1.43	0.72	2.15
50-54	0.82	0.44	1.26	0.30	0.06	0.36	1.12	0.50	1.62
55-59	0.61	0.31	0.92	0.20	0.04	0.23	0.81	0.35	1.16
60+	0.93	0.42	1.35	0.17	0.05	0.22	1.10	0.47	1.57
Total	**12.84**	**7.78**	**20.62**	**4.38**	**1.11**	**5.49**	**17.22**	**8.88**	**26.11**

Source: ibid

Projected Age-Sex MCWS Labour Force of Rajasthan in 2012 (in million)

Age Group	Rural			Urban			Rural + Urban		
	Male	Female	Person	Male	Female	Person	Male	Female	Person
0-4	0.00	0.00	0.00	0.00	0.00	0.00	0.00	0.00	0.00
5-9	0.00	0.00	0.00	0.00	0.00	0.00	0.00	0.00	0.00
10-14	0.00	0.12	0.12	0.07	0.00	0.07	0.07	0.13	0.19
15-19	1.33	1.04	2.37	0.32	0.12	0.44	1.65	1.16	2.81
20-24	2.52	1.24	3.76	0.71	0.18	0.89	3.23	1.42	4.65
25-29	2.15	1.11	3.26	0.80	0.16	0.97	2.95	1.27	4.23
30-34	1.71	1.01	2.72	0.73	0.21	0.95	2.44	1.23	3.67
35-39	1.48	1.03	2.51	0.60	0.18	0.78	2.08	1.21	3.29
40-44	1.35	0.88	2.23	0.53	0.15	0.68	1.87	1.03	2.91
45-49	1.19	0.76	1.95	0.45	0.12	0.57	1.64	0.88	2.52
50-54	0.98	0.55	1.53	0.38	0.08	0.45	1.36	0.62	1.98
55-59	0.74	0.39	1.13	0.25	0.05	0.30	0.99	0.44	1.43
60+	1.09	0.52	1.61	0.19	0.06	0.25	1.28	0.57	1.85
Total	**14.54**	**8.64**	**23.18**	**5.03**	**1.32**	**6.35**	**19.57**	**9.96**	**29.53**

Source: ibid

Projected Age-Sex MCWS Labour Force of Rajasthan in 2017 (in million)

Age Group	Rural			Urban			Rural + Urban		
	Male	Female	Person	Male	Female	Person	Male	Female	Person
0-4	0.00	0.00	0.00	0.00	0.00	0.00	0.00	0.00	0.00
5-9	0.00	0.00	0.00	0.00	0.00	0.00	0.00	0.00	0.00
10-14	0.00	0.00	0.00	0.06	0.00	0.06	0.06	0.00	0.06
15-19	1.20	0.98	2.18	0.31	0.12	0.43	1.51	1.10	2.61
20-24	2.75	1.38	4.14	0.72	0.19	0.91	3.47	1.57	5.05
25-29	2.68	1.39	4.06	0.88	0.19	1.07	3.55	1.58	5.13
30-34	2.10	1.16	3.26	0.84	0.24	1.08	2.94	1.40	4.34
35-39	1.67	1.09	2.75	0.72	0.20	0.92	2.38	1.29	3.67
40-44	1.44	0.96	2.40	0.61	0.16	0.77	2.05	1.12	3.17
45-49	1.29	0.87	2.16	0.50	0.13	0.63	1.79	1.00	2.79
50-54	1.13	0.66	1.79	0.43	0.09	0.52	1.56	0.75	2.31
55-59	0.88	0.47	1.35	0.31	0.06	0.37	1.19	0.53	1.72
60+	1.30	0.63	1.93	0.22	0.07	0.28	1.51	0.70	2.21
Total	**16.44**	**9.59**	**26.03**	**5.59**	**1.46**	**7.05**	**22.03**	**11.05**	**33.08**

Source: ibid

Projected Age-Sex MCWS Labour Force of Tamil Nadu in 2007 (in million)

Age Group	Rural			Urban			Rural + Urban		
	Male	Female	Person	Male	Female	Person	Male	Female	Person
0-4	0.00	0.00	0.00	0.00	0.00	0.00	0.00	0.00	0.00
5-9	0.00	0.00	0.00	0.00	0.00	0.00	0.00	0.00	0.00
10-14	0.00	0.01	0.01	0.02	0.03	0.05	0.02	0.04	0.06
15-19	0.67	0.59	1.25	0.60	0.30	0.90	1.26	0.89	2.15
20-24	1.18	0.66	1.84	1.44	0.52	1.96	2.62	1.18	3.81
25-29	1.22	0.68	1.90	1.56	0.51	2.07	2.78	1.19	3.97
30-34	1.16	0.86	2.01	1.43	0.57	2.00	2.58	1.43	4.01
35-39	1.07	0.89	1.96	1.30	0.48	1.78	2.37	1.37	3.74
40-44	1.02	0.88	1.90	1.15	0.40	1.55	2.18	1.28	3.46
45-49	0.93	0.77	1.70	0.99	0.34	1.33	1.92	1.11	3.03
50-54	0.80	0.64	1.44	0.81	0.27	1.07	1.60	0.91	2.51
55-59	0.62	0.47	1.09	0.54	0.15	0.68	1.16	0.61	1.77
60+	1.01	0.62	1.63	0.47	0.19	0.66	1.47	0.82	2.29
Total	**9.67**	**7.08**	**16.75**	**10.31**	**3.75**	**14.06**	**19.98**	**10.83**	**30.81**

Source: ibid

Projected Age-Sex MCWS Labour Force of Tamil Nadu in 2012 (in million)

Age Group	Rural			Urban			Rural + Urban		
	Male	Female	Person	Male	Female	Person	Male	Female	Person
0-4	0.00	0.00	0.00	0.00	0.00	0.00	0.00	0.00	0.00
5-9	0.00	0.00	0.00	0.00	0.00	0.00	0.00	0.00	0.00
10-14	0.00	0.00	0.00	0.00	0.01	0.01	0.00	0.01	0.01
15-19	0.46	0.45	0.91	0.57	0.31	0.88	1.03	0.77	1.80
20-24	0.87	0.50	1.37	1.62	0.63	2.25	2.50	1.13	3.62
25-29	1.07	0.47	1.54	1.82	0.62	2.43	2.89	1.08	3.98
30-34	1.12	0.79	1.91	1.64	0.71	2.35	2.76	1.51	4.27
35-39	1.02	0.92	1.93	1.53	0.63	2.16	2.54	1.55	4.09
40-44	0.97	0.95	1.91	1.34	0.46	1.81	2.31	1.41	3.72
45-49	0.93	0.91	1.84	1.17	0.43	1.60	2.10	1.34	3.44
50-54	0.84	0.77	1.61	0.94	0.32	1.27	1.78	1.09	2.88
55-59	0.69	0.57	1.26	0.65	0.18	0.83	1.34	0.75	2.09
60+	1.12	0.79	1.91	0.53	0.23	0.76	1.65	1.02	2.67
Total	**9.09**	**7.12**	**16.21**	**11.81**	**4.54**	**16.36**	**20.90**	**11.66**	**32.57**

Source: ibid

Projected Age-Sex MCWS Labour Force of Tamil Nadu in 2017 (in million)

Age Group	Rural			Urban			Rural + Urban		
	Male	Female	Person	Male	Female	Person	Male	Female	Person
0-4	0.00	0.00	0.00	0.00	0.00	0.00	0.00	0.00	0.00
5-9	0.00	0.00	0.00	0.00	0.00	0.00	0.00	0.00	0.00
10-14	0.00	0.00	0.00	0.00	0.00	0.00	0.00	0.00	0.00
15-19	0.27	0.31	0.58	0.55	0.33	0.88	0.81	0.65	1.46
20-24	0.45	0.27	0.73	1.85	0.70	2.54	2.30	0.97	3.27
25-29	0.84	0.21	1.05	2.01	0.71	2.72	2.85	0.92	3.77
30-34	1.06	0.65	1.71	1.81	0.76	2.57	2.87	1.42	4.28
35-39	1.01	0.91	1.92	1.72	0.69	2.41	2.72	1.60	4.33
40-44	0.95	1.02	1.98	1.52	0.53	2.05	2.47	1.55	4.02
45-49	0.91	1.01	1.91	1.32	0.49	1.81	2.23	1.50	3.72
50-54	0.86	0.92	1.79	1.09	0.37	1.46	1.95	1.30	3.25
55-59	0.75	0.68	1.43	0.76	0.22	0.98	1.51	0.90	2.41
60+	1.26	1.00	2.26	0.61	0.27	0.88	1.87	1.28	3.14
Total	**8.36**	**7.00**	**15.36**	**13.23**	**5.07**	**18.29**	**21.59**	**12.07**	**33.65**

Source: ibid

Projected Age-Sex MCWS Labour Force of Uttar Pradesh in 2007 (in million)

Age Group	Rural			Urban			Rural + Urban		
	Male	Female	Person	Male	Female	Person	Male	Female	Person
0-4	0.00	0.00	0.00	0.00	0.00	0.00	0.00	0.00	0.00
5-9	0.03	0.00	0.03	0.02	0.01	0.04	0.05	0.02	0.07
10-14	0.44	0.31	0.75	0.23	0.07	0.31	0.68	0.38	1.06
15-19	3.96	1.41	5.37	0.98	0.18	1.16	4.94	1.59	6.52
20-24	5.76	1.08	6.84	1.76	0.20	1.96	7.52	1.28	8.80
25-29	5.04	1.15	6.19	1.77	0.24	2.01	6.81	1.39	8.20
30-34	4.32	1.58	5.90	1.52	0.19	1.71	5.84	1.77	7.61
35-39	3.96	1.85	5.81	1.29	0.20	1.50	5.26	2.05	7.31
40-44	3.58	1.62	5.20	1.15	0.22	1.38	4.74	1.84	6.58
45-49	3.07	1.42	4.48	1.00	0.17	1.17	4.07	1.59	5.66
50-54	2.47	1.00	3.47	0.85	0.13	0.98	3.32	1.13	4.45
55-59	1.92	0.86	2.77	0.56	0.10	0.67	2.48	0.96	3.44
60+	3.73	1.17	4.90	0.55	0.11	0.66	4.28	1.28	5.56
Total	**38.28**	**13.44**	**51.72**	**11.69**	**1.84**	**13.52**	**49.97**	**15.27**	**65.24**

Source: ibid

Projected Age-Sex MCWS Labour Force of Uttar Pradesh in 2012 (in million)

Age Group	Rural			Urban			Rural + Urban		
	Male	Female	Person	Male	Female	Person	Male	Female	Person
0-4	0.00	0.00	0.00	0.00	0.00	0.00	0.00	0.00	0.00
5-9	0.00	0.00	0.00	0.03	0.01	0.05	0.03	0.01	0.05
10-14	0.14	0.18	0.31	0.21	0.03	0.24	0.34	0.20	0.55
15-19	3.87	1.68	5.55	0.88	0.20	1.08	4.76	1.88	6.63
20-24	7.17	1.47	8.64	1.90	0.26	2.17	9.07	1.74	10.81
25-29	6.29	1.33	7.62	2.14	0.30	2.44	8.43	1.63	10.06
30-34	4.82	1.67	6.49	1.95	0.24	2.18	6.77	1.91	8.68
35-39	4.11	2.05	6.16	1.57	0.23	1.80	5.68	2.28	7.96
40-44	3.76	1.95	5.70	1.28	0.25	1.54	5.04	2.20	7.24
45-49	3.45	1.80	5.26	1.10	0.18	1.28	4.56	1.98	6.54
50-54	2.86	1.28	4.14	1.01	0.17	1.18	3.87	1.45	5.32
55-59	2.25	1.10	3.35	0.71	0.14	0.85	2.97	1.24	4.20
60+	4.29	1.51	5.81	0.65	0.14	0.79	4.94	1.66	6.60
Total	**43.01**	**16.02**	**59.04**	**13.44**	**2.16**	**15.60**	56.46	**18.18**	**74.64**

Source: ibid

Projected Age-Sex MCWS Labour Force of Uttar Pradesh in 2017 (in million)

Age Group	Rural			Urban			Rural + Urban		
	Male	Female	Person	Male	Female	Person	Male	Female	Person
0-4	0.00	0.00	0.00	0.00	0.00	0.00	0.00	0.00	0.00
5-9	0.00	0.00	0.00	0.04	0.00	0.04	0.04	0.00	0.04
10-14	0.00	0.05	0.05	0.23	0.00	0.23	0.23	0.05	0.28
15-19	3.36	1.77	5.13	0.79	0.18	0.97	4.14	1.95	6.09
20-24	7.51	1.74	9.24	1.82	0.26	2.08	9.33	2.00	11.33
25-29	8.04	1.73	9.77	2.33	0.34	2.67	10.36	2.07	12.44
30-34	6.05	1.97	8.02	2.35	0.28	2.64	8.40	2.25	10.65
35-39	4.60	2.21	6.80	1.98	0.27	2.25	6.57	2.48	9.05
40-44	3.92	2.17	6.09	1.54	0.28	1.82	5.46	2.44	7.91
45-49	3.64	2.18	5.82	1.20	0.20	1.40	4.84	2.38	7.22
50-54	3.23	1.63	4.86	1.12	0.19	1.32	4.35	1.82	6.17
55-59	2.62	1.41	4.03	0.84	0.17	1.02	3.46	1.59	5.05
60+	5.02	1.96	6.98	0.78	0.18	0.95	5.80	2.14	7.93
Total	**47.97**	**18.81**	**66.78**	**15.03**	**2.35**	**17.38**	**63.00**	**21.17**	**84.16**

Source: ibid

Projected Age-Sex MCWS Labour Force of Uttarakhand in 2007 (in million)

Age Group	Rural			Urban			Rural + Urban		
	Male	Female	Person	Male	Female	Person	Male	Female	Person
0-4	0.00	0.00	0.00	0.00	0.00	0.00	0.00	0.00	0.00
5-9	0.00	0.00	0.00	0.00	0.00	0.00	0.00	0.00	0.00
10-14	0.02	0.00	0.02	0.00	0.00	0.00	0.02	0.00	0.02
15-19	0.11	0.10	0.21	0.05	0.01	0.05	0.16	0.11	0.26
20-24	0.28	0.16	0.44	0.11	0.02	0.13	0.39	0.18	0.57
25-29	0.24	0.14	0.38	0.12	0.02	0.14	0.36	0.16	0.53
30-34	0.19	0.14	0.33	0.11	0.02	0.13	0.30	0.16	0.47
35-39	0.17	0.13	0.30	0.10	0.02	0.12	0.27	0.15	0.43
40-44	0.16	0.10	0.26	0.09	0.01	0.09	0.25	0.11	0.36
45-49	0.14	0.08	0.22	0.07	0.02	0.09	0.22	0.10	0.32
50-54	0.12	0.08	0.20	0.06	0.01	0.07	0.18	0.10	0.27
55-59	0.09	0.08	0.17	0.04	0.01	0.05	0.14	0.08	0.22
60+	0.20	0.12	0.31	0.03	0.01	0.04	0.23	0.12	0.35
Total	**1.73**	**1.13**	**2.86**	**0.79**	**0.15**	**0.93**	**2.52**	**1.28**	**3.80**

Source: ibid

Projected Age-Sex MCWS Labour Force of Uttarakhand in 2012 (in million)

Age Group	Rural			Urban			Rural + Urban		
	Male	Female	Person	Male	Female	Person	Male	Female	Person
0-4	0.00	0.00	0.00	0.00	0.00	0.00	0.00	0.00	0.00
5-9	0.00	0.00	0.00	0.00	0.00	0.00	0.00	0.00	0.00
10-14	0.00	0.00	0.01	0.00	0.00	0.00	0.00	0.00	0.01
15-19	0.08	0.10	0.18	0.04	0.01	0.05	0.12	0.10	0.23
20-24	0.31	0.18	0.49	0.12	0.02	0.14	0.43	0.20	0.63
25-29	0.31	0.16	0.47	0.14	0.03	0.17	0.45	0.19	0.63
30-34	0.23	0.16	0.39	0.14	0.02	0.16	0.37	0.18	0.55
35-39	0.18	0.14	0.33	0.11	0.03	0.14	0.30	0.17	0.47
40-44	0.17	0.11	0.28	0.10	0.01	0.11	0.27	0.12	0.39
45-49	0.15	0.10	0.25	0.08	0.02	0.11	0.24	0.12	0.35
50-54	0.13	0.09	0.23	0.07	0.02	0.09	0.20	0.11	0.32
55-59	0.11	0.09	0.19	0.05	0.01	0.06	0.16	0.09	0.26
60+	0.22	0.13	0.36	0.05	0.01	0.06	0.27	0.14	0.41
Total	**1.90**	**1.26**	**3.17**	**0.91**	**0.17**	**1.08**	**2.81**	**1.44**	**4.25**

Source: ibid

Projected Age-Sex MCWS Labour Force of Uttarakhand in 2017 (in million)

Age Group	Rural			Urban			Rural + Urban		
	Male	Female	Person	Male	Female	Person	Male	Female	Person
0-4	0.00	0.00	0.00	0.00	0.00	0.00	0.00	0.00	0.00
5-9	0.00	0.00	0.00	0.00	0.00	0.00	0.00	0.00	0.00
10-14	0.00	0.00	0.00	0.00	0.00	0.00	0.00	0.00	0.00
15-19	0.05	0.09	0.14	0.04	0.01	0.04	0.09	0.10	0.18
20-24	0.31	0.23	0.54	0.12	0.02	0.14	0.42	0.26	0.68
25-29	0.36	0.24	0.60	0.15	0.03	0.18	0.50	0.27	0.78
30-34	0.30	0.23	0.53	0.16	0.03	0.18	0.46	0.26	0.71
35-39	0.22	0.19	0.42	0.14	0.03	0.17	0.36	0.23	0.59
40-44	0.18	0.16	0.34	0.11	0.01	0.13	0.29	0.17	0.46
45-49	0.16	0.14	0.30	0.09	0.02	0.12	0.25	0.17	0.42
50-54	0.14	0.13	0.28	0.08	0.02	0.10	0.23	0.15	0.38
55-59	0.12	0.12	0.24	0.07	0.01	0.08	0.19	0.13	0.31
60+	0.25	0.21	0.46	0.07	0.01	0.08	0.32	0.22	0.55
Total	**2.10**	**1.75**	**3.85**	**1.02**	**0.20**	**1.22**	**3.12**	**1.95**	**5.07**

Source: ibid

Projected Age-Sex MCWS Labour Force of West Bengal in 2007 (in million)

Age Group	Rural			Urban			Rural + Urban		
	Male	Female	Person	Male	Female	Person	Male	Female	Person
0-4	0.00	0.00	0.00	0.00	0.00	0.00	0.00	0.00	0.00
5-9	0.00	0.00	0.00	0.00	0.00	0.01	0.00	0.01	0.01
10-14	0.22	0.15	0.37	0.10	0.05	0.15	0.31	0.20	0.52
15-19	1.83	0.51	2.34	0.40	0.17	0.58	2.23	0.68	2.92
20-24	2.57	0.48	3.05	0.92	0.28	1.20	3.49	0.76	4.25
25-29	2.43	0.53	2.96	1.12	0.24	1.36	3.55	0.78	4.32
30-34	2.28	0.60	2.88	1.08	0.23	1.31	3.36	0.83	4.19
35-39	2.15	0.58	2.73	1.02	0.21	1.24	3.17	0.79	3.96
40-44	1.98	0.40	2.37	0.96	0.19	1.15	2.94	0.58	3.52
45-49	1.64	0.32	1.95	0.85	0.11	0.96	2.49	0.42	2.91
50-54	1.22	0.23	1.44	0.71	0.09	0.81	1.93	0.32	2.25
55-59	0.86	0.08	0.94	0.52	0.06	0.58	1.39	0.14	1.52
60+	1.11	0.13	1.24	0.35	0.02	0.37	1.46	0.16	1.62
Total	18.28	4.01	22.29	8.04	1.66	9.71	26.32	5.67	31.99

Source: ibid

Projected Age-Sex MCWS Labour Force of West Bengal in 2012 (in million)

Age Group	Rural			Urban			Rural + Urban		
	Male	Female	Person	Male	Female	Person	Male	Female	Person
0-4	0.00	0.00	0.00	0.00	0.00	0.00	0.00	0.00	0.00
5-9	0.00	0.00	0.00	0.01	0.00	0.01	0.01	0.00	0.01
10-14	0.11	0.14	0.25	0.09	0.04	0.13	0.20	0.18	0.38
15-19	1.79	0.54	2.32	0.34	0.17	0.51	2.13	0.70	2.83
20-24	2.99	0.58	3.57	0.91	0.29	1.20	3.89	0.87	4.76
25-29	2.78	0.59	3.37	1.18	0.27	1.45	3.96	0.86	4.82
30-34	2.38	0.63	3.01	1.17	0.26	1.42	3.54	0.89	4.44
35-39	2.19	0.65	2.84	1.09	0.23	1.32	3.28	0.87	4.16
40-44	2.12	0.48	2.59	1.02	0.21	1.22	3.14	0.68	3.82
45-49	1.89	0.43	2.33	0.93	0.12	1.05	2.82	0.55	3.38
50-54	1.52	0.29	1.80	0.82	0.11	0.93	2.33	0.40	2.73
55-59	1.10	0.08	1.18	0.64	0.08	0.72	1.75	0.15	1.90
60+	1.34	0.17	1.51	0.38	0.01	0.39	1.72	0.18	1.89
Total	**20.21**	**4.56**	**24.77**	**8.55**	**1.79**	**10.34**	**28.76**	**6.35**	**35.11**

Source: ibid

Projected Age-Sex MCWS Labour Force of West Bengal in 2017 (in million)

Age Group	Rural			Urban			Rural + Urban		
	Male	Female	Person	Male	Female	Person	Male	Female	Person
0-4	0.00	0.00	0.00	0.00	0.00	0.00	0.00	0.00	0.00
5-9	0.00	0.00	0.00	0.01	0.01	0.01	0.01	0.01	0.01
10-14	0.00	0.11	0.11	0.09	0.04	0.12	0.09	0.15	0.23
15-19	1.62	0.52	2.15	0.28	0.16	0.44	1.91	0.68	2.59
20-24	3.00	0.61	3.61	0.83	0.28	1.12	3.83	0.89	4.72
25-29	3.24	0.73	3.97	1.19	0.29	1.47	4.43	1.02	5.45
30-34	2.74	0.70	3.44	1.23	0.27	1.50	3.97	0.97	4.94
35-39	2.31	0.67	2.98	1.16	0.23	1.40	3.47	0.91	4.38
40-44	2.18	0.52	2.70	1.08	0.22	1.30	3.26	0.74	4.00
45-49	2.04	0.49	2.53	0.98	0.13	1.11	3.02	0.62	3.64
50-54	1.77	0.36	2.13	0.89	0.13	1.02	2.66	0.49	3.15
55-59	1.38	0.06	1.44	0.73	0.09	0.83	2.11	0.16	2.27
60+	1.67	0.21	1.88	0.41	0.00	0.41	2.07	0.21	2.28
Total	**21.94**	**4.99**	**26.93**	**8.88**	**1.84**	**10.73**	**30.83**	**6.83**	**37.66**

Source: ibid

Projected Age-Sex MCWS Labour Force of India in 2007 (in million)

Age Group	Rural			Urban			Rural + Urban		
	Male	Female	Person	Male	Female	Person	Male	Female	Person
0-4	0.00	0.00	0.00	0.00	0.00	0.00	0.00	0.00	0.00
5-9	0.04	0.04	0.08	0.04	0.02	0.06	0.08	0.06	0.14
10-14	2.15	2.05	4.20	0.71	0.35	1.06	2.86	2.40	5.26
15-19	21.98	10.28	32.26	6.35	1.89	8.24	28.33	12.17	40.50
20-24	32.50	11.47	43.97	13.81	3.45	17.26	46.31	14.92	61.23
25-29	29.48	11.85	41.33	15.77	3.46	19.23	45.25	15.31	60.56
30-34	26.35	12.34	38.69	14.24	3.47	17.71	40.59	15.81	56.40
35-39	24.44	13.59	38.02	12.66	3.49	16.15	37.09	17.08	54.17
40-44	22.38	12.01	34.39	11.15	2.98	14.14	33.53	14.99	48.53
45-49	19.03	9.69	28.72	9.51	2.12	11.63	28.54	11.82	40.36
50-54	15.12	6.94	22.06	7.50	1.60	9.10	22.63	8.54	31.17
55-59	11.28	5.14	16.42	4.87	0.95	5.82	16.15	6.09	22.24
60+	18.04	6.72	24.76	4.01	1.01	5.02	22.05	7.73	29.78
Total	**222.79**	**102.12**	**324.91**	**100.61**	**24.80**	**125.41**	**323.40**	**126.92**	**450.32**

Source: ibid

Projected Age-Sex MCWS Labour Force of India in 2012 (in million)

Age Group	Rural			Urban			Rural + Urban		
	Male	Female	Person	Male	Female	Person	Male	Female	Person
0-4	0.00	0.00	0.00	0.00	0.00	0.00	0.00	0.00	0.00
5-9	0.00	0.00	0.00	0.05	0.02	0.07	0.05	0.02	0.07
10-14	0.67	1.02	1.68	0.51	0.21	0.72	1.18	1.22	2.40
15-19	20.86	10.07	30.93	5.97	1.89	7.85	26.83	11.96	38.78
20-24	37.43	12.92	50.35	14.92	4.10	19.03	52.35	17.03	69.38
25-29	34.35	12.71	47.06	18.07	4.12	22.19	52.43	16.83	69.26
30-34	28.58	12.90	41.48	16.78	4.13	20.91	45.35	17.03	62.39
35-39	25.35	14.78	40.13	14.79	4.20	18.99	40.13	18.99	59.12
40-44	23.50	13.86	37.36	12.69	3.47	16.16	36.18	17.34	53.52
45-49	21.36	11.95	33.31	10.97	2.55	13.53	32.33	14.50	46.84
50-54	17.71	8.66	26.37	9.01	2.00	11.00	26.72	10.66	37.37
55-59	13.58	6.41	20.00	6.14	1.23	7.38	19.73	7.65	27.37
60+	20.70	8.24	28.94	4.60	1.16	5.76	25.30	9.40	34.70
Total	**244.09**	**113.54**	**357.63**	**114.49**	**29.08**	**143.58**	**358.58**	**142.62**	**501.20**

Source: ibid

Projected Age-Sex MCWS Labour Force of India in 2017 (in million)

Age Group	Rural			Urban			Rural + Urban		
	Male	Female	Person	Male	Female	Person	Male	Female	Person
0-4	0.00	0.00	0.00	0.00	0.00	0.00	0.00	0.00	0.00
5-9	0.00	0.00	0.00	0.06	0.01	0.06	0.06	0.01	0.07
10-14	0.14	0.35	0.49	0.44	0.14	0.59	0.59	0.49	1.08
15-19	18.33	9.20	27.52	5.63	1.86	7.49	23.96	11.06	35.01
20-24	37.54	13.14	50.67	15.42	4.44	19.85	52.95	17.57	70.53
25-29	40.20	14.76	54.97	19.54	4.70	24.24	59.75	19.46	79.21
30-34	33.63	14.52	48.16	18.85	4.62	23.47	52.48	19.14	71.63
35-39	27.66	15.87	43.52	17.11	4.75	21.86	44.77	20.62	65.38
40-44	24.53	15.33	39.87	14.55	3.93	18.48	39.08	19.26	58.34
45-49	22.51	13.95	36.47	12.26	2.90	15.16	34.77	16.85	51.63
50-54	19.97	10.81	30.78	10.28	2.40	12.68	30.25	13.21	43.46
55-59	15.98	8.18	24.17	7.28	1.52	8.79	23.26	9.70	32.96
60+	24.25	10.33	34.58	5.36	1.39	6.75	29.61	11.72	41.33
Total	**264.75**	**126.45**	**391.20**	**126.77**	**32.65**	**159.42**	**391.53**	**159.10**	**550.63**

Source: ibid

Annex 5.5: State-wise UPSS Labour Force by Educational Status, Sector and Sex as on 1st April of 2007, 2012 and 2017.

Table 1: Projected Rural UPSS Labour Force by Educational Status, Sector and Sex in 2007 (in million)

State/UT	Rural Male						Rural Female						Rural Total					
	IL	PB	M	S+H	G+	Total	IL	PB	M	S+H	G+	Total	IL	PB	M	S+H	G+	Total
Andhra Pradesh	8.05	4.45	2.66	2.61	0.64	18.41	10.24	2.38	0.87	0.72	0.09	14.30	18.29	6.82	3.53	3.33	0.73	32.70
Assam	1.24	3.12	1.65	0.97	0.18	7.16	0.63	1.15	0.54	0.23	0.03	2.58	1.87	4.26	2.20	1.20	0.21	9.74
Bihar	8.37	5.72	3.15	3.95	0.87	22.06	5.21	0.71	0.25	0.20	0.02	6.39	13.59	6.43	3.40	4.15	0.89	28.45
Chhattisgarh	1.44	1.94	0.87	0.56	0.20	5.01	2.62	1.07	0.26	0.08	0.03	4.07	4.06	3.02	1.12	0.65	0.23	9.08
Gujarat	2.54	3.14	2.65	1.80	0.36	10.49	4.15	1.39	0.80	0.53	0.07	6.94	6.69	4.53	3.45	2.33	0.43	17.43
Haryana	1.12	1.32	0.60	1.24	0.30	4.57	1.48	0.52	0.19	0.29	0.04	2.52	2.60	1.84	0.79	1.52	0.35	7.09
Himachal Pradesh	0.22	0.61	0.26	0.54	0.12	1.75	0.49	0.45	0.16	0.32	0.07	1.50	0.71	1.06	0.42	0.86	0.19	3.25
J&K	0.81	0.47	0.57	0.47	0.10	2.42	0.70	0.25	0.20	0.14	0.02	1.30	1.51	0.72	0.77	0.61	0.12	3.72
Jharkhand	2.33	1.97	1.07	0.75	0.19	6.30	2.64	0.46	0.20	0.08	0.01	3.40	4.96	2.43	1.27	0.83	0.20	9.70
Karnataka	4.15	3.14	2.21	1.54	0.34	11.39	5.06	1.55	0.98	0.46	0.09	8.13	9.21	4.69	3.19	2.01	0.43	19.53
Kerala	0.36	1.91	2.79	1.97	0.35	7.38	0.40	0.98	1.15	1.21	0.35	4.08	0.76	2.89	3.94	3.18	0.70	11.46
Maharashtra	3.61	4.21	4.50	4.13	0.93	17.38	6.51	2.99	2.50	1.24	0.16	13.39	10.11	7.20	7.00	5.36	1.09	30.76
Madhya Pradesh	4.98	4.84	2.06	1.40	0.45	13.73	6.89	1.42	0.31	0.16	0.04	8.81	11.86	6.26	2.37	1.56	0.49	22.55
Orissa	3.17	3.21	2.16	1.07	0.50	10.11	3.71	1.11	0.66	0.23	0.10	5.80	6.87	4.32	2.82	1.30	0.59	15.90
Punjab	1.53	1.37	0.70	1.44	0.16	5.19	1.12	0.66	0.27	0.54	0.05	2.64	2.65	2.02	0.97	1.98	0.22	7.83
Rajasthan	5.05	3.77	2.10	1.62	0.51	13.05	7.62	1.15	0.42	0.21	0.03	9.43	12.67	4.93	2.52	1.82	0.54	22.48
Tamil Nadu	2.48	3.65	1.89	1.51	0.39	9.91	3.85	2.11	0.80	0.63	0.13	7.51	6.33	5.76	2.69	2.13	0.52	17.43
Uttar Pradesh	14.26	9.27	7.94	6.40	2.03	39.89	12.83	2.01	1.08	0.62	0.12	16.67	27.08	11.28	9.02	7.02	2.16	56.56
Uttarakhand	0.42	0.38	0.51	0.44	0.13	1.88	0.73	0.32	0.21	0.20	0.04	1.50	1.15	0.70	0.73	0.63	0.16	3.38
West Bengal	5.48	7.74	2.91	2.01	0.72	18.86	3.00	1.72	0.42	0.28	0.07	5.49	8.48	9.46	3.33	2.29	0.80	24.36
Other NE	0.50	1.19	0.70	0.45	0.15	2.99	0.48	0.69	0.31	0.18	0.05	1.71	0.97	1.88	1.02	0.63	0.20	4.70
Other states	0.12	0.21	0.18	0.32	0.06	0.89	0.11	0.06	0.03	0.06	0.02	0.29	0.23	0.27	0.22	0.38	0.09	1.18
All India	72.20	67.63	44.13	37.18	9.69	230.83	80.45	25.14	12.63	8.60	1.63	128.44	152.65	92.77	56.75	45.79	11.31	359.27

Note: IL - Illiterate, PB - Primary and Below Primary, M - Middle, S+H - Secondary & Higher Secondary, G+ - Graduate and above
Source: ibid

Table 2: Projected Urban UPSS Labour Force by Educational Status, Sector and Sex in 2007 (in million)

State/UT	Urban Male						Urban Female						Urban Total					
	IL	PB	M	S+H	G+	Total	IL	PB	M	S+H	G+	Total	IL	PB	M	S+H	G+	Total
Andhra Pradesh	1.29	1.49	1.12	1.81	1.18	6.90	1.24	0.49	0.18	0.29	0.25	2.46	2.54	1.98	1.31	2.10	1.43	9.36
Assam	0.10	0.24	0.29	0.39	0.30	1.33	0.04	0.05	0.03	0.05	0.05	0.22	0.14	0.29	0.32	0.44	0.35	1.55
Bihar	0.45	0.46	0.34	0.66	0.69	2.60	0.26	0.07	0.01	0.03	0.03	0.40	0.72	0.52	0.35	0.68	0.72	2.99
Chhattisgarh	0.17	0.37	0.24	0.43	0.31	1.53	0.20	0.10	0.05	0.04	0.04	0.42	0.37	0.47	0.29	0.46	0.35	1.95
Gujarat	0.50	1.31	1.57	2.57	1.11	7.06	0.52	0.30	0.29	0.36	0.17	1.65	1.02	1.61	1.86	2.93	1.28	8.70
Haryana	0.40	0.61	0.32	0.96	0.37	2.66	0.14	0.05	0.04	0.12	0.12	0.47	0.55	0.66	0.35	1.08	0.49	3.13
Himachal Pradesh	0.04	0.06	0.02	0.10	0.04	0.25	0.03	0.02	0.00	0.02	0.02	0.08	0.07	0.08	0.02	0.12	0.05	0.34
J&K	0.22	0.18	0.21	0.27	0.09	0.96	0.05	0.02	0.03	0.03	0.04	0.17	0.27	0.20	0.23	0.30	0.13	1.13
Jharkhand	0.14	0.24	0.43	0.67	0.45	1.93	0.14	0.07	0.09	0.07	0.06	0.43	0.28	0.31	0.52	0.74	0.51	2.36
Karnataka	0.54	1.31	1.30	2.08	1.07	6.31	0.67	0.34	0.35	0.42	0.28	2.05	1.20	1.65	1.65	2.50	1.35	8.36
Kerala	0.08	0.54	0.86	0.78	0.33	2.60	0.09	0.23	0.27	0.43	0.30	1.31	0.17	0.76	1.13	1.21	0.63	3.91
Maharashtra	1.16	2.62	4.10	4.86	2.54	15.28	0.94	0.90	0.65	0.87	0.85	4.20	2.10	3.52	4.75	5.72	3.39	19.48
Madhya Pradesh	0.68	1.40	0.75	1.48	1.23	5.53	0.54	0.31	0.13	0.17	0.24	1.39	1.22	1.71	0.88	1.65	1.47	6.92
Orissa	0.27	0.42	0.37	0.52	0.38	1.97	0.22	0.10	0.07	0.08	0.09	0.57	0.50	0.53	0.44	0.60	0.47	2.54
Punjab	0.44	0.75	0.44	1.15	0.47	3.25	0.14	0.09	0.03	0.20	0.26	0.71	0.57	0.84	0.47	1.35	0.73	3.96
Rajasthan	0.87	1.14	0.78	0.96	0.66	4.42	0.79	0.17	0.13	0.11	0.14	1.34	1.67	1.31	0.91	1.07	0.80	5.76
Tamil Nadu	0.78	2.67	2.00	3.13	1.87	10.44	1.00	1.27	0.58	0.76	0.55	4.15	1.78	3.94	2.58	3.88	2.41	14.59
Uttar Pradesh	2.55	2.85	1.89	2.60	1.95	11.85	1.13	0.39	0.14	0.18	0.33	2.17	3.68	3.24	2.03	2.79	2.28	14.03
Uttarakhand	0.11	0.15	0.14	0.23	0.16	0.79	0.05	0.01	0.01	0.05	0.04	0.17	0.16	0.17	0.14	0.28	0.20	0.96
West Bengal	0.86	2.16	1.65	1.97	1.51	8.16	0.43	0.51	0.28	0.32	0.38	1.91	1.29	2.67	1.92	2.30	1.89	10.07
Other NE	0.05	0.16	0.19	0.26	0.17	0.83	0.04	0.06	0.07	0.11	0.08	0.35	0.09	0.22	0.26	0.37	0.24	1.18
Other states	0.37	1.15	0.99	1.68	1.47	5.67	0.21	0.13	0.06	0.18	0.34	0.92	0.58	1.28	1.06	1.86	1.81	6.59
All India	12.10	22.29	20.02	29.55	18.36	102.31	8.87	5.67	3.47	4.89	4.64	27.55	20.97	27.96	23.49	34.44	23.01	129.86

Source: ibid

Table 3: Projected UPSS Labour Force by Educational Status, Sector and Sex in 2007 (in million)

State/UT	Male						Female						Total					
	IL	PB	M	S+H	G+	Total	IL	PB	M	S+H	G+	Total	IL	PB	M	S+H	G+	Total
Andhra Pradesh	9.34	5.94	3.79	4.42	1.82	25.30	11.48	2.87	1.05	1.01	0.34	16.76	20.83	8.80	4.84	5.43	2.16	42.07
Assam	1.34	3.36	1.95	1.36	0.48	8.48	0.67	1.19	0.57	0.28	0.08	2.80	2.01	4.55	2.52	1.64	0.56	11.28
Bihar	8.83	6.18	3.49	4.60	1.56	24.66	5.47	0.77	0.26	0.23	0.05	6.79	14.30	6.95	3.75	4.83	1.61	31.45
Chhattisgarh	1.61	2.32	1.10	0.99	0.52	6.54	2.82	1.17	0.31	0.12	0.07	4.49	4.43	3.49	1.41	1.11	0.59	11.03
Gujarat	3.03	4.45	4.22	4.37	1.47	17.55	4.67	1.69	1.10	0.89	0.24	8.59	7.71	6.14	5.31	5.26	1.71	26.13
Haryana	1.52	1.92	0.91	2.20	0.68	7.23	1.62	0.57	0.23	0.41	0.16	2.99	3.14	2.50	1.14	2.61	0.83	10.22
Himachal Pradesh	0.26	0.67	0.27	0.64	0.16	2.00	0.51	0.47	0.17	0.34	0.09	1.58	0.78	1.14	0.44	0.98	0.24	3.58
J&K	1.03	0.65	0.77	0.74	0.19	3.39	0.75	0.27	0.23	0.17	0.06	1.47	1.78	0.92	1.00	0.91	0.25	4.86
Jharkhand	2.47	2.20	1.50	1.42	0.64	8.23	2.78	0.54	0.29	0.15	0.07	3.82	5.25	2.74	1.79	1.57	0.71	12.06
Karnataka	4.69	4.46	3.52	3.62	1.41	17.70	5.72	1.88	1.33	0.88	0.37	10.19	10.41	6.34	4.85	4.51	1.78	27.89
Kerala	0.44	2.45	3.65	2.75	0.68	9.98	0.49	1.20	1.41	1.64	0.65	5.39	0.93	3.65	5.07	4.39	1.33	15.37
Maharashtra	4.77	6.83	8.60	8.98	3.47	32.66	7.44	3.89	3.14	2.10	1.01	17.59	12.21	10.72	11.75	11.09	4.49	50.24
Madhya Pradesh	5.65	6.23	2.81	2.88	1.68	19.26	7.43	1.73	0.44	0.32	0.28	10.21	13.08	7.96	3.26	3.20	1.96	29.47
Orissa	3.44	3.64	2.53	1.59	0.88	12.07	3.93	1.21	0.73	0.31	0.19	6.37	7.37	4.85	3.26	1.90	1.06	18.44
Punjab	1.96	2.12	1.14	2.59	0.64	8.45	1.26	0.74	0.30	0.74	0.31	3.35	3.22	2.86	1.44	3.33	0.95	11.79
Rajasthan	5.92	4.91	2.89	2.58	1.17	17.47	8.41	1.33	0.54	0.31	0.17	10.76	14.33	6.24	3.43	2.89	1.34	28.24
Tamil Nadu	3.26	6.31	3.90	4.63	2.26	20.36	4.85	3.38	1.37	1.38	0.67	11.66	8.11	9.70	5.27	6.02	2.93	32.02
Uttar Pradesh	16.81	12.12	9.83	9.00	3.98	51.74	13.96	2.40	1.22	0.80	0.45	18.84	30.77	14.52	11.06	9.80	4.44	70.59
Uttarakhand	0.54	0.53	0.65	0.66	0.29	2.67	0.78	0.34	0.22	0.25	0.08	1.67	1.31	0.87	0.87	0.91	0.37	4.33
West Bengal	6.34	9.90	4.56	3.98	2.24	27.02	3.43	2.22	0.70	0.61	0.45	7.40	9.77	12.12	5.26	4.59	2.69	34.42
Other NE	0.54	1.35	0.90	0.71	0.32	3.82	0.52	0.75	0.38	0.29	0.12	2.06	1.06	2.11	1.27	1.00	0.44	5.88
Other states	0.49	1.36	1.18	2.00	1.54	6.56	0.32	0.19	0.10	0.24	0.36	1.21	0.81	1.55	1.27	2.24	1.90	7.77
All India	84.29	89.91	64.14	66.74	28.05	333.14	89.32	30.81	16.10	13.49	6.27	155.99	173.62	120.72	80.24	80.23	34.32	489.13

Source: ibid

Table 4: Projected Rural UPSS Labour Force by Educational Status, Sector and Sex in 2012 (in million)

State/UT	Rural Male						Rural Female						Rural Total					
	IL	PB	M	S+H	G+	Total	IL	PB	M	S+H	G+	Total	IL	PB	M	S+H	G+	Total
Andhra Pradesh	7.83	4.57	3.22	3.26	0.82	19.70	10.32	2.73	1.09	0.95	0.12	15.21	18.15	7.29	4.31	4.21	0.95	34.91
Assam	1.04	3.60	2.00	1.15	0.20	7.99	0.37	1.58	0.79	0.30	0.04	3.07	1.40	5.18	2.79	1.46	0.23	11.05
Bihar	8.03	6.88	3.90	5.08	1.00	24.89	5.03	0.87	0.28	0.26	0.02	6.47	13.05	7.76	4.18	5.34	1.03	31.36
Chhattisgarh	1.11	2.25	1.15	0.67	0.27	5.45	2.50	1.32	0.35	0.11	0.05	4.32	3.61	3.57	1.51	0.77	0.32	9.77
Gujarat	2.32	3.18	3.40	2.10	0.41	11.42	4.22	1.53	1.03	0.67	0.09	7.54	6.55	4.71	4.43	2.77	0.50	18.96
Haryana	1.02	1.43	0.70	1.48	0.42	5.03	1.57	0.65	0.25	0.40	0.07	2.95	2.59	2.08	0.95	1.88	0.49	7.99
Himachal Pradesh	0.14	0.68	0.28	0.64	0.16	1.89	0.42	0.52	0.19	0.41	0.10	1.63	0.55	1.19	0.47	1.05	0.25	3.52
J&K	0.83	0.49	0.63	0.53	0.14	2.61	0.64	0.27	0.24	0.18	0.03	1.36	1.47	0.75	0.87	0.71	0.16	3.96
Jharkhand	2.05	2.64	1.34	0.92	0.23	7.18	2.71	0.62	0.28	0.11	0.02	3.73	4.76	3.26	1.61	1.04	0.24	10.91
Karnataka	3.93	3.38	2.68	1.77	0.39	12.15	4.97	1.76	1.26	0.60	0.11	8.71	8.90	5.13	3.94	2.38	0.50	20.85
Kerala	0.35	1.70	3.03	2.32	0.40	7.79	0.36	0.77	1.25	1.33	0.40	4.11	0.71	2.47	4.28	3.64	0.80	11.90
Maharashtra	3.02	3.98	5.10	5.20	1.22	18.53	6.14	3.18	2.93	1.57	0.21	14.03	9.17	7.17	8.02	6.77	1.44	32.57
Madhya Pradesh	4.63	5.57	2.72	1.68	0.62	15.22	7.06	1.68	0.40	0.22	0.06	9.42	11.70	7.25	3.12	1.90	0.68	24.64
Orissa	2.78	3.37	2.58	1.39	0.67	10.80	3.61	1.41	0.92	0.32	0.14	6.39	6.39	4.78	3.50	1.71	0.81	17.18
Punjab	1.33	1.50	0.75	1.69	0.19	5.46	1.03	0.75	0.31	0.65	0.06	2.80	2.36	2.25	1.06	2.34	0.25	8.26
Rajasthan	4.88	4.37	2.63	2.14	0.68	14.71	8.03	1.41	0.57	0.29	0.04	10.34	12.91	5.78	3.20	2.44	0.72	25.05
Tamil Nadu	2.28	3.34	1.86	1.43	0.38	9.30	3.71	2.00	0.73	0.57	0.12	7.13	5.99	5.34	2.59	2.00	0.50	16.43
Uttar Pradesh	13.89	10.43	9.76	7.77	2.72	44.57	13.91	2.51	1.53	0.89	0.19	19.03	27.80	12.94	11.29	8.65	2.91	63.59
Uttarakhand	0.42	0.31	0.66	0.57	0.13	2.08	0.67	0.39	0.27	0.27	0.05	1.65	1.09	0.69	0.93	0.84	0.18	3.73
West Bengal	5.62	8.62	3.27	2.44	0.86	20.81	2.83	1.99	0.50	0.35	0.09	5.77	8.45	10.61	3.77	2.80	0.95	26.58
Other NE	0.43	1.38	0.89	0.56	0.19	3.44	0.36	0.92	0.45	0.26	0.06	2.06	0.79	2.30	1.33	0.82	0.25	5.50
Other states	0.10	0.21	0.22	0.38	0.08	0.99	0.10	0.07	0.04	0.08	0.03	0.33	0.20	0.28	0.26	0.46	0.11	1.33
All India	68.04	73.86	52.76	45.16	12.19	252.00	80.57	28.93	15.66	10.80	2.09	138.04	148.60	102.79	68.42	55.96	14.28	390.04

Source: ibid

Table 5: Projected Urban UPSS Labour Force by Educational Status, Sector and Sex in 2012 (in million)

State/UT	Urban Male						Urban Female						Urban Total					
	IL	PB	M	S+H	G+	Total	IL	PB	M	S+H	G+	Total	IL	PB	M	S+H	G+	Total
Andhra Pradesh	1.22	1.47	1.22	2.03	1.43	7.38	1.31	0.53	0.23	0.39	0.31	2.77	2.54	2.00	1.45	2.42	1.75	10.15
Assam	0.11	0.26	0.33	0.47	0.39	1.56	0.05	0.05	0.04	0.06	0.07	0.28	0.16	0.31	0.37	0.53	0.47	1.84
Bihar	0.41	0.49	0.36	0.78	0.88	2.93	0.30	0.07	0.01	0.04	0.04	0.45	0.71	0.55	0.36	0.82	0.92	3.37
Chhattisgarh	0.20	0.39	0.31	0.51	0.41	1.81	0.21	0.13	0.08	0.04	0.05	0.50	0.40	0.52	0.38	0.55	0.45	2.31
Gujarat	0.38	1.11	1.92	3.31	1.35	8.07	0.46	0.30	0.39	0.46	0.22	1.83	0.85	1.41	2.31	3.76	1.57	9.90
Haryana	0.39	0.69	0.33	1.27	0.48	3.16	0.15	0.06	0.04	0.16	0.16	0.57	0.53	0.75	0.37	1.43	0.64	3.72
Himachal Pradesh	0.05	0.08	0.02	0.11	0.04	0.30	0.03	0.02	0.01	0.02	0.02	0.10	0.08	0.10	0.02	0.13	0.06	0.40
J&K	0.31	0.22	0.25	0.26	0.07	1.11	0.04	0.02	0.04	0.04	0.05	0.19	0.35	0.24	0.28	0.31	0.12	1.30
Jharkhand	0.10	0.19	0.47	0.82	0.58	2.15	0.12	0.08	0.11	0.09	0.07	0.48	0.22	0.27	0.58	0.91	0.65	2.63
Karnataka	0.41	1.50	1.48	2.40	1.30	7.09	0.61	0.36	0.44	0.48	0.35	2.24	1.02	1.86	1.92	2.88	1.65	9.33
Kerala	0.09	0.44	0.91	0.88	0.37	2.69	0.08	0.18	0.27	0.46	0.36	1.34	0.17	0.62	1.18	1.34	0.73	4.04
Maharashtra	1.07	2.63	4.88	5.77	3.07	17.41	0.78	1.13	0.81	1.11	1.12	4.96	1.86	3.76	5.69	6.88	4.19	22.38
Madhya Pradesh	0.61	1.46	0.90	1.78	1.66	6.41	0.52	0.40	0.19	0.22	0.30	1.63	1.13	1.86	1.09	2.00	1.96	8.04
Orissa	0.28	0.45	0.39	0.62	0.47	2.21	0.22	0.15	0.11	0.12	0.13	0.73	0.50	0.60	0.50	0.74	0.60	2.93
Punjab	0.42	0.87	0.48	1.42	0.59	3.78	0.12	0.10	0.02	0.24	0.34	0.83	0.54	0.97	0.50	1.66	0.94	4.61
Rajasthan	0.95	1.32	0.90	1.12	0.77	5.06	0.91	0.19	0.17	0.13	0.17	1.56	1.85	1.51	1.08	1.25	0.94	6.62
Tamil Nadu	0.67	2.65	2.28	3.81	2.52	11.93	0.88	1.51	0.73	0.96	0.75	4.83	1.55	4.16	3.01	4.77	3.27	16.76
Uttar Pradesh	2.60	3.31	2.18	3.12	2.36	13.57	1.21	0.45	0.18	0.22	0.46	2.51	3.80	3.76	2.37	3.34	2.82	16.09
Uttarakhand	0.15	0.18	0.17	0.26	0.16	0.91	0.05	0.02	0.01	0.07	0.05	0.20	0.20	0.19	0.18	0.33	0.21	1.11
West Bengal	0.80	2.16	1.82	2.19	1.71	8.67	0.38	0.54	0.34	0.38	0.44	2.07	1.17	2.69	2.16	2.57	2.14	10.74
Other NE	0.05	0.17	0.21	0.31	0.21	0.94	0.03	0.06	0.08	0.14	0.11	0.41	0.08	0.23	0.29	0.45	0.31	1.36
Other states	0.19	1.40	1.35	2.16	1.85	6.96	0.23	0.16	0.08	0.20	0.39	1.07	0.42	1.56	1.43	2.37	2.24	8.02
All India	11.45	23.42	23.18	35.40	22.68	116.12	8.70	6.50	4.36	6.04	5.96	31.55	20.15	29.92	27.53	41.44	28.63	147.67

Source: ibid

Table 6: Projected UPSS Labour Force by Educational Status, Sector and Sex in 2012 (in million)

State/UT	Male						Female						Total					
	IL	PB	M	S+H	G+	Total	IL	PB	M	S+H	G+	Total	IL	PB	M	S+H	G+	Total
Andhra Pradesh	9.06	6.04	4.44	5.29	2.26	27.09	11.63	3.26	1.31	1.34	0.43	17.98	20.69	9.29	5.76	6.63	2.69	45.06
Assam	1.15	3.86	2.33	1.62	0.59	9.55	0.42	1.63	0.83	0.36	0.11	3.35	1.57	5.49	3.16	1.98	0.70	12.89
Bihar	8.44	7.37	4.25	5.87	1.89	27.82	5.32	0.94	0.29	0.29	0.06	6.91	13.77	8.31	4.54	6.16	1.95	34.73
Chhattisgarh	1.30	2.64	1.46	1.18	0.68	7.26	2.71	1.45	0.43	0.14	0.09	4.82	4.01	4.09	1.89	1.32	0.77	12.08
Gujarat	2.71	4.30	5.33	5.41	1.76	19.50	4.69	1.83	1.41	1.12	0.32	9.37	7.39	6.12	6.74	6.53	2.08	28.87
Haryana	1.41	2.12	1.02	2.75	0.89	8.19	1.72	0.71	0.30	0.56	0.23	3.52	3.12	2.83	1.32	3.31	1.13	11.71
Himachal Pradesh	0.19	0.75	0.29	0.75	0.20	2.18	0.45	0.54	0.20	0.43	0.12	1.73	0.64	1.29	0.49	1.18	0.32	3.91
J&K	1.14	0.71	0.87	0.79	0.21	3.72	0.68	0.29	0.28	0.22	0.07	1.54	1.82	0.99	1.15	1.01	0.28	5.26
Jharkhand	2.15	2.82	1.81	1.74	0.81	9.33	2.84	0.70	0.39	0.21	0.09	4.21	4.99	3.52	2.20	1.95	0.89	13.54
Karnataka	4.34	4.88	4.16	4.17	1.69	19.24	5.58	2.12	1.70	1.09	0.46	10.94	9.92	6.99	5.86	5.26	2.15	30.18
Kerala	0.44	2.14	3.94	3.20	0.77	10.48	0.43	0.96	1.51	1.79	0.77	5.46	0.88	3.10	5.45	4.98	1.53	15.94
Maharashtra	4.10	6.61	9.98	10.97	4.29	35.95	6.93	4.31	3.74	2.68	1.34	19.00	11.02	10.93	13.72	13.65	5.63	54.94
Madhya Pradesh	5.25	7.03	3.62	3.46	2.28	21.63	7.58	2.08	0.59	0.44	0.36	11.04	12.83	9.11	4.21	3.89	2.64	32.68
Orissa	3.06	3.82	2.98	2.01	1.14	13.00	3.83	1.56	1.02	0.43	0.26	7.11	6.89	5.38	4.00	2.44	1.41	20.12
Punjab	1.74	2.37	1.23	3.10	0.79	9.24	1.15	0.85	0.33	0.89	0.40	3.63	2.90	3.22	1.56	4.00	1.19	12.87
Rajasthan	5.82	5.69	3.54	3.26	1.45	19.77	8.94	1.59	0.74	0.43	0.20	11.90	14.76	7.29	4.28	3.69	1.66	31.67
Tamil Nadu	2.95	5.99	4.14	5.24	2.90	21.23	4.58	3.51	1.47	1.53	0.87	11.96	7.54	9.51	5.61	6.77	3.77	33.19
Uttar Pradesh	16.49	13.74	11.95	10.89	5.08	58.14	15.12	2.96	1.71	1.11	0.64	21.54	31.61	16.70	13.66	12.00	5.73	79.68
Uttarakhand	0.57	0.48	0.82	0.83	0.29	2.99	0.72	0.41	0.28	0.34	0.10	1.85	1.29	0.89	1.10	1.17	0.39	4.84
West Bengal	6.42	10.77	5.09	4.63	2.56	29.48	3.21	2.53	0.84	0.73	0.52	7.84	9.63	13.30	5.94	5.36	3.09	37.32
Other NE	0.48	1.54	1.10	0.87	0.40	4.39	0.39	0.98	0.52	0.40	0.17	2.47	0.87	2.53	1.62	1.27	0.57	6.86
Other states	0.29	1.61	1.58	2.54	1.93	7.95	0.34	0.24	0.12	0.29	0.42	1.40	0.63	1.85	1.69	2.83	2.35	9.35
All India	79.49	97.28	75.93	80.55	34.87	368.12	89.26	35.43	20.02	16.84	8.04	169.59	168.75	132.71	95.95	97.39	42.91	537.71

Source: ibid

Table 7: Projected Rural UPSS Labour Force by Educational Status, Sector and Sex in 2017 (in million)

State/UT	Rural Male						Rural Female						Rural Total					
	IL	PB	M	S+H	G+	Total	IL	PB	M	S+H	G+	Total	IL	PB	M	S+H	G+	Total
Andhra Pradesh	7.54	4.64	3.77	3.87	1.03	20.86	10.36	3.05	1.28	1.13	0.16	15.99	17.90	7.69	5.06	5.01	1.19	36.85
Assam	0.80	4.10	2.32	1.31	0.23	8.76	0.00	2.07	1.08	0.38	0.04	3.56	0.80	6.16	3.40	1.69	0.27	12.33
Bihar	7.51	8.09	4.72	6.42	1.14	27.88	4.88	1.01	0.27	0.33	0.03	6.52	12.40	9.10	4.99	6.74	1.17	34.39
Chhattisgarh	0.70	2.59	1.48	0.78	0.35	5.90	2.41	1.54	0.44	0.12	0.06	4.58	3.11	4.13	1.92	0.91	0.41	10.47
Gujarat	2.15	3.18	4.13	2.37	0.47	12.30	4.30	1.70	1.24	0.80	0.12	8.17	6.45	4.88	5.38	3.18	0.59	20.48
Haryana	0.97	1.51	0.76	1.69	0.53	5.46	1.71	0.78	0.32	0.51	0.10	3.42	2.68	2.28	1.08	2.20	0.63	8.87
Himachal Pradesh	0.09	0.73	0.29	0.71	0.19	2.01	0.38	0.57	0.22	0.45	0.11	1.73	0.47	1.31	0.50	1.16	0.30	3.74
J&K	0.85	0.52	0.70	0.60	0.18	2.85	0.59	0.30	0.30	0.23	0.03	1.46	1.43	0.82	1.00	0.84	0.21	4.30
Jharkhand	1.86	3.25	1.51	1.18	0.29	8.08	2.81	0.81	0.39	0.17	0.02	4.20	4.67	4.06	1.89	1.35	0.31	12.28
Karnataka	3.58	3.55	3.13	1.98	0.44	12.68	4.84	1.98	1.58	0.76	0.13	9.28	8.42	5.53	4.70	2.74	0.57	21.96
Kerala	0.35	1.48	3.22	2.65	0.44	8.14	0.35	0.63	1.38	1.43	0.46	4.25	0.69	2.12	4.60	4.08	0.89	12.39
Maharashtra	2.43	3.79	5.66	6.24	1.53	19.65	5.97	3.48	3.26	1.81	0.26	14.78	8.41	7.27	8.92	8.05	1.80	34.44
Madhya Pradesh	4.26	6.29	3.43	2.03	0.84	16.85	7.31	1.98	0.51	0.27	0.08	10.15	11.57	8.27	3.94	2.30	0.92	27.00
Orissa	2.34	3.51	2.97	1.71	0.88	11.42	3.47	1.71	1.14	0.40	0.18	6.90	5.81	5.22	4.11	2.11	1.06	18.31
Punjab	1.20	1.61	0.75	1.90	0.22	5.68	0.93	0.85	0.34	0.73	0.06	2.91	2.12	2.46	1.09	2.64	0.28	8.59
Rajasthan	4.66	5.05	3.26	2.74	0.90	16.61	8.58	1.70	0.74	0.39	0.05	11.45	13.24	6.74	3.99	3.13	0.95	28.06
Tamil Nadu	2.21	2.94	1.73	1.26	0.36	8.50	3.68	1.76	0.60	0.44	0.10	6.57	5.90	4.69	2.32	1.70	0.46	15.07
Uttar Pradesh	13.36	11.40	11.71	9.35	3.51	49.32	14.87	3.02	1.94	1.19	0.26	21.28	28.23	14.41	13.66	10.54	3.77	70.60
Uttarakhand	0.39	0.27	0.78	0.69	0.13	2.26	0.64	0.46	0.30	0.33	0.06	1.79	1.03	0.73	1.08	1.02	0.19	4.05
West Bengal	5.72	9.36	3.63	2.87	1.01	22.59	2.62	2.25	0.57	0.42	0.11	5.97	8.34	11.61	4.21	3.29	1.11	28.56
Other NE	0.38	1.51	1.06	0.65	0.24	3.85	0.18	1.19	0.60	0.35	0.08	2.40	0.56	2.70	1.67	1.01	0.32	6.25
Other states	0.09	0.21	0.27	0.42	0.10	1.08	0.08	0.08	0.04	0.10	0.04	0.33	0.17	0.29	0.31	0.51	0.13	1.41
All India	63.44	79.56	61.27	53.45	14.99	272.72	80.96	32.91	18.54	12.74	2.54	147.68	144.40	112.48	79.81	66.19	17.53	420.40

Source: ibid

Table 8: Projected Urban UPSS Labour Force by Educational Status, Sector and Sex in 2017 (in million)

State/UT	Urban Male						Urban Female						Urban Total					
	IL	PB	M	S+H	G+	Total	IL	PB	M	S+H	G+	Total	IL	PB	M	S+H	G+	Total
Andhra Pradesh	1.12	1.42	1.30	2.25	1.69	7.78	1.34	0.53	0.26	0.46	0.34	2.94	2.46	1.95	1.57	2.71	2.04	10.72
Assam	0.13	0.26	0.37	0.53	0.48	1.77	0.05	0.06	0.05	0.06	0.09	0.32	0.18	0.33	0.41	0.60	0.57	2.09
Bihar	0.35	0.53	0.36	0.89	1.06	3.19	0.34	0.07	0.01	0.04	0.05	0.51	0.69	0.60	0.37	0.93	1.11	3.70
Chhattisgarh	0.22	0.41	0.38	0.58	0.49	2.08	0.22	0.17	0.10	0.04	0.06	0.58	0.44	0.58	0.48	0.62	0.55	2.66
Gujarat	0.30	0.96	2.22	3.98	1.52	8.99	0.42	0.31	0.49	0.55	0.27	2.02	0.72	1.26	2.71	4.53	1.79	11.01
Haryana	0.36	0.78	0.37	1.57	0.57	3.65	0.15	0.05	0.05	0.19	0.22	0.67	0.51	0.84	0.42	1.76	0.79	4.32
Himachal Pradesh	0.06	0.09	0.02	0.11	0.05	0.33	0.03	0.02	0.01	0.02	0.02	0.11	0.10	0.12	0.02	0.13	0.07	0.44
J&K	0.39	0.25	0.28	0.25	0.06	1.23	0.04	0.02	0.05	0.05	0.05	0.20	0.43	0.27	0.33	0.30	0.10	1.43
Jharkhand	0.10	0.17	0.50	0.93	0.67	2.37	0.10	0.10	0.14	0.12	0.08	0.54	0.21	0.26	0.64	1.05	0.75	2.91
Karnataka	0.30	1.66	1.63	2.72	1.48	7.79	0.58	0.40	0.52	0.54	0.42	2.47	0.88	2.06	2.15	3.26	1.91	10.26
Kerala	0.10	0.33	0.96	0.98	0.41	2.77	0.08	0.14	0.26	0.46	0.40	1.35	0.18	0.47	1.21	1.44	0.81	4.12
Maharashtra	0.98	2.54	5.64	6.66	3.59	19.40	0.62	1.32	0.94	1.31	1.32	5.51	1.61	3.86	6.58	7.97	4.91	24.92
Madhya Pradesh	0.58	1.46	1.03	2.03	2.11	7.21	0.52	0.45	0.21	0.26	0.36	1.81	1.09	1.92	1.25	2.29	2.47	9.02
Orissa	0.28	0.46	0.40	0.72	0.55	2.40	0.20	0.19	0.13	0.14	0.16	0.83	0.48	0.65	0.53	0.86	0.72	3.23
Punjab	0.37	0.98	0.51	1.69	0.71	4.26	0.13	0.12	0.00	0.26	0.42	0.94	0.50	1.10	0.51	1.95	1.13	5.20
Rajasthan	1.01	1.46	1.00	1.27	0.87	5.61	0.97	0.18	0.21	0.16	0.20	1.71	1.98	1.64	1.21	1.42	1.07	7.32
Tamil Nadu	0.66	2.54	2.52	4.45	3.19	13.36	0.75	1.70	0.87	1.14	0.93	5.39	1.41	4.25	3.39	5.58	4.12	18.75
Uttar Pradesh	2.56	3.75	2.42	3.63	2.76	15.12	1.23	0.48	0.22	0.26	0.56	2.76	3.80	4.23	2.65	3.89	3.32	17.89
Uttarakhand	0.19	0.19	0.20	0.29	0.16	1.03	0.05	0.02	0.01	0.08	0.06	0.22	0.24	0.21	0.21	0.37	0.22	1.25
West Bengal	0.72	2.10	1.96	2.35	1.88	9.01	0.33	0.53	0.38	0.41	0.47	2.12	1.05	2.63	2.34	2.76	2.34	11.13
Other NE	0.04	0.17	0.23	0.36	0.25	1.06	0.04	0.05	0.09	0.17	0.14	0.49	0.08	0.23	0.31	0.54	0.38	1.54
Other states	0.17	1.53	1.63	2.51	2.14	7.98	0.25	0.20	0.10	0.21	0.43	1.19	0.42	1.73	1.73	2.73	2.57	9.17
All India	11.00	24.04	25.93	40.74	26.69	128.40	8.46	7.13	5.09	6.96	7.04	34.69	19.46	31.17	31.02	47.70	33.74	163.09

Source: ibid

Table 9: Projected UPSS Labour Force by Educational Status, Sector and Sex in 2017 (in million)

State/UT	Male						Female						Total					
	IL	PB	M	S+H	G+	Total	IL	PB	M	S+H	G+	Total	IL	PB	M	S+H	G+	Total
Andhra Pradesh	8.66	6.06	5.08	6.12	2.72	28.64	11.70	3.58	1.55	1.60	0.50	18.93	20.37	9.64	6.62	7.72	3.22	47.57
Assam	0.93	4.36	2.69	1.85	0.71	10.53	0.05	2.13	1.12	0.44	0.13	3.88	0.99	6.49	3.81	2.29	0.84	14.42
Bihar	7.86	8.62	5.08	7.31	2.20	31.07	5.22	1.08	0.28	0.37	0.08	7.03	13.09	9.70	5.36	7.68	2.27	38.10
Chhattisgarh	0.92	3.00	1.86	1.36	0.84	7.98	2.63	1.71	0.54	0.17	0.12	5.16	3.55	4.71	2.39	1.52	0.96	13.14
Gujarat	2.45	4.14	6.35	6.36	1.99	21.29	4.72	2.01	1.73	1.35	0.39	10.20	7.17	6.15	8.09	7.71	2.38	31.49
Haryana	1.33	2.29	1.13	3.26	1.10	9.11	1.87	0.83	0.37	0.70	0.32	4.08	3.19	3.12	1.50	3.96	1.42	13.19
Himachal Pradesh	0.15	0.82	0.30	0.83	0.24	2.34	0.41	0.60	0.22	0.47	0.13	1.84	0.56	1.42	0.53	1.30	0.37	4.18
J&K	1.24	0.77	0.98	0.86	0.24	4.08	0.63	0.32	0.35	0.28	0.08	1.65	1.86	1.09	1.33	1.14	0.32	5.73
Jharkhand	1.96	3.41	2.01	2.11	0.96	10.45	2.91	0.91	0.52	0.29	0.10	4.74	4.87	4.32	2.53	2.40	1.06	15.19
Karnataka	3.88	5.21	4.76	4.69	1.92	20.47	5.42	2.38	2.10	1.31	0.55	11.76	9.30	7.59	6.86	6.00	2.48	32.22
Kerala	0.44	1.82	4.18	3.63	0.85	10.92	0.43	0.78	1.64	1.89	0.86	5.59	0.87	2.59	5.82	5.52	1.71	16.51
Maharashtra	3.42	6.32	11.30	12.90	5.12	39.06	6.59	4.80	4.21	3.12	1.58	20.30	10.01	11.13	15.50	16.01	6.70	59.36
Madhya Pradesh	4.84	7.75	4.47	4.06	2.95	24.06	7.82	2.44	0.72	0.54	0.44	11.96	12.66	10.19	5.19	4.60	3.39	36.02
Orissa	2.62	3.96	3.37	2.43	1.43	13.82	3.67	1.90	1.27	0.54	0.34	7.73	6.29	5.86	4.65	2.97	1.78	21.55
Punjab	1.57	2.59	1.26	3.59	0.93	9.94	1.06	0.97	0.34	0.99	0.48	3.84	2.63	3.56	1.60	4.59	1.41	13.78
Rajasthan	5.67	6.51	4.26	4.01	1.78	22.22	9.55	1.88	0.94	0.55	0.24	13.16	15.22	8.38	5.20	4.56	2.02	35.38
Tamil Nadu	2.87	5.48	4.24	5.71	3.55	21.85	4.44	3.46	1.47	1.58	1.03	11.97	7.31	8.94	5.71	7.29	4.58	33.82
Uttar Pradesh	15.92	15.15	14.13	12.98	6.27	64.45	16.11	3.50	2.17	1.45	0.82	24.04	32.03	18.65	16.30	14.43	7.09	88.49
Uttarakhand	0.58	0.47	0.98	0.98	0.29	3.29	0.69	0.48	0.32	0.41	0.11	2.01	1.27	0.94	1.29	1.39	0.40	5.30
West Bengal	6.44	11.46	5.59	5.23	2.88	31.60	2.96	2.78	0.95	0.83	0.57	8.09	9.40	14.24	6.55	6.05	3.46	39.69
Other NE	0.43	1.68	1.29	1.02	0.48	4.90	0.21	1.24	0.69	0.52	0.22	2.89	0.64	2.92	1.98	1.54	0.70	7.79
Other states	0.26	1.74	1.90	2.93	2.23	9.06	0.33	0.27	0.14	0.31	0.47	1.52	0.59	2.01	2.04	3.24	2.70	10.58
All India	74.44	103.60	87.21	94.20	41.68	401.12	89.42	40.04	23.63	19.70	9.58	182.37	163.86	143.64	110.83	113.89	51.26	583.49

Source: ibid

Annex 5.6: State-wise MCWS Labour Force by Educational Status, Sector and Sex as on 1st April of 2007, 2012 and 2017.

Table 1: Projected Rural MCWS Labour Force by Educational Status, Sector and Sex in 2007 (in million)

State/UT	Rural Male						Rural Female						Rural Total					
	IL	PB	M	S+H	G+	Total	IL	PB	M	S+H	G+	Total	IL	PB	M	S+H	G+	Total
Andhra Pradesh	7.74	4.27	2.56	2.51	0.61	17.70	8.68	2.02	0.74	0.61	0.08	12.12	16.42	6.29	3.30	3.12	0.69	29.82
Assam	1.21	3.05	1.62	0.95	0.17	7.00	0.40	0.73	0.35	0.15	0.02	1.64	1.61	3.78	1.96	1.10	0.19	8.64
Bihar	8.14	5.56	3.06	3.84	0.84	21.45	3.55	0.48	0.17	0.14	0.01	4.36	11.69	6.05	3.23	3.97	0.86	25.81
Chhattisgarh	1.39	1.87	0.83	0.54	0.19	4.83	2.48	1.01	0.24	0.08	0.03	3.84	3.86	2.89	1.08	0.62	0.22	8.67
Gujarat	2.48	3.07	2.59	1.76	0.35	10.25	3.46	1.16	0.67	0.44	0.05	5.79	5.95	4.23	3.26	2.20	0.41	16.04
Haryana	1.09	1.29	0.59	1.21	0.30	4.48	1.30	0.46	0.17	0.25	0.04	2.22	2.40	1.75	0.75	1.46	0.33	6.69
Himachal Pradesh	0.21	0.58	0.24	0.51	0.11	1.66	0.41	0.38	0.14	0.27	0.06	1.25	0.62	0.96	0.38	0.78	0.17	2.91
J&K	0.79	0.46	0.55	0.46	0.10	2.36	0.43	0.15	0.12	0.08	0.01	0.80	1.22	0.61	0.67	0.54	0.11	3.16
Jharkhand	2.23	1.89	1.02	0.72	0.18	6.05	1.53	0.27	0.12	0.04	0.01	1.97	3.76	2.16	1.14	0.76	0.19	8.01
Karnataka	3.99	3.02	2.13	1.48	0.33	10.96	4.20	1.28	0.81	0.38	0.07	6.76	8.20	4.31	2.94	1.87	0.40	17.72
Kerala	0.34	1.80	2.63	1.85	0.33	6.94	0.31	0.76	0.89	0.94	0.27	3.17	0.65	2.56	3.51	2.79	0.60	10.11
Maharashtra	3.46	4.04	4.31	3.96	0.89	16.66	4.98	2.28	1.91	0.95	0.12	10.24	8.43	6.32	6.22	4.90	1.02	26.90
Madhya Pradesh	4.79	4.65	1.99	1.35	0.44	13.21	5.00	1.03	0.22	0.11	0.03	6.39	9.78	5.68	2.21	1.46	0.47	19.60
Orissa	2.99	3.03	2.03	1.01	0.47	9.53	2.33	0.70	0.42	0.14	0.06	3.65	5.32	3.73	2.45	1.16	0.53	13.18
Punjab	1.51	1.35	0.69	1.42	0.16	5.13	1.19	0.69	0.29	0.57	0.05	2.79	2.70	2.04	0.97	1.99	0.22	7.92
Rajasthan	4.97	3.71	2.07	1.59	0.50	12.84	6.29	0.95	0.34	0.17	0.02	7.78	11.26	4.66	2.41	1.76	0.52	20.62
Tamil Nadu	2.42	3.56	1.85	1.47	0.38	9.67	3.63	1.99	0.75	0.59	0.12	7.08	6.05	5.55	2.60	2.06	0.50	16.75
Uttar Pradesh	13.68	8.89	7.62	6.14	1.95	38.28	10.34	1.62	0.87	0.50	0.10	13.44	24.02	10.51	8.49	6.64	2.05	51.72
Uttarakhand	0.39	0.35	0.47	0.40	0.12	1.73	0.55	0.24	0.16	0.15	0.03	1.13	0.94	0.59	0.63	0.55	0.15	2.86
West Bengal	5.31	7.50	2.82	1.95	0.70	18.28	2.19	1.25	0.31	0.21	0.05	4.01	7.49	8.75	3.13	2.15	0.75	22.29
Other NE	0.48	1.16	0.69	0.44	0.15	2.91	0.42	0.61	0.27	0.16	0.04	1.50	0.90	1.77	0.96	0.60	0.19	4.41
Other states	0.12	0.21	0.18	0.32	0.06	0.88	0.08	0.04	0.02	0.04	0.02	0.20	0.19	0.25	0.20	0.36	0.08	1.08
All India	69.72	65.32	42.53	35.89	9.34	222.79	63.73	20.11	9.99	6.98	1.30	102.11	133.45	85.43	52.52	42.87	10.64	324.91

Note: IL - Illiterate, PB - Primary and Below Primary, M - Middle, S+H - Secondary & Higher Secondary, G+ - Graduate and above
Source: ibid

Table 2: Projected Urban MCWS Labour Force by Educational Status, Sector and Sex in 2007 (in million)

State/UT	Urban Male						Urban Female						Urban Total					
	IL	PB	M	S+H	G+	Total	IL	PB	M	S+H	G+	Total	IL	PB	M	S+H	G+	Total
Andhra Pradesh	1.27	1.46	1.10	1.77	1.16	6.77	1.24	0.49	0.18	0.29	0.25	2.45	2.51	1.95	1.29	2.07	1.41	9.22
Assam	0.10	0.24	0.29	0.39	0.30	1.31	0.04	0.04	0.03	0.04	0.04	0.19	0.14	0.28	0.32	0.43	0.34	1.50
Bihar	0.45	0.46	0.34	0.66	0.69	2.59	0.22	0.06	0.01	0.02	0.03	0.34	0.68	0.51	0.34	0.68	0.72	2.93
Chhattisgarh	0.17	0.36	0.23	0.41	0.30	1.47	0.17	0.08	0.04	0.03	0.03	0.36	0.34	0.44	0.27	0.44	0.34	1.84
Gujarat	0.49	1.31	1.56	2.55	1.10	7.01	0.47	0.27	0.27	0.33	0.16	1.50	0.97	1.58	1.82	2.88	1.26	8.51
Haryana	0.35	0.53	0.27	0.84	0.32	2.31	0.13	0.05	0.03	0.11	0.10	0.42	0.48	0.58	0.31	0.95	0.43	2.73
Himachal Pradesh	0.04	0.06	0.02	0.09	0.04	0.24	0.02	0.02	0.00	0.02	0.02	0.07	0.06	0.07	0.02	0.11	0.05	0.32
J&K	0.22	0.18	0.20	0.26	0.09	0.95	0.04	0.02	0.03	0.03	0.04	0.16	0.26	0.20	0.23	0.29	0.13	1.11
Jharkhand	0.14	0.23	0.42	0.65	0.44	1.87	0.12	0.06	0.07	0.06	0.05	0.35	0.25	0.29	0.49	0.70	0.48	2.22
Karnataka	0.53	1.29	1.28	2.05	1.05	6.21	0.57	0.29	0.30	0.36	0.24	1.77	1.10	1.58	1.58	2.41	1.30	7.98
Kerala	0.08	0.51	0.81	0.74	0.31	2.43	0.08	0.19	0.23	0.37	0.26	1.13	0.15	0.70	1.04	1.10	0.57	3.56
Maharashtra	1.15	2.59	4.07	4.81	2.52	15.14	0.92	0.88	0.63	0.85	0.84	4.11	2.07	3.47	4.70	5.66	3.35	19.26
Madhya Pradesh	0.67	1.38	0.74	1.46	1.21	5.44	0.45	0.26	0.11	0.14	0.20	1.15	1.12	1.63	0.85	1.60	1.41	6.60
Orissa	0.27	0.42	0.36	0.50	0.37	1.92	0.17	0.08	0.05	0.07	0.07	0.45	0.44	0.50	0.42	0.57	0.44	2.37
Punjab	0.43	0.75	0.44	1.14	0.47	3.24	0.12	0.08	0.02	0.18	0.23	0.63	0.55	0.82	0.47	1.33	0.70	3.87
Rajasthan	0.87	1.13	0.78	0.95	0.66	4.38	0.65	0.14	0.10	0.09	0.12	1.11	1.52	1.27	0.88	1.04	0.77	5.49
Tamil Nadu	0.77	2.63	1.98	3.09	1.84	10.31	0.91	1.15	0.52	0.68	0.49	3.75	1.67	3.78	2.50	3.77	2.33	14.06
Uttar Pradesh	2.52	2.81	1.87	2.57	1.92	11.69	0.95	0.33	0.12	0.15	0.28	1.84	3.47	3.14	1.99	2.72	2.20	13.52
Uttarakhand	0.11	0.15	0.13	0.23	0.16	0.79	0.05	0.01	0.01	0.04	0.04	0.15	0.16	0.17	0.14	0.27	0.20	0.93
West Bengal	0.85	2.13	1.62	1.95	1.49	8.04	0.37	0.44	0.24	0.28	0.33	1.66	1.22	2.57	1.86	2.23	1.82	9.71
Other NE	0.05	0.16	0.19	0.26	0.16	0.82	0.04	0.06	0.06	0.10	0.07	0.33	0.09	0.22	0.25	0.36	0.24	1.15
Other states	0.37	1.15	0.99	1.68	1.47	5.66	0.20	0.12	0.06	0.17	0.33	0.89	0.57	1.27	1.05	1.85	1.80	6.55
All India	11.89	21.91	19.69	29.04	18.08	100.61	7.94	5.12	3.13	4.42	4.20	24.80	19.83	27.03	22.82	33.46	22.27	125.41

Source: ibid

Table 3: Projected MCWS Labour Force by Educational Status, Sector and Sex in 2007 (in million)

State/UT	Male						Female						Total					
	IL	PB	M	S+H	G+	Total	IL	PB	M	S+H	G+	Total	IL	PB	M	S+H	G+	Total
Andhra Pradesh	9.01	5.74	3.66	4.29	1.77	24.47	9.92	2.50	0.92	0.90	0.33	14.57	18.93	8.24	4.58	5.19	2.10	39.04
Assam	1.31	3.28	1.91	1.34	0.47	8.31	0.44	0.77	0.37	0.19	0.06	1.83	1.75	4.05	2.28	1.53	0.53	10.14
Bihar	8.59	6.02	3.40	4.49	1.53	24.04	3.78	0.54	0.18	0.16	0.04	4.70	12.37	6.56	3.58	4.65	1.58	28.73
Chhattisgarh	1.55	2.23	1.06	0.95	0.50	6.30	2.65	1.10	0.29	0.11	0.06	4.21	4.20	3.33	1.35	1.06	0.56	10.51
Gujarat	2.97	4.37	4.15	4.32	1.46	17.26	3.94	1.43	0.94	0.77	0.21	7.29	6.91	5.80	5.08	5.08	1.67	24.55
Haryana	1.44	1.82	0.86	2.05	0.62	6.79	1.43	0.50	0.20	0.36	0.14	2.64	2.87	2.32	1.06	2.41	0.76	9.43
Himachal Pradesh	0.25	0.63	0.26	0.61	0.15	1.90	0.43	0.39	0.14	0.29	0.07	1.32	0.68	1.03	0.40	0.89	0.22	3.22
J&K	1.01	0.64	0.76	0.72	0.19	3.31	0.47	0.17	0.15	0.11	0.05	0.95	1.48	0.81	0.90	0.83	0.24	4.26
Jharkhand	2.37	2.12	1.44	1.37	0.62	7.92	1.64	0.33	0.19	0.10	0.05	2.31	4.01	2.44	1.63	1.47	0.67	10.23
Karnataka	4.52	4.32	3.41	3.53	1.38	17.17	4.78	1.57	1.12	0.75	0.31	8.53	9.30	5.89	4.53	4.28	1.69	25.69
Kerala	0.42	2.30	3.44	2.59	0.64	9.38	0.38	0.95	1.12	1.31	0.53	4.30	0.80	3.26	4.55	3.90	1.17	13.67
Maharashtra	4.61	6.63	8.38	8.77	3.41	31.80	5.89	3.16	2.54	1.79	0.96	14.35	10.50	9.80	10.92	10.56	4.37	46.15
Madhya Pradesh	5.45	6.03	2.72	2.80	1.65	18.65	5.44	1.29	0.34	0.25	0.23	7.54	10.90	7.31	3.06	3.06	1.87	26.20
Orissa	3.25	3.45	2.40	1.52	0.84	11.46	2.50	0.78	0.47	0.21	0.13	4.10	5.76	4.23	2.87	1.73	0.97	15.55
Punjab	1.94	2.10	1.13	2.57	0.63	8.37	1.31	0.77	0.31	0.75	0.28	3.42	3.25	2.87	1.44	3.32	0.92	11.79
Rajasthan	5.83	4.84	2.85	2.55	1.15	17.22	6.94	1.10	0.45	0.26	0.14	8.88	12.78	5.94	3.29	2.80	1.29	26.11
Tamil Nadu	3.19	6.19	3.82	4.56	2.22	19.98	4.54	3.14	1.27	1.27	0.61	10.83	7.72	9.33	5.09	5.83	2.83	30.81
Uttar Pradesh	16.20	11.70	9.49	8.71	3.88	49.97	11.29	1.95	0.99	0.65	0.38	15.27	27.49	13.66	10.48	9.36	4.25	65.24
Uttarakhand	0.50	0.50	0.61	0.63	0.28	2.51	0.59	0.26	0.17	0.19	0.06	1.28	1.10	0.76	0.78	0.82	0.34	3.80
West Bengal	6.16	9.63	4.44	3.89	2.19	26.32	2.56	1.69	0.55	0.49	0.38	5.67	8.72	11.33	4.99	4.38	2.57	31.99
Other NE	0.53	1.32	0.88	0.69	0.31	3.73	0.46	0.67	0.34	0.26	0.11	1.84	0.99	1.98	1.21	0.96	0.42	5.56
Other states	0.49	1.36	1.17	1.99	1.53	6.54	0.28	0.17	0.08	0.22	0.34	1.09	0.77	1.52	1.26	2.21	1.88	7.63
All India	81.61	87.23	62.22	64.93	27.42	323.40	71.67	25.23	13.11	11.41	5.50	126.91	153.27	112.46	75.34	76.33	32.91	450.32

Source: ibid

Table 4: Projected Rural MCWS Labour Force by Educational Status, Sector and Sex in 2012 (in million)

State/UT	Rural Male						Rural Female						Rural Total					
	IL	PB	M	S+H	G+	Total	IL	PB	M	S+H	G+	Total	IL	PB	M	S+H	G+	Total
Andhra Pradesh	7.60	4.43	3.12	3.16	0.80	19.10	8.97	2.37	0.94	0.82	0.11	13.21	16.56	6.80	4.07	3.98	0.90	32.31
Assam	1.02	3.52	1.96	1.13	0.19	7.82	0.23	1.01	0.50	0.19	0.02	1.96	1.25	4.53	2.46	1.32	0.21	9.78
Bihar	7.81	6.70	3.79	4.95	0.98	24.23	3.53	0.61	0.20	0.18	0.02	4.55	11.34	7.31	3.99	5.13	0.99	28.77
Chhattisgarh	1.07	2.17	1.11	0.64	0.26	5.26	2.37	1.25	0.33	0.10	0.04	4.09	3.43	3.42	1.45	0.74	0.31	9.35
Gujarat	2.28	3.13	3.34	2.06	0.40	11.22	3.64	1.32	0.88	0.57	0.08	6.49	5.92	4.44	4.23	2.64	0.48	17.71
Haryana	1.00	1.40	0.68	1.45	0.41	4.94	1.48	0.62	0.24	0.38	0.07	2.79	2.48	2.02	0.92	1.83	0.47	7.73
Himachal Pradesh	0.13	0.64	0.26	0.61	0.15	1.78	0.35	0.44	0.16	0.35	0.08	1.38	0.48	1.08	0.42	0.95	0.23	3.17
J&K	0.81	0.47	0.61	0.51	0.13	2.54	0.39	0.17	0.15	0.11	0.02	0.84	1.20	0.64	0.76	0.63	0.15	3.38
Jharkhand	1.96	2.53	1.28	0.88	0.22	6.87	1.64	0.37	0.17	0.07	0.01	2.25	3.60	2.90	1.45	0.95	0.23	9.12
Karnataka	3.80	3.26	2.59	1.71	0.38	11.74	4.26	1.50	1.08	0.52	0.09	7.45	8.05	4.77	3.67	2.23	0.47	19.19
Kerala	0.33	1.61	2.86	2.19	0.37	7.36	0.30	0.64	1.04	1.10	0.34	3.41	0.63	2.25	3.90	3.29	0.71	10.78
Maharashtra	2.92	3.85	4.93	5.03	1.18	17.92	4.92	2.55	2.35	1.26	0.17	11.25	7.85	6.41	7.28	6.29	1.35	29.17
Madhya Pradesh	4.47	5.38	2.62	1.62	0.60	14.70	5.10	1.21	0.29	0.16	0.04	6.79	9.57	6.59	2.92	1.78	0.64	21.49
Orissa	2.60	3.15	2.41	1.30	0.63	10.10	2.24	0.88	0.57	0.20	0.08	3.97	4.85	4.03	2.98	1.50	0.71	14.07
Punjab	1.32	1.48	0.74	1.67	0.19	5.41	1.25	0.91	0.38	0.79	0.07	3.40	2.57	2.39	1.12	2.46	0.26	8.81
Rajasthan	4.82	4.32	2.60	2.12	0.68	14.54	6.71	1.18	0.47	0.25	0.03	8.64	11.54	5.50	3.08	2.36	0.71	23.18
Tamil Nadu	2.23	3.27	1.82	1.40	0.37	9.09	3.70	2.00	0.73	0.57	0.12	7.12	5.93	5.26	2.55	1.97	0.50	16.21
Uttar Pradesh	13.41	10.06	9.42	7.50	2.63	43.01	11.72	2.12	1.29	0.75	0.16	16.02	25.12	12.18	10.71	8.24	2.78	59.04
Uttarakhand	0.38	0.28	0.60	0.52	0.12	1.90	0.51	0.30	0.21	0.21	0.04	1.26	0.89	0.58	0.81	0.73	0.16	3.17
West Bengal	5.46	8.37	3.18	2.37	0.83	20.21	2.24	1.57	0.40	0.28	0.07	4.56	7.70	9.94	3.57	2.65	0.90	24.77
Other NE	0.42	1.34	0.87	0.54	0.19	3.35	0.32	0.81	0.39	0.23	0.06	1.81	0.74	2.15	1.26	0.77	0.24	5.17
Other states	0.10	0.21	0.22	0.37	0.08	0.99	0.08	0.06	0.03	0.07	0.03	0.26	0.18	0.27	0.25	0.44	0.11	1.25
All India	65.94	71.57	51.03	43.74	11.79	244.08	65.95	23.87	12.81	9.15	1.74	113.52	131.89	95.45	63.84	52.89	13.53	357.61

Source: ibid

Table 5: Projected Urban MCWS Labour Force by Educational Status, Sector and Sex in 2012 (in million)

State/UT	Urban Male						Urban Female						Urban Total					
	IL	PB	M	S+H	G+	Total	IL	PB	M	S+H	G+	Total	IL	PB	M	S+H	G+	Total
Andhra Pradesh	1.21	1.45	1.21	2.00	1.41	7.28	1.34	0.54	0.23	0.40	0.32	2.83	2.55	1.99	1.44	2.40	1.73	10.11
Assam	0.11	0.25	0.33	0.46	0.39	1.54	0.04	0.05	0.03	0.05	0.06	0.24	0.16	0.30	0.36	0.51	0.45	1.79
Bihar	0.41	0.49	0.36	0.78	0.88	2.93	0.26	0.06	0.01	0.03	0.03	0.39	0.67	0.55	0.36	0.82	0.92	3.31
Chhattisgarh	0.19	0.37	0.29	0.48	0.39	1.72	0.18	0.12	0.07	0.04	0.04	0.45	0.37	0.49	0.36	0.52	0.43	2.17
Gujarat	0.38	1.11	1.92	3.30	1.35	8.06	0.44	0.28	0.36	0.43	0.21	1.72	0.82	1.39	2.28	3.73	1.56	9.78
Haryana	0.34	0.60	0.29	1.11	0.42	2.76	0.13	0.05	0.04	0.14	0.15	0.52	0.47	0.65	0.33	1.26	0.57	3.28
Himachal Pradesh	0.05	0.07	0.02	0.10	0.04	0.28	0.03	0.02	0.01	0.02	0.02	0.09	0.08	0.09	0.02	0.12	0.06	0.37
J&K	0.30	0.22	0.24	0.26	0.07	1.10	0.04	0.01	0.03	0.04	0.04	0.16	0.34	0.24	0.28	0.30	0.11	1.26
Jharkhand	0.10	0.18	0.46	0.79	0.56	2.08	0.10	0.07	0.09	0.08	0.06	0.40	0.20	0.25	0.55	0.86	0.61	2.47
Karnataka	0.41	1.48	1.47	2.38	1.29	7.02	0.54	0.32	0.39	0.43	0.31	2.00	0.95	1.81	1.86	2.81	1.60	9.02
Kerala	0.09	0.41	0.86	0.83	0.35	2.53	0.07	0.16	0.24	0.42	0.33	1.23	0.16	0.58	1.10	1.25	0.68	3.76
Maharashtra	1.07	2.61	4.85	5.73	3.05	17.31	0.78	1.13	0.81	1.11	1.12	4.97	1.85	3.74	5.66	6.85	4.17	22.27
Madhya Pradesh	0.61	1.45	0.89	1.76	1.64	6.34	0.43	0.33	0.16	0.19	0.25	1.36	1.04	1.78	1.05	1.94	1.89	7.70
Orissa	0.27	0.44	0.38	0.60	0.46	2.15	0.17	0.12	0,08	0.09	0.10	0.56	0.44	0.55	0.47	0.69	0.56	2.71
Punjab	0.41	0.87	0.48	1.41	0.59	3.77	0.11	0.09	0.02	0.22	0.32	0.76	0.53	0.96	0.50	1.63	0.91	4.53
Rajasthan	0.94	1.31	0.90	1.11	0.77	5.03	0.76	0.16	0.15	0.11	0.14	1.31	1.70	1.47	1.04	1.22	0.91	6.35
Tamil Nadu	0.66	2.62	2.26	3.77	2.49	11.81	0.82	1.42	0.69	0.90	0.70	4.54	1.49	4.05	2.95	4.68	3.20	16.36
Uttar Pradesh	2.57	3.28	2.16	3.09	2.34	13.44	1.04	0.38	0.16	0.19	0.39	2.16	3.61	3.66	2.32	3.28	2.73	15.60
Uttarakhand	0.15	0.18	0.16	0.26	0.16	0.91	0.05	0.02	0.01	0.06	0.04	0.17	0.20	0.19	0.17	0.32	0.20	1.08
West Bengal	0.78	2.13	1.80	2.16	1.68	8.55	0.33	0.47	0.29	0.33	0.38	1.79	1.11	2.59	2.09	2.49	2.06	10.34
Other NE	0.05	0.17	0.21	0.31	0.20	0.93	0.03	0.06	0.07	0.13	0.10	0.39	0.08	0.22	0.28	0.44	0.30	1.32
Other states	0.19	1.40	1.35	2.16	1.85	6.94	0.23	0.16	0.08	0.20	0.38	1.04	0.42	1.56	1.43	2.36	2.23	7.99
All India	11.28	23.09	22.87	34.87	22.37	114.49	7.94	6.01	4.02	5.61	5.50	29.08	19.22	29.10	26.89	40.48	27.88	143.57

Source: ibid

Table 6: Projected MCWS Labour Force by Educational Status, Sector and Sex in 2012 (in million)

State/UT	Male						Female						Total					
	IL	PB	M	S+H	G+	Total	IL	PB	M	S+H	G+	Total	IL	PB	M	S+H	G+	Total
Andhra Pradesh	8.80	5.87	4.33	5.16	2.21	26.38	10.31	2.91	1.18	1.22	0.43	16.04	19.11	8.78	5.51	6.38	2.64	42.42
Assam	1.13	3.78	2.28	1.59	0.58	9.36	0.28	1.05	0.54	0.24	0.09	2.20	1.41	4.83	2.82	1.84	0.67	11.56
Bihar	8.23	7.19	4.15	5.73	1.86	27.15	3.79	0.67	0.20	0.21	0.05	4.93	12.02	7.86	4.35	5.94	1.91	32.08
Chhattisgarh	1.25	2.54	1.40	1.13	0.65	6.98	2.55	1.36	0.40	0.13	0.08	4.54	3.81	3.91	1.81	1.26	0.74	11.52
Gujarat	2.66	4.24	5.26	5.36	1.75	19.28	4.07	1.60	1.25	1.00	0.29	8.21	6.74	5.83	6.51	6.37	2.04	27.49
Haryana	1.34	2.00	0.97	2.56	0.83	7.70	1.62	0.67	0.28	0.53	0.22	3.31	2.95	2.67	1.25	3.09	1.04	11.01
Himachal Pradesh	0.18	0.71	0.28	0.71	0.19	2.06	0.38	0.46	0.17	0.37	0.10	1.47	0.56	1.17	0.45	1.07	0.29	3.53
J&K	1.11	0.69	0.85	0.77	0.21	3.64	0.43	0.18	0.18	0.15	0.05	1.00	1.54	0.87	1.04	0.92	0.26	4.63
Jharkhand	2.06	2.70	1.74	1.67	0.77	8.94	1.74	0.44	0.26	0.14	0.07	2.65	3.80	3.14	1.99	1.82	0.84	11.59
Karnataka	4.20	4.75	4.05	4.09	1.67	18.76	4.80	1.82	1.47	0.95	0.41	9.45	9.00	6.57	5.53	5.04	2.07	28.21
Kerala	0.42	2.02	3.72	3.02	0.72	9.90	0.37	0.81	1.28	1.52	0.67	4.64	0.79	2.83	5.00	4.54	1.39	14.54
Maharashtra	3.99	6.47	9.78	10.76	4.23	35.23	5.71	3.68	3.16	2.37	1.29	16.22	9.70	10.15	12.94	13.13	5.53	51.45
Madhya Pradesh	5.08	6.82	3.51	3.38	2.24	21.04	5.53	1.54	0.45	0.34	0.30	8.15	10.61	8.37	3.96	3.72	2.54	29.19
Orissa	2.87	3.59	2.80	1.90	1.09	12.25	2.42	0.99	0.65	0.29	0.18	4.53	5.29	4.58	3.45	2.19	1.27	16.78
Punjab	1.73	2.35	1.23	3.08	0.79	9.18	1.37	1.00	0.39	1.01	0.39	4.16	3.10	3.36	1.62	4.10	1.17	13.35
Rajasthan	5.76	5.64	3.50	3.23	1.44	19.57	7.48	1.33	0.62	0.36	0.17	9.96	13.24	6.97	4.12	3.59	1.61	29.53
Tamil Nadu	2.90	5.89	4.08	5.17	2.87	20.90	4.52	3.42	1.42	1.47	0.83	11.66	7.42	9.31	5.50	6.64	3.69	32.57
Uttar Pradesh	15.98	13.34	11.59	10.58	4.97	56.46	12.75	2.50	1.44	0.94	0.55	18.18	28.73	15.84	13.03	11.52	5.52	74.64
Uttarakhand	0.53	0.46	0.77	0.78	0.28	2.81	0.56	0.31	0.22	0.27	0.08	1.44	1.09	0.77	0.98	1.05	0.36	4.25
West Bengal	6.25	10.49	4.97	4.53	2.52	28.76	2.57	2.04	0.69	0.61	0.45	6.35	8.81	12.54	5.67	5.14	2.96	35.11
Other NE	0.47	1.51	1.07	0.85	0.39	4.29	0.35	0.87	0.47	0.36	0.16	2.20	0.82	2.38	1.54	1.21	0.55	6.49
Other states	0.29	1.61	1.57	2.53	1.93	7.93	0.31	0.22	0.11	0.27	0.41	1.31	0.60	1.82	1.68	2.80	2.33	9.24
All India	77.22	94.66	73.91	78.61	34.17	358.57	73.88	29.89	16.83	14.76	7.24	142.60	151.11	124.55	90.74	93.37	41.41	501.17

Source: ibid

Table 7: Projected Rural MCWS Labour Force by Educational Status, Sector and Sex in 2017 (in million)

State/UT	Rural Male						Rural Female						Rural Total					
	IL	PB	M	S+H	G+	Total	IL	PB	M	S+H	G+	Total	IL	PB	M	S+H	G+	Total
Andhra Pradesh	7.32	4.51	3.66	3.76	1.00	20.25	9.04	2.66	1.12	0.99	0.14	13.95	16.36	7.17	4.78	4.75	1.14	34.20
Assam	0.79	4.03	2.29	1.29	0.22	8.63	0.00	1.32	0.69	0.24	0.03	2.28	0.79	5.36	2.98	1.54	0.25	10.91
Bihar	7.31	7.87	4.59	6.24	1.11	27.11	3.58	0.74	0.20	0.24	0.02	4.78	10.89	8.61	4.79	6.48	1.13	31.89
Chhattisgarh	0.67	2.49	1.42	0.75	0.34	5.68	2.32	1.48	0.42	0.12	0.06	4.40	2.99	3.97	1.84	0.87	0.40	10.07
Gujarat	2.11	3.12	4.05	2.33	0.46	12.06	3.80	1.50	1.10	0.71	0.11	7.22	5.90	4.62	5.15	3.04	0.57	19.28
Haryana	0.95	1.48	0.74	1.66	0.52	5.34	1.71	0.77	0.32	0.50	0.10	3.40	2.65	2.25	1.06	2.16	0.62	8.74
Himachal Pradesh	0.09	0.69	0.27	0.68	0.18	1.91	0.32	0.49	0.18	0.38	0.10	1.47	0.41	1.18	0.46	1.06	0.28	3.38
J&K	0.83	0.51	0.68	0.59	0.18	2.78	0.37	0.19	0.19	0.15	0.02	0.91	1.19	0.69	0.87	0.73	0.20	3.69
Jharkhand	1.77	3.10	1.44	1.13	0.27	7.71	2.72	0.79	0.37	0.17	0.02	4.07	4.49	3.89	1.81	1.29	0.30	11.78
Karnataka	3.46	3.43	3.02	1.91	0.42	12.25	4.23	1.73	1.38	0.67	0.11	8.13	7.69	5.16	4.40	2.58	0.54	20.38
Kerala	0.33	1.40	3.04	2.50	0.41	7.68	0.29	0.52	1.14	1.18	0.38	3.51	0.61	1.92	4.18	3.68	0.79	11.19
Maharashtra	2.36	3.67	5.48	6.04	1.49	19.04	4.91	2.87	2.68	1.49	0.21	12.17	7.27	6.54	8.16	7.53	1.70	31.20
Madhya Pradesh	4.11	6.07	3.32	1.96	0.81	16.28	5.25	1.42	0.36	0.20	0.06	7.29	9.36	7.50	3.68	2.16	0.87	23.57
Orissa	2.21	3.31	2.80	1.61	0.83	10.76	2.14	1.05	0.70	0.25	0.11	4.25	4.34	4.36	3.51	1.86	0.94	15.00
Punjab	1.19	1.60	0.75	1.89	0.22	5.64	1.28	1.18	0.47	1.01	0.08	4.02	2.47	2.77	1.21	2.90	0.30	9.66
Rajasthan	4.61	5.00	3.22	2.71	0.89	16.44	7.19	1.42	0.62	0.33	0.04	9.59	11.80	6.42	3.84	3.04	0.93	26.03
Tamil Nadu	2.18	2.89	1.70	1.24	0.35	8.36	3.92	1.87	0.64	0.47	0.10	7.00	6.10	4.76	2.34	1.71	0.46	15.36
Uttar Pradesh	12.99	11.08	11.39	9.09	3.41	47.97	13.15	2.67	1.72	1.05	0.23	18.81	26.14	13.75	13.11	10.14	3.64	66.78
Uttarakhand	0.36	0.25	0.72	0.64	0.12	2.10	0.63	0.45	0.30	0.32	0.06	1.75	0.99	0.70	1.02	0.96	0.17	3.85
West Bengal	5.56	9.09	3.53	2.79	0.98	21.94	2.19	1.88	0.48	0.35	0.09	4.99	7.75	10.97	4.01	3.14	1.07	26.93
Other NE	0.38	1.47	1.04	0.64	0.23	3.75	0.16	1.05	0.53	0.31	0.07	2.13	0.53	2.52	1.57	0.95	0.30	5.88
Other states	0.09	0.21	0.27	0.42	0.10	1.08	0.08	0.07	0.04	0.09	0.04	0.32	0.17	0.29	0.31	0.51	0.13	1.40
All India	61.65	77.27	59.42	51.88	14.54	264.75	69.26	28.13	15.65	11.21	2.18	126.42	130.91	105.40	75.07	63.08	16.72	391.18

Source: ibid

Table 8: Projected Urban MCWS Labour Force by Educational Status, Sector and Sex in 2017 (in million)

State/UT	Urban Male						Urban Female						Urban Total					
	IL	PB	M	S+H	G+	Total	IL	PB	M	S+H	G+	Total	IL	PB	M	S+H	G+	Total
Andhra Pradesh	1.11	1.40	1.28	2.21	1.66	7.66	1.44	0.57	0.28	0.49	0.37	3.15	2.54	1.96	1.56	2.71	2.03	10.81
Assam	0.13	0.26	0.36	0.53	0.48	1.75	0.05	0.05	0.04	0.05	0.08	0.27	0.17	0.31	0.40	0.58	0.56	2.03
Bihar	0.35	0.53	0.37	0.90	1.06	3.21	0.29	0.06	0.01	0.04	0.04	0.44	0.65	0.59	0.37	0.93	1.11	3.65
Chhattisgarh	0.22	0.39	0.36	0.55	0.47	1.99	0.19	0.15	0.09	0.04	0.05	0.52	0.41	0.54	0.45	0.59	0.52	2.51
Gujarat	0.30	0.95	2.22	3.98	1.52	8.98	0.40	0.29	0.47	0.52	0.25	1.94	0.70	1.25	2.69	4.51	1.77	10.92
Haryana	0.32	0.69	0.33	1.38	0.50	3.21	0.14	0.05	0.04	0.17	0.20	0.61	0.46	0.74	0.37	1.55	0.70	3.82
Himachal Pradesh	0.06	0.09	0.01	0.10	0.05	0.31	0.03	0.02	0.01	0.02	0.02	0.09	0.09	0.11	0.02	0.12	0.07	0.41
J&K	0.39	0.25	0.28	0.25	0.06	1.22	0.03	0.01	0.04	0.04	0.04	0.17	0.42	0.26	0.32	0.29	0.10	1.39
Jharkhand	0.10	0.16	0.48	0.90	0.65	2.28	0.10	0.10	0.13	0.12	0.08	0.54	0.20	0.26	0.62	1.02	0.73	2.82
Karnataka	0.30	1.64	1.62	2.69	1.47	7.71	0.52	0.36	0.47	0.48	0.38	2.20	0.82	2.00	2.08	3.17	1.85	9.92
Kerala	0.09	0.31	0.90	0.92	0.38	2.60	0.08	0.14	0.25	0.45	0.39	1.31	0.17	0.45	1.15	1.37	0.78	3.91
Maharashtra	0.98	2.52	5.60	6.61	3.57	19.28	0.66	1.40	1.00	1.39	1.40	5.83	1.64	3.92	6.60	8.00	4.96	25.12
Madhya Pradesh	0.57	1.45	1.02	2.01	2.09	7.15	0.43	0.38	0.18	0.22	0.30	1.52	1.01	1.83	1.20	2.23	2.39	8.67
Orissa	0.27	0.45	0.39	0.70	0.54	2.35	0.16	0.15	0.10	0.11	0.13	0.64	0.43	0.59	0.49	0.81	0.67	2.99
Punjab	0.37	0.98	0.51	1.68	0.71	4.24	0.12	0.11	0.00	0.24	0.38	0.84	0.49	1.08	0.51	1.92	1.09	5.09
Rajasthan	1.00	1.46	1.00	1.26	0.87	5.59	0.83	0.15	0.18	0.13	0.17	1.46	1.83	1.61	1.18	1.40	1.04	7.05
Tamil Nadu	0.65	2.52	2.49	4.40	3.16	13.23	0.71	1.60	0.82	1.07	0.87	5.07	1.36	4.12	3.31	5.47	4.03	18.29
Uttar Pradesh	2.55	3.73	2.41	3.61	2.74	15.03	1.05	0.41	0.19	0.22	0.48	2.35	3.60	4.14	2.60	3.83	3.22	17.38
Uttarakhand	0.19	0.19	0.19	0.29	0.16	1.02	0.05	0.02	0.01	0.07	0.05	0.20	0.23	0.21	0.21	0.36	0.21	1.22
West Bengal	0.71	2.07	1.93	2.32	1.85	8.88	0.29	0.46	0.33	0.36	0.40	1.84	1.00	2.53	2.26	2.67	2.25	10.72
Other NE	0.04	0.17	0.22	0.36	0.24	1.04	0.03	0.05	0.08	0.16	0.13	0.46	0.08	0.22	0.31	0.52	0.37	1.50
Other states	0.17	1.53	1.63	2.51	2.14	7.98	0.24	0.19	0.10	0.21	0.42	1.16	0.42	1.72	1.72	2.72	2.56	9.14
All India	10.85	23.72	25.62	40.17	26.37	126.74	7.83	6.72	4.81	6.61	6.63	32.60	18.69	30.45	30.43	46.78	33.00	159.35

Source: ibid

Table 9: Projected MCWS Labour Force by Educational Status, Sector and Sex in 2017 (in million)

State/UT	Male						Female						Total					
	IL	PB	M	S+H	G+	Total	IL	PB	M	S+H	G+	Total	IL	PB	M	S+H	G+	Total
Andhra Pradesh	8.43	5.91	4.95	5.97	2.66	27.91	10.48	3.23	1.40	1.49	0.51	17.10	18.90	9.13	6.35	7.46	3.17	45.01
Assam	0.92	4.29	2.65	1.82	0.70	10.38	0.05	1.38	0.73	0.30	0.11	2.56	0.96	5.67	3.38	2.12	0.80	12.94
Bihar	7.66	8.40	4.96	7.14	2.17	30.32	3.87	0.80	0.20	0.28	0.06	5.22	11.53	9.20	5.16	7.41	2.23	35.54
Chhattisgarh	0.89	2.88	1.78	1.30	0.81	7.67	2.51	1.63	0.51	0.16	0.11	4.91	3.40	4.51	2.29	1.46	0.92	12.58
Gujarat	2.41	4.08	6.27	6.31	1.98	21.04	4.20	1.80	1.56	1.23	0.36	9.15	6.60	5.87	7.84	7.54	2.34	30.20
Haryana	1.26	2.17	1.07	3.04	1.02	8.55	1.85	0.82	0.36	0.68	0.30	4.01	3.11	2.99	1.43	3.71	1.32	12.57
Himachal Pradesh	0.14	0.78	0.29	0.78	0.23	2.22	0.35	0.51	0.19	0.40	0.11	1.57	0.49	1.29	0.48	1.18	0.34	3.79
J&K	1.21	0.75	0.96	0.84	0.23	4.00	0.40	0.20	0.23	0.19	0.06	1.08	1.61	0.96	1.19	1.03	0.29	5.07
Jharkhand	1.87	3.26	1.92	2.02	0.92	10.00	2.82	0.88	0.51	0.29	0.10	4.61	4.69	4.15	2.43	2.31	1.02	14.60
Karnataka	3.76	5.07	4.64	4.60	1.89	19.97	4.75	2.09	1.85	1.15	0.49	10.33	8.51	7.16	6.48	5.75	2.39	30.29
Kerala	0.42	1.71	3.94	3.42	0.80	10.28	0.36	0.66	1.39	1.63	0.77	4.82	0.78	2.37	5.33	5.05	1.57	15.10
Maharashtra	3.34	6.19	11.08	12.66	5.05	38.32	5.57	4.26	3.68	2.87	1.61	18.00	8.91	10.45	14.77	15.53	6.66	56.32
Madhya Pradesh	4.69	7.52	4.34	3.97	2.91	23.43	5.68	1.81	0.54	0.42	0.36	8.81	10.37	9.33	4.88	4.39	3.27	32.24
Orissa	2.48	3.75	3.19	2.31	1.37	13.11	2.29	1.20	0.81	0.35	0.24	4.89	4.77	4.95	4.00	2.67	1.61	18.00
Punjab	1.55	2.57	1.26	3.57	0.93	9.88	1.40	1.29	0.47	1.25	0.46	4.86	2.96	3.86	1.72	4.82	1.39	14.74
Rajasthan	5.62	6.45	4.22	3.98	1.76	22.03	8.01	1.57	0.79	0.46	0.21	11.05	13.63	8.02	5.02	4.44	1.97	33.08
Tamil Nadu	2.83	5.41	4.19	5.64	3.51	21.59	4.63	3.47	1.45	1.54	0.98	12.07	7.46	8.88	5.65	7.18	4.49	33.65
Uttar Pradesh	15.54	14.81	13.80	12.70	6.15	63.00	14.20	3.07	1.91	1.27	0.71	21.17	29.74	17.89	15.71	13.97	6.86	84.16
Uttarakhand	0.55	0.45	0.92	0.93	0.28	3.12	0.67	0.47	0.31	0.39	0.11	1.95	1.22	0.91	1.23	1.32	0.38	5.07
West Bengal	6.27	11.16	5.46	5.11	2.83	30.83	2.48	2.34	0.81	0.70	0.49	6.83	8.75	13.50	6.27	5.81	3.32	37.65
Other NE	0.42	1.64	1.26	1.00	0.47	4.80	0.19	1.10	0.62	0.48	0.20	2.59	0.61	2.75	1.88	1.47	0.68	7.39
Other states	0.26	1.74	1.90	2.93	2.23	9.06	0.33	0.27	0.13	0.30	0.46	1.48	0.59	2.01	2.03	3.23	2.69	10.54
All India	72.50	100.99	85.04	92.05	40.91	391.50	77.09	34.86	20.46	17.82	8.80	159.03	149.59	135.85	105.50	109.87	49.72	550.53

Source: ibid